WRESTLING WITH ASIA

A MEMOIR

FRANK MOUNT

Published in 2012 by Connor Court Publishing Pty Ltd.

Reprinted in 2025

Copyright © Frank Mount 2012, 2025

ALL RIGHTS RESERVED. This book contains material protected under International and Federal Copyright Laws and Treaties. Any unauthorized reprint or use of this material is prohibited. No part of this book may be reproduced or transmitted in any form or by any means, electronic or mechanical, including photocopying, recording, or by any information storage and retrieval system without express written permission from the publisher.

Connor Court Publishing Pty Ltd.
PO BOX 7257
REDLAND BAY QLD 4165

sales@connorcourt.com
www.connorcourt.com

ISBN: 9781923568112

Cover design by Ian James

Cover picture: Frank Mount in the Mekong Delta with a South Vietnamese riverine patrol

Printed in Australia

*This book is lovingly dedicated to my
immediate family
Eileen, Patrick and Lucy*

TABLE OF CONTENTS

Acknowledgements   v
Maps   vi, vii

Part One:

THE VIETNAM WAR and THE PACIFIC INSTITUTE

1. Introduction   3
2. Into Asia, 1967: *Manila, Saigon, Phnom Penh, Bangkok, Vientiane, Calcutta, Colombo, Singapore, Kuala Lumpur*   13
3. Round the Region Again: *Manila, Saigon, Bangkok, Songkhla, Penang, Kuala Lumpur, Singapore, Kuching, Jesselton, Manila*   57
4. Indonesia 1968   111
5. The PI Conference 1967   135
6. Back to Melbourne   139
7. On My Bike Again   155
8. The 1968 Tet Offensive and its Aftermath   163
9. The 1968 PI Conference and on to APEC 1989   183
10. Living in Saigon   201
11. Eight Scenarios   215
12. The Fall of Saigon   221
13. Life In Manila   229
14. From Manila to Melbourne   237

Part Two:

ADDENDA, VIGNETTES and ANECDOTES

1. The Burchett Case, Saigon and the CIA   245
2. The Beek Organisation in Indonesia   253
3. Ali Moertopo and Abu Bakar Bashir, 1978   265
4. The 1975 Invasion and 1999 Liberation of East Timor: Some Points   269
5. The Overthrow of Soeharto, May 21, 1998   279
6. With Ali Moertopo in Bandung   293
7. On the Cushions with Soedjono Hoemardani   297
8. Soeharto Visits Australia, 1972; A Brief for Soeharto   301
9. Flight to Phnom Penh   303
10. Whitlam, Khemlani and the CIA   307
11. Santamaria and Malcolm Fraser   311
12. A Champagne Breakfast with Lon Nol and Sirik Matak   317
13. My Take on the 1981 NCC Split   323
14. Asia Pacific Report and George Bush   325
15. For the Good Times   329
16. Jesuits in Asia   331
17. Two Adventures:
    I. "The Human Fly" Escapes in Bangkok   337
    II. A Pen-Pal "Bride"   341
18. Why I Parted Company with Santamaria   343

Select Bibliography   349

Photographs   129-134, 231-236

(All are from the Mount Collection unless otherwise stated)

Index   367

ACKNOWLEDGMENTS

I was encouraged to write this book by Patrick Morgan after he'd finished editing the first of his two books on B.A. Santamaria's documents. He suggested I should write about the Pacific Institute and the project expanded from there to a work of selected memoirs. Without his encouragement, and subsequent advice, there would be no book. Then a few years later, Connor Court Publishing's Anthony Cappello examined the manuscript and kindly and courageously agreed to publish it, with a few editorial adjustments, of course.

I'd like to thank Celia Parham for her invaluable professional editorial advice and suggestions, Ian James for his excellent and patient work in the cover design and the Connor Court proof readers and staff. I greatly appreciated their enthusiastic support. Many hours were spent checking the facts and dates in the book and all responsibility for their accuracy rests with me.

Finally, I'd like to thank my wife Eileen, who shared many of my experiences in Asia, and whose encouragement and patience also made it possible.

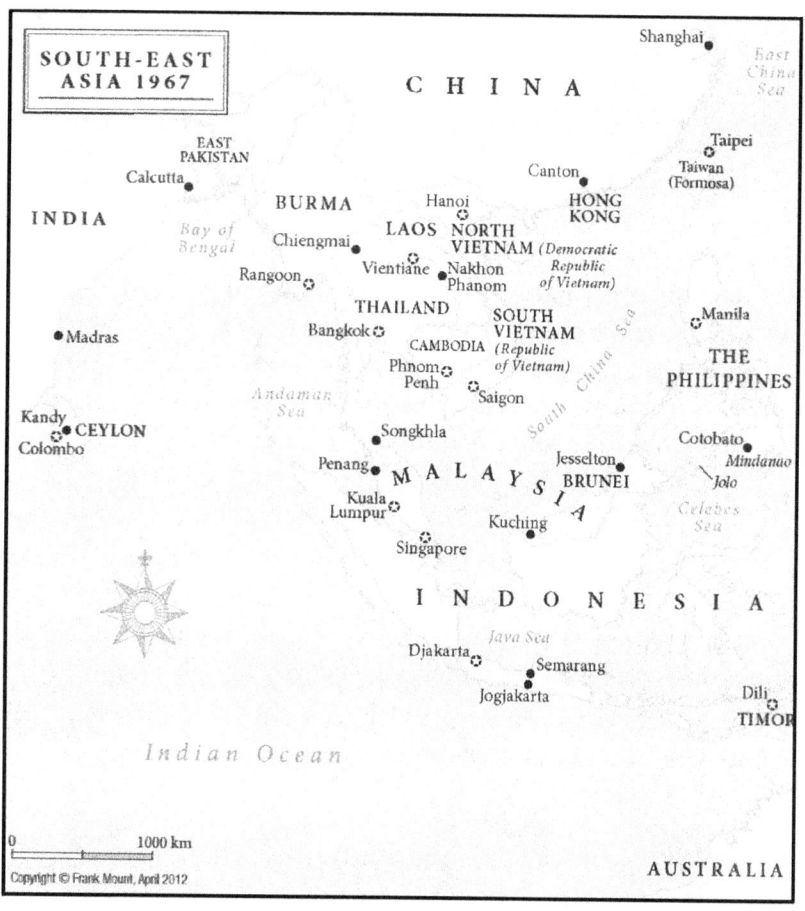

Map of South-East Asia 1967 by Demap (www.demap.com.au)

South Vietnam with provinces and Corps areas. Map courtesy of US Army Center of Military History.

PART ONE

The Vietnam War and the Pacific Institute

2

1
Introduction

I was born a city rat and a political animal with a voracious appetite for knowledge and a love for action in the world. At a very young age, between eight and twelve, I'd developed a romantic interest in Asian and international affairs and even intelligence matters because of the defections of Burgess and Maclean in the early fifties and British thriller movies of the time. This came from my reading newspapers from about eight years of age (my father said I'd get up at 6am, bring in the delivered papers and read the international articles) listening to radio news crackling in from places with exotic, musical names like Kuala Lumpur, Addis Ababa, Paris, Dubrovnik, Singapore, Hong Kong and Luang Prabang. I was James Bond before he was thought of.

There is, perhaps, no better place to start this memoir than from the day in February 1967 when Bob Santamaria, the head of the anti-communist National Civic Council (NCC), or "The Movement" as it was known, invited me to lunch at the venerable Latin Cafe in Melbourne and asked if I'd like to travel around Southeast Asia for a few months reporting to him on what was happening in the region, how we might better help our anti-communist friends there and promote his Pacific Community concept while writing articles for the NCC's *News Weekly* and any other publications I'd like to do a deal with. He said he had funding for this from a number of Melbourne businessmen and prominent NCC supporters.

From previous comments he had made to me, I understood that he trusted my political judgements from what he had observed of my political operations on the Melbourne University campus and within the Australian Democratic Labor Party (DLP) which at that time held the balance of power in the Australian Federal Parliament, I being a member of the DLP Victorian State Executive. He also knew that in my capacities as National Secretary of the Defend Australia Committee (DAC) and National President of the Wheat for India Campaign, I had already held foreign policy and political discussions with politicians and federal cabinet ministers at various places around Australia, Melbourne and the Mornington Peninsula. Along with that I had written over a number of years many articles for *News Weekly*, numerous research papers for Bob, while he, the NCC generally and I had worked together on many political operations including the DLP, the DAC and Wheat for India. So by 1967 Bob and I were close friends and political mates and it's worth keeping in mind that I was always a political activist and something of an international strategist long before I was a serious journalist.

Bob suggested I go away and think about his Southeast Asian proposal because, he said, it could change my life for ever. It could be a career-influencing matter, he said. But I didn't have to think about it and simply asked, "When do I start?" That turned out to be a couple of months later which saw me travelling around Southeast Asia for six months.

Bob had been aware in the early sixties of my passionate interest in Asia and heard from one of my friends that I had read every book on Southeast Asian history and politics I could lay my hands on by the age of 16. That interest in Asia, sparked romantically early, was intensified in my teens by the communist threat to the Western world and the region, widely seen by me and others as emanating from Russia and China. Bob also knew that I was a long-standing student of counter-insurgency and international conflict, and that I had travelled extensively in the Asian region at my own expense in late 1965-66 and again over Christmas in 1966-67, on both occasions spending a lot of time looking at the war in Vietnam, the Vietnamese themselves and their American 'colonisers'. He knew that I could handle myself in tight situations.

My first personal involvement with Asia, however, was an indirect one. Sometime in 1964, before I ever went overseas, Bob had asked me to help him obtain some financial and other support for some of "our friends" in Asia. Those he was most involved with at that time were based in the Philippines and Indonesia and included Senator Raul Manglapus, who ran the Philippine Christian Social Movement (CSM), Professor Jeremias Montemayor, who headed the Philippine Federation of Free Farmers (FFF) and a Dutch Jesuit in Indonesia, Fr. Joseph (Joop) Beek SJ, who trained and ran a network of political/intelligence cadres which I eventually called The Beek Organisation as it was otherwise nameless (see The Beek Organisation, Part II, Chapter 2). Bob had described these and other friends in the region as running similar sorts of anti-communist movements as his own National Civic Council. This exercise brought me into personal contact with a number of people I was to be involved with for years to come, including Manglapus himself who visited Melbourne in September 1966. We put on a dinner for the crew-cutted Raul in an upstairs private room at the Latin which enabled us to introduce him to a number of our own 'heavyweight' anti-communist intellectual colleagues and associates including the conservative Catholic poet James McAuley, DLP Senator Frank McManus, British economist Colin Clark, liberal Catholic poet Vincent Buckley, agnostic Jewish philosopher Frank Knopfelmacher and Indian agnostic Brahmin Professor of Indian Studies Sibnarayan Ray with the long term aim of improving our leverage with him in the Philippines.

Bob's Asian interests were cast within the context of a grand regional strategic approach centred on the concept of an Asia Pacific

Community or "confederation" which apart from promoting strategic regional co-operation along the lines of today's Association of South East Asian Nations (ASEAN) and APEC (Asia Pacific Economic Co-operation), involved promoting liberal democratic ideas, principles and institutions wherever possible. Bob had outlined his idea of a Pacific Community in an article titled "A Pacific Confederation" which appeared in the Summer 1962 issue of *Quadrant*. The following year, he and a Jesuit friend, W.G. 'Bill' Smith SJ, the Director of the Institute of Social Order, organised a Christian Social Week at Melbourne University around the theme of a Pacific Community, inviting some prominent academics to express their opinions about the idea. One of its invited critics was Dr. Herb Feith, a renowned expert on Indonesia at Monash University, who thought the very idea of regional co-operation to be naive and unrealistic and said so bluntly.

Early on, we saw that one of the strategic objectives of this Pacific Community was the protection of the sea lanes of communication (SLOCs), that is, the trade routes running though the Indonesian and South Pacific waterways connecting the Indian and Pacific oceans.

On a number of occasions from the early sixties on, I can remember standing with Bob in the front room of his office building in Hawthorn in Melbourne before a huge map of the world centred on Australia discussing regional and global strategic and security matters affecting Australia and the regional balance of power. I realised then that he had a good geo-strategic mind and a sound grasp of matters concerning Europe, the Mediterranean, the Persian Gulf and East and Southeast Asia.

As Australians on an island continent we both had a firm appreciation of the importance of Australia's trade routes running through the Indonesian waterways to Singapore, Japan and Europe and through the Pacific Islands to the US. We also realised that 90% of Japan and China's oil supplies flowed through these waterways and the South China Sea from the Middle East. Their protection, effected through co-operation with our allies, mainly the US, Japan, the UK and France, was seen by us to be a major objective. That, in turn, required a stable, peaceful and prosperous Southeast Asia which, we hoped, might be brought about through closer regional co-operation. It should be remembered that even in the mid-sixties Southeast Asia was still an unstable region containing mostly poor, developing nations leading many to believe that its future was bleak and the prospect of co-operation among its nations even bleaker. As late as 1970 the eminent Australian academic, Milton Osborne, wrote a book titled *Region of Revolt: Focus on Southeast Asia* (Pergamon Press, Australia 1970) about what he saw as the endemic and intractable instability and inter-nation conflict in the region.

The establishment of ASEAN in late 1967, and the support every nation in the region received through the sixties directly from the US, Japan, Taiwan and international bodies like the UN, the Asian Development Bank (ADB) and the World Bank – and indirectly from the Vietnam War because of the enormous amounts of money that flowed into the region because of that war – were to be major factors transforming the region from one of revolt and conflict to one of harmony and prosperity.

Standing before that map Bob and I also contemplated China. We knew that long ago in history it was the centre of the world and that we had all lived on the periphery. Even in the early sixties we knew it was coming again and while it was a totalitarian communist state our best approach was to bring it into the community of nations through some sort of regional mechanism. So, even then, both Bob and I were thinking about what was to become APEC, for that is and always has been one of APEC's primary strategic purposes.

At the end of 1967, following my first six month trip around the region for Bob, we formed the Pacific Institute at a conference in Manila to among other things promote the Pacific Community.

Attending this gathering was an illustrious group of Filipinos including Senator Raul Manglapus, Jerry Montemayor, Johnny Tan who led the Federation of Free Workers (FFW) and Fr. Horacio de la Costa SJ, one of the nation's leading historians, Indonesia's Fr. Beek SJ, who many people believed was a major force behind the strategy and grass roots structure of the Soeharto's Golkar Party, Dr. Colin Clark, one of the world's greatest economists and demographers, and South Vietnam's Ngo Khac Tinh, a future acting foreign minister and a Confucian cousin of President Nguyen Van Thieu. Tinh was to be my major partner in assisting the development of an important liberal social democratic party across South Vietnam called the Vietnam Nhan-Xa Cach Mang Dang or Vietnam Social Humanist Revolutionary Party (Nhan-Xa Party).

We all knew that central to the entire endeavour of encouraging regional co-operation and liberal democracy in the region was the war in Vietnam. It was central because the communist totalitarian threat it represented helped us unify the people we were bringing together across Southeast Asia. There was a two-sided operation here. On the one hand we were bringing our regional associates together to support the Vietnam War against communism, and on the other we were using the Vietnam War to bring Southeast Asian nations together for long term strategic, security and economic reasons. Whatever the war's ultimate outcome, and no one was ever sure, it bought us time to build institutions like ASEAN, just as it bought us time to defeat the PKI in Indonesia and contain threatening radical Islamic extremist forces in Indonesia and Malaysia.

In one of my early conversations in Saigon with the Australian Colonel Francis Philip 'Ted' Serong in 1967, the father of the 'infamous' Phoenix program, he told me of his now well known conversation with General Sir Walter 'Bill' Cawthorn, the Director General of the Australian Secret Intelligence Service (ASIS) in the Melbourne Club in 1964. Standing by the swimming pool in his CIA funded villa Serong told me that Cawthorn had said to him: "Get me ten years in Vietnam, Ted, and we'll build something in Southeast Asia". Cawthorn obviously had a great geopolitical-strategic mind which is what attracted Serong, Santamaria, and me, to him. Serong then said to me in his often hubristic style with a smile and a pat on my back: "I'll run the war, you run the politics, keep me informed, and build the regional Southeast Asian architecture."

Serong was casual with me in a way he wasn't with some others because the Serong, Mount, Santamaria, Maynes and some other families with a practical interest in Vietnam had known each other for decades in Melbourne, many of us attending the same schools. Despite our at times cuttingly real differences of temperament, education and 'profession', he being a senior soldier of repute and myself a young inexperienced civilian in a war zone, we intuitively understood each other to a considerable degree.

Supporting our efforts in Vietnam and against communist influence in Asia generally were a number of organisations we set up in Australia including the Congress for the Defence of Australia at Melbourne University in 1964 and later the Defend Australia Committee (DAC) in 1965. These organisations enabled us to participate in what became known as the Vietnam Debate. In the early sixties this had hardly begun but its nature was already predictable from the arguments coming out of people like Dr. Jim Cairns and other members of the pro-communist left that what was happening in South Vietnam was really just a civil war between US-supported neo-colonialists on the one hand and a liberating force of democratic nationalists and agrarian reformers on the other. North Vietnam and China, they said, had no involvement directly or indirectly. Communisn was not an issue. I had already appeared on Australian television programs like *Fighting Words* and *Four Corners* debating and discussing these very issues with Cairns and others.

In early 1966 we sought to broaden our efforts in Australia

with the establishment of a loosely knit, sometimes 'bohemian' grouping of academics and intellectuals called Peace with Freedom (PWF), through which we involved in the Vietnam debate, and other matters, a number of people not comfortable with the more highly organised DAC. Through the DAC and PWF we were able to feature an impressive array of speakers at seminars around Australia over the next six or seven years which were organised by hundreds of supporters of the South Vietnamese cause, the vast majority of them being members or associates of the NCC. Many of these speakers went from our seminars to appearing on national television programs and debates.

In support of this effort, I wrote a pamphlet arguing the case for the war titled *Vietnam* for the NCC which was published in June 1966 as a Supplement to *News Weekly*. It was commercially distributed through newsagents across the country and sold around 40,000 copies giving it one of the largest circulations of any political pamphlet ever written in Australia. It was also widely circulated among our friends in Asia, the US and Europe and was very well received everywhere.

So by the time I set out on my first trip for Bob on May 22, 1967, just before my 26th birthday, I already had a substantial network of contacts, even in places I hadn't been to before, and was reasonably well known in many circles. In those days you could buy a discounted 'open' around the region airline ticket as long as you kept "going forward" as they put it. That is, you could easily change dates, places and flights as long as you kept going forward. At my own discretion, and it was totally up to me where I went and when, I planned a six month trip that would take me around the region twice. The itinerary read Melbourne-Manila-Hong Kong-Saigon-Phnom Penh-Bangkok-Vientiane-Bangkok-Calcutta-Colombo-Singapore-Kuala Lumpur-Singapore-Manila-Saigon-Bangkok-Songkhla-Penang-Kuala Lumpur-Singapore-Manila-Melbourne. In the event, I added to this by visiting Songkhla between Bangkok and Penang, and Kuching and

Jesselton between Singapore and Manila at the end. It was designed to culminate in the first Pacific Institute conference in the Philippines in early-mid November. One of my many tasks was to persuade people to attend the conference as I travelled the region and to organise the conference itself. Part I is structured around this 1967 trip casting backwards and forwards in time in each city or country as seems appropriate and a lot of it is based on my diaries and reports to Bob Santamaria.

So there I was about to set out on a mission to Asia which would take me through the humid war zones of Vietnam, Laos and Cambodia, the guerrilla-infested areas of Thailand, Malaysia and the Philippines and the exotic capital cities across the region. I was totally my own boss. Bob Santamaria had in effect handed me a bag full of money and simply said "go and report". No one oversaw my mission and activities in any shape or form. I was totally free to do as I liked, and once I stepped on the plane was almost incommunicado. My major responsibilities were to write articles for *News Weekly* and any other publications I liked; to send Bob Santamaria even more detailed and highly confidential reports on the region; to advance the ideas of the Pacific Community regional co-operation concept; to support liberal democratic organisations everywhere; and to do whatever else I thought appropriate in Australia's interest as Bob and his friend Cawthorn put it. I couldn't get there fast enough.

2
Into Asia, 1967

MANILA

Sowing Seeds

I arrived from Melbourne on a Qantas 707 and booked into the old Filipinas Hotel on the bayside strip then called Dewey Boulevard and today Roxas Boulevard. I spent every day of a three week visit making appointments and talking with as many politicians, political activists, journalists, trade unionists and others of a social or Christian democratic persuasion as I could. As well as Manglapus, Tan and Montemayor, who helped me with introductions to many people, they included a couple of legendary Jesuit backroom operators, Francisco Araneta and the famed historian Horacio de la Costa who was to become, like Tan and Manglapus, an important member of the Pacific Institute.

Before flying out to Hong Kong on Friday, June 9th, I had long sessions with Manglapus and Tan the day before. We discussed at length the need for a good social democratic party or movement in the Philippines. We also talked about the need for greater regional co-operation. One of the Philippines' problems was that it always looked strategically east across the Pacific to the United States, its former colonial overlord. I, and quite a few Americans in fact, constantly tried to encourage the Filipinos to look west and south to their Asian neighbours. Manglapus, fortunately, did not need much encouragement in this regard as he had played a significant role when he was acting foreign secretary (that is acting foreign minister), under President Diosdado Macapagal, in the formation of Maphilindo, linking Malaysia, the Philippines and Indonesia. However, Manglapus' interest was limited because he looked mainly not to the US or Southest East Asia but to Europe where he hankered after the German Christian Democrats.

If this sounds confusing, it was, because the good-looking, charismatic Manglapus was himself confused. Like his fellow Jesuit-trained political activists Tan and Montemayor, he was at heart a social democrat, or at least sounded like one policy-wise, but he preferred to move in more 'cultured', elite and wealthy Christian circles in Manila where his strange 'Boston-style' accent was more acceptable. He was all for land reform and workers' rights, but personal involvement with trade unions and rural barrios was not for him. He was never sure what he was or what he wanted. But on regional co-operation he was, on balance, a plus. As we shall see later, at this very time our Indonesian friends, closely associated with President Soeharto and his assistant Major General Ali Moertopo, were working hard with their Malaysian associates led by Tan Sri Ghazali Shafie, the head of the Foreign Affairs Department, to foster stronger regional co-operation and later in the year were largely responsible for the creation of the fledgling ASEAN in Kuala Lumpur in August of that year, 1967. No one knew how long it could last, or what could be built from it. But more then 40 years later it's still going strong, performing central strategic functions. Many other pieces of regional economic and strategic architecture, including PECC (Pacific Economic Co-operation Council), ARF (ASEAN Regional Forum), APEC (Asia Pacific Economic Co-operation) and most recently EAS (East Asia Summit) have been built from it. APEC and EAS would never have come into existence without ASEAN.

SAIGON

Serong and the Phoenix Program

It's a magical place – or was to me in the sixties. I don't know it well enough today to say how much it has changed, but a recent visit suggests that despite the old Marxist oppressors its real heart still beats.

When I arrived on the June 19, 1967, I was met at Tan Son Nhat airport by Tran Van Lam, a former ambassador to Australia where I'd first met him and by the year's end to be President of the Senate, and an Australian Army major sent separately by the ever reliable Colonel Ted Serong. On many future occasions, Ted would meet me himself with a folder of recent newspaper cuttings and numerous reports of varying security classifications including "Top Secret" to, in his words, "bring me up to date on current political and military developments". I always greatly appreciated that.

Lam and the major delivered me to the wonderful old downtown French colonial Continental Palace Hotel, where, as it turned out, I was to spend many weeks, if not months, over the next eight years. The next evening I dined with Serong at one of his favourite cosy French restaurants, Romuncho, which was owned by former general Ton That Dinh, a man he disliked, even hated, because he had been a leader of the coup against Ngo Dinh Diem in 1963, but whose food Serong approved. We were shortly joined, although very briefly, by Colonel Algernon Montague 'Monty' Rodulfo, a stocky, slightly overweight and moustachioed West Indian-born very British Army and MI6 officer who had been seconded to Serong by the British.

Monty and I hit it off immediately and we were to be friends for many years until he died of a heart attack one day in August 1971 in a dirty dingy flat in Hong Kong's Wanchai district escaping Vietnam demons. (These were not of his own making as they were to do with corruption involving some high level US military officers which he'd discovered while conducting an operation for Serong). The next day, on Ted's instructions to "save you money", Monty moved me out of the Continental into one of "Ted's" Police Field Force (PFF) apartments just below his own in a four story apartment building up a narrow, dead end lane a stone's throw from the Dakao bridge, made famous in Graham Greene's novel *The Quiet American*. On the ground floor below me was the fledgling, unofficial office of the controversial Phoenix Progam which Serong had created and at that time ran as part of the overall Pacification Program.

On many days, I lunched with Monty whose favourite restaurant was a comfortable old Castillion joint called Le Castel right below the apartment in which Graham Greene lived on Tu Do Street, now called Dong Khoi and in Greene's day Rue Catinat. When Saigon fell in 1975 these and many other French and European restaurants, run in many cases by the Corsican mafia, simply disappeared. As my reports to Santamaria show, I formed the opinion after talking to countless people on the political scene that South Vietnam lacked even one soundly based civilian political party remotely capable of ruling the country. So we put our minds together and directed our resources to rectifying that. If grappling with Philippine politics was like wading though a dog's breakfast, South Vietnam's was like trying to grab hold of a jellyfish and sometimes a spiked one if you can imagine any such thing existing.

* * *

At this point, I can see some readers in Australia and elsewhere asking who are these men Santamaria and Serong? What are their backgrounds? Where did they come from?

Well, they both came from Melbourne and for a time went to school together. And both their families were well known to my family, to my father in particular who knew both of their fathers. But there is no need to go back that far in any detail in this book. For the purposes of this book, which is an international story, Bob Santamaria was the President of the National Civic Council, an overwhelmingly Catholic anti-communist organisation which within Australia helped organise groups to fight communist power in the trade unions and elsewhere and was consequently the backbone of the Democratic Labor Party (DLP) which was created following a major split in the mid-fifties in the Australian Labor Party (ALP) over the issue of communist influence in the latter (See Robert Murray, *The Split: Australian Labor in the Fifties*, F.W. Cheshire Publishing, Melbourne, 1970). The NCC was by far the most effective anti-communist, liberal democratic organisation or movement in the country which is why I joined up with it.

The young Santamaria's initial interest in socio-political matters was fired, like mine, by the social papal encyclicals which led him into the field of Catholic Action and opposition to the excesses of capitalism and the totalitarianism of both communism and Nazism. This in turn sparked a concern with international politics and strategic affairs which went naturally with his almost innate interest in Italian and European affairs. A cosmopolitan and chubby Italian intellectual with a yen for political action, he was compared by Frank Knopfelmacher to the Christian democratic European statesmen Alcide de Gasperi, Robert Schumann and Konrad Adenauer. (For more on Santamaria see Patrick Morgan (Ed.), *B.A. Santamaria, Your Most Obedient Servant; Select Letters: 1938-1996*, The Miegunyah Press, Melbourne 2007 and Patrick Morgan (Ed.), *B.A. Santamaria, Running The Show; Select Documents: 1939-1996*, The Miegunyah Press, Melbourne, 2008).

The young compact Ted Serong always wanted to be a soldier and in the end became one of Australia's finest. He was the founder of the Australian Army's modern Jungle Training Centre at Canungra in Queensland and there, with a well selected band of fellow officers, including Lt. Col. George Warfe and Major Frederick Lomas, developed the renowned counter-guerrilla and counter-insurgency techniques and practices that proved so successful in Malaya and other places, including Iraq during the 2007 'surge'. The US Commander in Iraq, General David Petreaus, had the benefit of the advice of Australia's Colonel David Kilcullen, who is extremely well versed in these Australian techniques and practices.

In the late fifties and from 1960 to early 1962, Serong was posted to Burma advising the Burmese Army on counter-insurgency. Not only were the Burmese impressed, so were Rangoon-based CIA officers and as a result the US asked for him to be sent to South Vietnam to be seconded to the CIA as an Australian colonel to advise the CIA and the US command on jungle warfare matters. Out of this grew Ted's idea of the Australian Army Training Team Vietnam (AATTV) to advise CIA forces and South Vietnamese units such as the Popular and Regional Forces on counter-insurgency. Serong was its first commander. He personally selected the initial 30 members of this force and after it arrived in South Vietnam in August 1962, he placed them around South Vietnam following hard fought discussions with the Americans and South Vietnamese. The AATTV, which would eventually deploy nearly a thousand Australian military advisors and commanders in South Vietnam, was to become one of Australia's most remarkable military units and the most highly decorated. Before long, Serong's time was largely consumed in Saigon personally advising the US Commander General Paul Harkins, the Ambassador Frederick Nolting and his successor Henry Cabot Lodge, the CIA command and South Vietnamese generals. He was relieved of his direct AATTV command in late 1964. Four books in particular illuminate Serong's effort and influence in Vietnam: in chronological order of publication they are Anne Blair, *There to the Bitter End: Ted Serong in Vietnam*, Allen and Unwin, Sydney, 2001; Anne Blair, *Ted Serong: The Life of an Australian Counter-Insurgency Expert*, Oxford University

Press, 2002; Bruce Davies and Gary McKay, *The Men Who Persevered*, Allen & Unwin, 2005; and Paul Ham, *Vietnam: The Australian War*, Harper Collins, 2007. In August 1968, at the age of 52, he took early retirement from the Australian Army and was promoted to the rank of brigadier. In a chapter devoted to Serong, Paul Ham describes him as among the most powerful and influential people in the CIA in Saigon and Vietnam right through until at least the 1968 Tet Offensive. Australian journalist Kate Webb, who covered Vietnam as a war correspondent for United Press International (UPI) and whom I had known from my Melbourne University days, and who saw Serong at close quarters and under great pressure during both the 1968 Tet Offensive and the fall of Saigon in 1975, described him as the "toughest, calmest and most courageous man under fire". He was just "tough, tough, tough", she said to me after the war.

Blair's books are based on Serong's diaries for he was quite old and his memory failing badly when she interviewed him for the book. He had no recollection at all for example of Kate Webb or of another journalist, the novelist, Robert Elegant, whom he knew well. Nowhere in her book, nor I suspect the diaries, am I mentioned, which is quite extraordinary. But, then, as with Webb and Elegant, neither were many other people who had significant dealings with him, mainly Australians, but also some extremely important Vietnamese figures (and Vietnamese organisations like the Nhan-Xa Party). In fact, unlike Ham's book, little is said about the activities of Australian military forces and individuals in South Vietnam and nothing at all about our political activities even though I regularly briefed him about them. In the early seventies we made him, at his request, Chairman of the Saigon branch of the Pacific Institute so that he might have even better access to certain elements in the Saigon elite. I not only attended every branch meeting, I organised most of them.

It seems that Ted's diaries were a rough record of his encounter with the US in Vietnam, and in this he was illuminating. He didn't like Americans, believing himself to have had some sort of Franco-Irish origin, the name Serong deriving from the French Seron. (He was actually of Portuguese descent). It seems his Saigon diaries were largely concerned with his meetings with the Americans in Vietnam and the infighting that went on between their various agencies about, as he put it, overall control of the war or parts of it. This saw battles for control of the war between the White House, the Pentagon, the State Department, the US Ambassador in Saigon, the US Commander in Vietnam, the CIA, MACV (US Military Assistance Command Vietnam, that is US Army Headquarters), Cords (US Civilian Operations and Revolutionary Development Support), and so on. As he said to me on one occasion, "If they fought the enemy as well as they fight among themselves, we'll win the war".

Despite what he said publicly, he was always pessimistic about the outcome of the war. This was not because of the bureaucratic infighting, but because of America's lack of jungle warfare experience and general counter-insurgency expertise. He was appalled at the way they fought the war, substituting firepower for strategic thought. Complicating matters, as he pointed out at more than one Pacific Institute conference, was the fact, to which I can personally attest, that the US army at the time was thoroughly drug-ridden, racially divided and its command in the field seriously corrupt in part. In his judgement, it could hardly put one effective division into the field. (It should be said that none of these things are true of the US military today). Despite all of that, Ted insisted that the US never lost the war militarily against the North Vietnamese (and it had been the North Vietnamese, not the VC, from the very start, as Ham clearly reveals, backed by 300,000 People's Liberation Army (PLA) Chinese troops in North Vietnam). In his view, and mine, it was lost politically in Washington as a consequence of Watergate which paralysed the US administrative and military bureaucracies thoroughly undermining Henry Kissinger's admittedly seriously flawed but otherwise adequate 1972 Paris Agreement.

***

During my two weeks in Serong's Dakao flat I met an array of interesting characters hired by Serong to advise his creations the Police Field Force (PFF) and the Phoenix Program and who, once again, are either not mentioned at all or just in passing in the books on Serong. Two of these characters, a roughly elegant English rake, Lionel Hitchcock, and the overly neat Anglo-Burmese ex-Burmese Army officer, Patrick Pohla, were professional assassins. Of Pohla, Serong said he had never known anyone who could kill as efficiently with his bare hands. Hitchcock, he said, preferred a knife or a garrote. These two assassins were major advisors to the Phoenix Program which I will say more about later rather than now in the interests of the Pacific Institute's regional co-operation narrative. It suffices to say at this stage that despite its bad reputation in the Western Press, Phoenix was an essential part of any sound counter-insurgency program against the VC infrastructure (VCI). Paul Ham in his book claims that Serong was Phoenix, but this is a vast exaggeration, for having created it, it took on a US and ARVN life of its own. What is certain is that not only was Phoenix an essential counter-insurgency (CI) tool against a ruthless, cruel and bloodthirsty enemy which like Pol Pot in Cambodia indiscriminately killed teachers, doctors, nurses, local officials and mothers in villages every night, it was an integral, if not controlling, part of the overall successful Pacification/Vietnamisation process. (One AATTV officer is on record as saying that VC atrocities regularly and commonly involved night-time torturing, beheading and disembowelling to sow fear among the people.)

The North Vietnamese understood the value and effectiveness of Phoenix telling journalist/historian Stanley Karnow after the war that Phoenix inflicted more damage on the VC/NVA complex that anything else (see Stanley Karnow, *Vietnam, A History: The First Complete Account of Vietnam at War*, The Viking Press, New York, 1983, pp 602-603). That alone places Ted Serong as one of Australia's greatest and most effective military leaders. I took the opportunity of talking with Pohla and Hitchcock as often as I could in the hope of learning something about the mind of an assassin. I didn't learn much but came to the conclusion that they were people of little or no substance. They didn't believe in anything. The pathetic, mumbling Hitchcock had no views on anything. Neither of them ever read a newspaper or a book. They were morose, alienated people. They were also regular patrons of a sleazy girly bar down the road called the Purple Cow and kept bringing back to the flat a line of not very attractive uneducated girls wearing plain Western blouses and the then fashionable feet-hugging stirrup slacks. Monty held them in contempt. I kept a few notes and tried to use their characters in an unpublished novel of mine in the eighties.

The people in the comfortable but basic Dakao apartment could be split, perhaps, into two vaguely distinguishable groups: those training Phoenix counter terror cadre, including Pohla and Hitchcock, and those advising the PFF among them Rodulfo, Commander Tommy Wright, formerly of the Burmese Navy, and two retired Australian commandos from the Canungra Jungle Training Centre, Colonel George Warfe and Major Fred Lomas. Monty had an additional function: to collect Intelligence on the Chinese community in Cholon and its knowledge of local communist activity as he had long experience in the field elsewhere. He spoke Chinese languages fluently having been a UK Foreign Service specialist in Yunnan, the south-west province of China. He maintained a close liaison with Taiwanese Intelligence in Saigon and to further aid his mission, he took up with a quite delightful, highly cultured Chinese mistress who held degrees in Chinese literature and history. She came and stayed with him often, while her family lived in Cholon. He'd been in and out of Vietnam since 1947; had fought in Burma and Malaya; and had operated as a British Secret Intelligence Service (SIS, i.e., MI6) agent in Cuba, Norway and India and probably other places. I came to regard very highly his knowledge of Intelligence and counter-insurgency and ranked him second only behind Serong. He was a cultured gentleman, widely read in history and anthropology and a dab hand with a paint brush. At one time or another in the Vietnam War, all of these officers, including Serong, could be described as mercenaries.

When Monty showed me into my bedroom, he pointed to a double-barrelled combination rifle/shotgun standing in a corner and said in his neat clipped British accent which matched his equally neatly clipped moustache: "Always keep it loaded and ready for action. The wardrobe is full of ammunition. This is war. We are the PFF and below us is the Phoenix office which Ted also runs. The enemy knows this. Keep the door locked when you go to bed. After dinner, I'll come back and have a sherry with you." I was to remember this when in February the next year the NVA/VC struck with the Tet Offensive and thousands of 'guerrillas' streamed over the Dakao bridge and up the lane to attack the apartment. The ensuing battle went on for days, but all of my mates, if not the apartment block, somehow miraculously survived.

The day after moving into the flat, Monty, Patrick Pohla and I, all of us well armed with automatic weapons, drove out in a green and white PFF jeep to Cu Chi to inspect a number of PFF outposts in the area. They seemed to be happy with what they saw, but the Vietnamese PFF looked like an uninterested, unhappy rabble to me, as I reported to both Serong and Santamaria. As we know, if only from the Ham book, countless millions of South Vietnamese were caught between being loyal to the South Vietnamese Government (GVN) and the nightly terror of the VC/NVA. The test came in the Tet Offensive of February 1968. Hanoi expected that the South Vietnamese population would rise up and overthrow the South Vietnamese regime. But they didn't, they backed Saigon and the VC was totally destroyed forever.

*　*　*

While staying at the flat I would walk all over town through graceful tree lined streets spoiled only by the blue pollution of loud, heavy US Army vehicles churning through the city. After dawn I would knock on the doors of various people I wanted to talk to – politicians, journalists, diplomats, generals and knowledgable Jesuits while in the Wagnerian political background Air Vice-Marshal Nguyen Cao Ky and General Nguyen Van Thieu tussled for control of the country with the cunning, Catholic Thieu ultimately winning out (see my Reports to Santamaria, Frank Mount Papers). Among the many people I met up with, thanks I think to Serong, was the erudite Malaysian charge d'affaires Jack de Silva who was of Malaccan Portuguese descent. At out first meeting, we hit it off immediately and after more than a few Johnny Walkers and a good meal we headed downtown. As we were about to drive into red light district so to speak, he carefully instructed the driver of his embassy Mercedes to wrap up the Malaysian flag that was fluttering on the front mudguard. This was the beginning of a long and very pleasant and rewarding friendship over many years. Later that same year, he was to introduce me, in his Saigon colonial residence, to a then largely unknown Indonesian Colonel named Benny Moerdani who was staying with him. Moerdani was then a very low key charge d'affaires at the Indonesian embassy in Kuala Lumpur.

Among Moerdani's tasks was to report on Vietnam and Cambodia to Brig. Gen. Ali Moertopo, then the Deputy Head of BAKIN (the Indonesian State Intelligence Co-ordinating Board) and the Head of the Army's Special Operations organisation (OPSUS). Indonesia had no diplomatic relations with South Vietnam so Moerdani secretly entered South Vietnam, with the knowledge of the Vietnamese authorities, and stayed with de Silva. I knew more about them all than they thought, and in time they were all to become associates of mine, having an input, directly or indirectly, into the Pacific Institute over the years. Imperceptibly, I was already beginning to build what was to become a remarkable network throughout the region. Concerning Moerdani and the Malaysian link, de Silva explained over a few drinks that Malaysia would always, in the end, follow Indonesia. Indonesia, he said, was the leading nation of Southeast Asia. This gave Indonesian generals like Soeharto and Ali Moertopo and now Moerdani great influence in the region if only through the military networks and in fact there was lot more commercially, diplomatically and politically. These generals had their own personal appointees in embassies and other places throughout the region who reported back to them personally and not to the Foreign Affairs, Defence or Trade departments which might officially employ them. This observation held me in good stead for at least a couple of decades.

Before I flew out of Saigon for Phnom Penh I had a few sessions with Tran Van Lam and other friendly political figures including Bishop (later Cardinal) Franciscus Xaverius Nguyen Van Thuan, a nephew of the slain President Ngo Dinh Diem, Ngo Khac Tinh, a cousin of President Thieu and later a cabinet minister, and Truong Cong Cuu a former leader of the Can Lao Party. Apart from seeking their views on current developments including the capabilities of President Thieu and his new cabinet, we spoke about the future and the need to build a new grass roots political party and, as in the Philippines, we said we'd work on it and talk about it again when I returned later in the year. This was to be the beginning of the Vietnam Nhan-Xa Cach Mang Dang (Vietnam Social Humanist Revolutionary Party) or Nhan-Xa Party which I would be intimately involved with for a number of years, visiting its branches throughout the country. (None of these Vietnamese seem to have been mentioned in any significant way in Ted's diaries).

PHNOM PENH

Sihanouk's Pleasure

I landed in Phnom Penh on July 11th but wasn't allowed into the country. I was told that while Australian tourists didn't need visas, my Australian passport said I was a journalist and they needed special and personal approval from Prince Sihanouk before they could enter. And sure enough every Australian passport in those days carried inside the front cover a notation as to one's occupation and other matters. They said I had to get back on the plane. Luckily, it was a Thai International flight going on to Bangkok and not Aeroflot going to Moscow. I reported this back to Bob Santamaria in Melbourne who contacted his friends in Canberra and from that day to this you won't find occupations listed in a Commonwealth passport. So the charms of Phnom Penh and Cambodia had to wait another day until well after I'd been required to write to Prince Sihanouk through the Cambodian embassy a disgustingly obsequious letter humbly requested a special visa and he'd replied inviting me to enjoy his personal hospitality during the next Water Festival. Such is the reign of princes!

BANGKOK and THAILAND

Rescuing John Myint

Apart from writing articles and reports on what I thought was happening politically, economically and militarily wherever I went, and reading magazines like the *Far Eastern Economic Review* to know what questions to ask, which I did late into the night every night, I had a special private mission when I arrived in steamy Bangkok on July 11. This was to rescue Captain Kaw Swa 'John' Myint, a 38 year old Burmese Army intelligence officer, from the claws of that socialist tyrant General Ne Win, the President of Burma in Rangoon. Myint had been Ne Win's Aide d'Camp and favourite 'son'. But Myint had decided that the Burman general and his gang were leading the country down the drain, treating ethnic minorities like dirt and ripping the nation off financially while they spent much of the year in England enjoying themselves at the Ascot races during the day and John Profumo style Gaslight bars in the evenings. So John and a few of his friends decided in mid-1965 that they would overthrow Ne Win by assassinating him. They failed badly and luckily escaped into the hills north of Rangoon.

I was on this mission to rescue John because of his vivacious and much younger sister Terry. I had known her for years as a student at Melbourne University and as a regular attendee at the Asian Student Centre in Melbourne, run by friends of Santamaria's and where Bob and I occasionally gave lectures. She was also attracted to the NCC itself because it was anti-communist, pro-democracy and by extension anti-Ne Win. One day in late 1965 she told me what her brother had done and that he was now stuck in the mountains with the Karennis near the Thai border. She asked if I could help get him out to Melbourne. At the time I had no idea what that might involve and I knew little of the Karennis. But that soon changed and a week later we were in discussion about the matter with Bob Santamaria and DLP Senator Frank McManus and through them with various people in the Australian government and its intelligence agencies. It was decided that we'd try to get John out. This was not only because of a desire to help Terry's family but because it was thought that John might bring with him some very valuable intelligence concerning Ne Win's modus operandi, palace intrigue, the Burmese Army's foreign operations and other matters. Bob clearly saw that if this was successful, it would boost his reputation and leverage with some senior Liberal Party ministers and senior foreign policy and intelligence bureaucrats in Canberra and Melbourne. As a first step towards our objective I made a special visit in early 1966 to Bangkok and the northern mountain town of Chiengmai to talk with people in indirect contact with John through Catholic Church and Shan State Army people to tell him to come across the border to Chiengmai where he would be protected by the Thai authorities. No one had any confidence in this, but it was the only way to go. Eventually he came, and as he told me eighteen months later he was nearly killed by a bunch of hired Thai killers.

So here I was now to contact him in Bangkok, arriving one week early, thanks to being put back on the plane in Phnom Penh, with no idea how to go about it or even where he might be. I arrived in Bangkok on July 11th, just under a week ahead of schedule. At the airport I booked into a city hotel which I knew quite well. At about 8pm in the evening I thought I would go for a stroll along the street. I had just walked out onto the footpath and was about to make my way across the road when I heard a voice shouting to me 'hey you", "hey you". I looked around and saw a chap half-running towards me from amongst the dozen or so taxis and other operators who usually accumulate around cosmopolitan Asian hotels. He had a prodigious lump on his right jaw. He said to me in broken English, "You want to see my friend John?"

I said, "Who?"

"My friend John."

I asked him, "John who?'

He said some name I didn't understand and I replied, "Don't know him". (Had he said the right name I had no intention of giving any indication it meant anything to me. If he represented anybody, it was an extremely clumsy approach. I suspected him when he was ten yards away.)

He continued the conversation, "You come from Saigon?"

I said, "Yes".

The conversation lapsed for a few seconds, we just looked at one another and then he said, "We go to dinner". I told him I had already eaten.

He then asked if I would like a nice girl. I politely declined, told him he had the wrong man, and casually walked back into the hotel. Actually, I felt like quickening the pace as the two figures I could just see converging behind me towards the hotel door were, as far as I was concerned, potential enemies. In fact, they were American tourists.

Once inside the hotel, I thought over the incident. Was he really one of John's friends, which was hard to believe; was he a Burmese agent who thought I might know John's whereabouts; or was he simply a pimp or propositioner with a rather unique approach?

If he was one of John's friends, I would be contacted again through an address I had given him via his sister in Melbourne and her network. So I was not concerned about that.

However, if he was a Burmese agent, how did he know I was coming and that I was staying at this particular hotel? They couldn't possibly have someone watching every hotel in Bangkok and asking every foreign tourist who came from Saigon whether he wanted to see 'John'.

Later on in the evening I went back onto the street to see if the fellow was still there. He had gone. I did not really think it was likely he was a Burmese agent, even a clumsy one, but decided to take precautions anyway.

The next morning I rang a good contact of mine, Leck Vanich Angkhul, a Muslim member of the Thai Senate and asked if he could arrange accommodation for me at a quiet, relatively cheap, out-of-the-way little place that I knew he was connected with called the Tung Mahamek Guesthouse. A quarter of an hour later his chauffer-driven Mercedes picked me up and I headed off into obscurity.

A week later, it took Thai Intelligence three days to find me. On Tuesday 18th, I had dinner with Alice, a Thai girl who had studied in Melbourne and whose address I had sent to John. She told me that the previous afternoon a Thai gentlemen, driving a Mercedes Benz, had called at her rather palatial house enquiring after me. Alice was not at home. He said he would call again and left his name and address. I had never heard of him and was uncertain as to who he might be and what he might represent. I did not know at that stage that John was under permanent Thai protection. I could do nothing else but to tell Alice to let him know where I was living should he call again.

The next morning I had some friends check out the name and address he had left. It was false. I then decided to go to see a number of people including the young and beautiful Princess Ying, an exiled Shan member of royalty, on the chance that she might be in contact with John. She'd heard, along with some others I spoke with, that he was under Thai government protection.

I now knew that the fellow looking for me was most likely from Thai Intelligence. However, I could not be certain. He eventually found me through Alice on Thursday 20th and came to see me at Tung Mahamek on the same day. He said his name was Peter which I didn't believe. From the manner of our introduction it seemed he had seen either me or my photograph before. The latter turned out to be the case as he had checked my 'immigration' file which he claimed held newspaper articles on and by me featuring my photograph. He said that 'the boss' had told him to find me and arrange a date for a meeting with John. He wouldn't tell me who the boss was and he was reluctant to tell me where he himself came from. Eventually, he told me he was from the Special Branch of the CID and upon request produced a card in Thai with his photograph on it. This didn't mean very much to me. He said he had been instructed simply to find me. As he had not been told to tell me anything, he was hesitant to do so. When he left I still had a few doubts in my mind.

On the day of the arranged meeting he picked me up in the early evening and we drove off into a dark, rainy night. I was uneasy about it and left a message at the guesthouse that if I didn't return by midnight for them to contact the Australian Embassy. In answer to my questions Peter told me his real name was Pisak, that 'the boss' was General Chat Chavangkul, the head of Special Branch, and the name of the street where the boss lived which was where I was to meet John. On top of this he said he had never met John and did not know who he was. All of this was probably true, but it hardly did anything to remove the tension and few remaining doubts I had as to his bona fides.

I was not completely happy until I was alone with John and we began our conversation. As this was held in an annex to the general's home, it may have been taped. If so, nothing could have been done to avoid it and in any case we did not say anything to cause concern. When I walked in John was seated at an ornate table in the middle of the room with some papers in front of him. He stood up, welcomed me with a handshake and asked me in excellent English to sit down at the table. He was a good-looking Eurasian of medium height and build and we looked cautiously at each other. He was unsure of me and I'd never been in this situation before. There was fear and uncertainty in his soft brown eyes. I spoke quietly to him saying something about Terry and reassuring him that we were doing everything possible to get him to Australia. He spoke even more softly, his round face and short cropped hair nodding in appreciation. He said he was staying here in the general's annexe where he had a nice bedroom and was being well fed and looked after. But he said he was very anxious to move out and asked if I could pass this on to Terry and others. Until now he had had no contact with any of Terry's friends. He said while the general was good to him, he'd been here for months now and with a shake of his head and fine hands said he feared the general might lose patience and do something drastic to get rid of him. I asked John very quietly about Ne Win and the coup attempt, but he shook his head scribbling "not here" on a pad in front of him. He spoke about his months with the Karennis which he enjoyed greatly. But when he came over to Chiengmai he didn't feel as comfortable. He stayed in a small Catholic convent where he was supposed to be under the protection of the Thai Special Branch. One day he had just walked out of the convent when he spotted four riders on two motorcycles coming towards him. His instinct told him this was danger and he ran into the house of a local parishioner, just getting in the door as the bullets hit the house. (I was later to discover in Australia that he had unbelievable powers of observation and memory). Towards the end of our meeting I expected him to give me a letter or something for Terry, but for some reason he didn't. As he escorted me to the door he shook my hand and thanked me, his eyes looking straight into mine saying please do something.

The Myint saga was to go on for months, with my meeting him many times, usually in the general's home, before we got him to Australia in July the following year. The delay was caused by Australian bureaucratic ineptitude and probably hostility, despite high level approaches to the Liberal Party cabinet ministers involved. As the months ticked by the general became increasingly impatient and John relayed to me through secret contacts that he feared he might dump him in the Chao Prya River. Suddenly in late June 1968 the general produced a Laotian passport with John's photograph in it under a false name along with a genuine Australian visa stamped inside, presumably issued by some corrupted or planted member in the Australian embassy. This shook up the Australians and within days they issued a Certificate of Identity to John which enabled us to have him put on a plane to Melbourne. There, the various Australian intelligence and other agencies, having done little or nothing to help him, were all over him like a rash, debriefing him for days. He also told me about the coup plan which, as far as I could understand it, given the local logistical circumstances, was hopeless. It was a pity for him and the future of Burma that he never had a chance to discuss it with people like Serong or Patrick Pohla. Had he succeeded at that time, he might have saved Burma a lot of pain. He moved into a bedroom in my parents' house where I lived when in Melbourne and one way or another stayed there for a couple of years. After he moved out and began studying at La Trobe University he introduced me on a blind date at the Windsor Hotel to a pretty student named Eileen Gleeson who was later to become my wife.

The day after my first meeting with John, I flew to Chiengmai which in those days had little electricity and no traffic lights. There I met up with some of John's friends in the Shan State Army and was able to do a useful assessment of the insurgencies in the region on and over the Thai-Burmese border. I was also brought up to date on the local opium poppy trade by Australia's David Wilson at the Tribal Research Centre and remade my acquaintance with a former British consul, Donald Gibson. Gibson was one of the great characters of my time in Asia. A stocky hunchback with an insatiable thirst for Scotch whisky he had retired to the outskirts of Chiengmai with a harem of surprisingly unattractive young Thai girls. However, while he might drink half a bottle of scotch before dinner and try to get you to do the same, his knowledge of regional insurgencies, politics and tribal conflicts was unsurpassed and I listened carefully. He also had a private aircraft which he used to fly lobsters from Hong Kong into the black markets of Laos, Thailand and Burma and occasionally to carry friends to Bangkok for golf parties.

I took an overnight train back to Bangkok and a few days later another to Ubol Ratchathani, a little town way out east on the flat, dry and hot Korat Plateau. Apart from there being an incipient insurgency in the region, the US had at least three or four airbases there at places like Ubol, Udorn Thani, and Nakhon Phanom engaged in reconnaissance and rescue missions over Vietnam, Laos and Cambodia. On the train from Bangkok I met an American in a dark suit in the bar-restaurant who said he was selling drink and pinball machines to the bases. While he fanned himself in the humidity, we had a few drinks together before retiring to bed. If you're ever tempted to try Thailand's Mekong whisky, don't. They run the trains on it. The next morning my suited, beautifully groomed friend met me over breakfast and said he'd had a terrible night. He explained that when he got to his steamy, hot, grimy compartment, there were a few mosquitoes buzzing about. Before getting on the bed naked and turning out the lights he thoroughly sprayed the room with insecticide for fear of getting malaria. In the early hours of the morning he awoke in the dark and felt himself sweating all over. But when he turned on the lights, he wasn't sweating – he was covered in thousands of cockroaches. The spray had chased them out from under his bed, some of them almost as big as mice with tiny ones crawling into his nose and ears.

Wherever I went in these sorts of places whether in Thailand, Indo-China or elsewhere, I set out to meet as many local officials, politicians and military officers as I could. The local governor was invariably a military officer and the local government was largely a military run affair. Apart from them, I sought out foreign missionaries of various denominations some of whom could be excellent sources of information especially if they'd lived in the area for years, sometimes decades, and had a reliable feel for politics. I also visited locally based American and other foreign officers and personnel whether they be in the military or with USAID, USIS, the CIA or some other outfit. Some of them were medicos in military and local civilian hospitals. I spent most of the evenings writing reports.

From Ubol I caught a Thai Airways DC3 daily mail run through the region to Nakhon Phanom, a pretty little town further north on the banks of the mighty Mekong River. By the time we reached Nakhon Phanom it was getting late in the afternoon, dark and beginning to rain. I was the only passenger on board. We circled the airport a couple of times to chase stray buffalo off the dirt strip and landed in the drizzle. Without turning off the engines, they opened the door at the rear, I jumped out, they handed me my typewriter, threw my luggage on the ground, slammed the door shut and took off. I don't think they even came to a halt. I looked up and as far as I could see I was in effect stranded alone in the middle of a field with not a building to be seen and no idea where to head. Then I noticed in the distance some lights moving along and thought that must be a road. I picked up the typewriter, my overnight bag and suitcase and trudged off. As I got near the road, I passed what looked like a small bus stop shelter with the words "Thai Airways Terminal" painted on it. I didn't have to wait long before a samlor came peddling along. No, it wasn't Norman Gunston, but he certainly resembled him. With my billowing short-sleeved shirt sopping wet, I hopped into the seat with the luggage and he peddled me six kilometres to the best hotel in town. He could have cut my throat and taken my luggage and money at any time.

The best restaurant in town turned out to be built out over the raging Mekong. It was an expansive girlie bar-restaurant in which the food was good and the girls rather ordinary. Across the river was Laos and it rose, seemingly from the banks of the river itself, in an unbelievably spectacular, straight up wall of blue cathedral mountains known as the Annamite Cordillera. It was a ravishing sight to behold. On one side of the river, a flat Thai plateau, on the other the Himalayas. As I gazed across the river while lunching and occasionally contemplating the interview notes I'd taken that morning, it struck me that through or beyond those forbidding jungle covered mountains ran the Ho Chi Minh Trail. Right now somewhere over there North Vietnamese soldiers were working their way down those tracks. It seemed surrealistic and so was the thought that the US Air Force was trying to interdict the Trail through bombing from Vietnam, Guam, and perhaps Thailand. I already knew from Serong that bombing the Trail was more or less a waste of time, but sitting there on the other side of the Mekong brought it home to me.

It was while in this restaurant and others like it as I travelled nearly every inch of train line in Thailand that I contemplated the nature of Thai politics. The country was ruled then by a military dictatorship led by generals Thanom Kittickachorn and Prapat Charusatien whom I always thought of as being humane, but tough, inflexible, illiberal types with no understanding of what a political party might be. Certainly, there were no national political parties anywhere in Thailand nor any trade union movement to speak of and few national church or charitable bodies. I came to see that one of the reasons for this was that there were no grass roots socio-political and socio-economic institutions of practically any kind. There was a virtual civilian institutional vacuum across the county. The nation was Buddhist and Buddhism generally doesn't produce the kinds of institutions that Christian and Islamic societies do. The only national, hierarchical institution in Thailand – and most other Southeast Asian nations at the time – was the military. And while it might not have been truly national, because the military broke down into fiefdoms or cliques, it was the only institution in which members developed a significant degree of trust among each other. Consequently, not only were nearly all Thai province chiefs military officers, but most of the nation's civil service bureaucracy was staffed by military and ex-military officers.

Even when the military government of Thanom and Prapat was overthrown and replaced by a succession of civilian governments, the military was never very far away and the civilians never managed to build any political parties of any lasting significance. In the nineteen sixties, when national political, administrative and social institutions in Thailand were weak and national communications were very slow or non-existent I used to think then that you could march a large army down through the middle of Thailand without resistance and almost unnoticed (which is what some people think the Japanese did in WWII). Thailand was politically a dead polity run by sterile bureaucratic cliques who staged little regional, ethnic and fratricidal coups among themselves. The bureaucracy was not directed by a governing cabinet because the cabinets themselves were made up of bureaucrats and technocrats. Fred Riggs called this a "bureaucratic polity" (see Fred W. Riggs, *Thailand, The Modernization of a Bureaucratic*

Polity, East-West Center Press, Honolulu, 1966). One might ask why hasn't someone tried to take over this sterile bureaucracy? The short answer is because there are no real political parties or ideological or totalitarian movements in Thailand. And the reason for that seems to have been the absence of colonising Europeans. And that in turn appears to have been an historical accident. Despite the recent dramas and riots involving pro-Thaksin Shinawatra Red Shirts and the supposedly royalist Yellow Shirts, nothing seems to have changed much despite mobile phones, the internet and other advances in communications (Thaksin's 'party' would disappear without the Thaksin money). In the sixties, I was once asked how I saw Thailand. Flippantly I said, "stable instability". That will still do.

From Nakhon Phanom, I made my way further up the river to Nong Khai where after a couple of days I crossed the river into Laos at Thadeua and then took a cyclo into Vientiane. I was to do this and vice versa many times over the next few years. The mighty, majestic river rises on the top of the world and flows thousands of kilometres to the Mekong Delta and the South China Sea. For over 800 kilometres it is the border between Laos and Thailand. Crossing it at Nong Khai took some getting used to. At this time of the year, the height of the rainy season, it was about 900 metres wide and running fast with a lot of large commercial traffic and debris in the water including submerged logs which could do considerable damage to large boats let alone to one of the longtail taxis boats I had to climb into. These boats were narrow and had room only for the driver, me and my luggage piled in front of me. When the river was running as it was in this July, the driver pointed his boat due upstream, gunned to full engine speed, hung on for dear life to the long metal pole to which the propeller was attached and we moved slowly sideways and slightly downstream across the river.

VIENTIANE, LAOS

A Nine to Five War in a Francophile Idyll

I always liked Vientiane. It was usually hot and wet when I was there, but I liked its wide streets and boulevards, its wats and temples and lazy, slow moving languid life. Mangy dogs and cats roamed the streets along with shuffling grey and saffron robed monks and members of royalty. There were so many princes and princesses in the place that it was said that if you stood on a street corner and threw a stone down the road you'd hit either a dog, a monk or a prince. Among the things I really looked forward to in Vientiane, and many other places in French Indo-China including Saigon and Phnom Penh, were the little French bars. Most of these were run by members of the Corsican mafia who until the mid-sixties were serviced by a Corsican airline that flew into Indo-China regularly. From the intriguing, happy Corsicans and their cheery female companions you could always get a bowl of wonderful and cheap French onion soup, a baguette and a bottle of decent red, or if it was too hot and humid for that, a cold bottle of "33" beer brewed by the French in Saigon. The bars were also useful places to pick up a few tips on the local culture and politics.

When I arrived from Nong Khai on my first visit, I had the cyclo driver take me straight to the Lane Xang Hotel on the Mekong River close to the centre of town. It was an old, slightly seedy, run down rambling colonial hostelry of a kind of which I was rather fond. In the mid-sixties these sorts of hotels could be found throughout Asia and at one time or another I stayed in nearly all of them – The Manila in the Philippines, The Cockpit and The Adelphi in Singapore, The Eastern and Oriental (the E & O) in Penang, the Le Royal in Phnom Penh, the Continental Palace in Saigon and The Oriental in Bangkok. Today, they have either disappeared or been restored and renovated like The Manila or cleaned up and rebuilt like the Lane Xang which is now excellent tourist value. In July '67 I was shown into a spacious two bedroom suite with a balcony looking out over the Mekong. Being covered in sweat, I immediately took a long shower. There was a nice sized writing desk against a wall. I pulled it in front of the balcony and sat down to type out a few reports to Bob Santamaria in Melbourne, including detailed accounts of my meeting with John Myint and my findings in North Eastern Thailand. I was to do a lot of writing over the next few days. Usually I typed direct from notes I'd jotted down in a small Spirax pad following each conversation I'd had that day. If the information was sensitive, I used my own hieroglyphics and codes which I carried in my head. I made it a practice never to take notes during an interview or conversation with anyone. I wanted to put them at ease and encourage them to confide in me which some of them did, astoundingly in a few cases. In every instance I had carefully worked out precisely what I wanted to ask, for I very strongly believed that you will never get the right answers if you don't ask the right questions. Very rarely will anyone volunteer you any information of real value or great confidentiality. I often jotted down in the notebook the main points I wanted to ask, but I would never produce it in front of the person or persons I was talking with.

Knowing what to ask required a great deal of study, research, careful listening, endless hours of silent contemplation lying in bed early in the morning with the blood flowing to the brain, and the application to the subject of an innate political animal instinct. That same instinct guides you through the conversations and hopefully enables you to recognise a gem when you hear it. The only times I produced a notebook were during press conferences or one-on-one formal media interviews. I conducted many of the latter over the years, including a series for Dutch Television in which I interviewed a number of foreign ministers starting with Adam Malik in Jakarta and then Thanat Khoman of Thailand, Sinathamby Rajaratnam in Singapore, and Carlos Romulo in Manila.

After a couple of hours work it was late in the afternoon and time for a drink at the bar downstairs. There I met up with my first real contact in Laos – an aging English writer and journalist named Estelle Holt. She was a small woman of fine features, who had been pretty in her youth, but was now about 50 years of age, had seen a lot of the world and was obviously still keen on a drink. I found her valuable and entertaining company. Despite some of the nonsenses we got up to, including midnight cyclo races from Prince Panya Souvanna Phouma's Third Eye Disco back to the hotel, she was a serious person who had written an interesting book on her travels in India and Pakistan in the fifties called *Asia and I* (Estelle Holt, *Asia and I*, Putnam & Company Limited, London, 1960).

Importantly from my point of view, she had lived in Laos for over six years and knew just about everybody of any significance in the country, including the prime minister of the supposedly neutralist government, Prince Souvanna Phouma. She promised to set up appointments – and she did. She said the first person I had to meet was the "beautiful, darling, General Oudone Sananikone". He was the 46 year old Chief of Staff of the Royal Laotian Government (RLG) Army, and according to my diaries I met him two days later in his office. He was as tall and charming as Estelle had said and he gave me a wonderful run down on the war at that time, the details of which are of interest today only the most arcane of military historians. I was later to learn from Estelle and others that because Laos had been declared "neutral" in the on-going Vietnam-Indo China War by the 1962 Geneva Agreement, which had been orchestrated by Averell Harriman to protect US interests in Europe, the 'Rightist' anti-communist Laotian generals, including Oudone, took an unusual approach to the war against the communist Pathet Lao. They and the Pathet Lao had decided to fight just a 9 to 5 war, without too much contact or bloodshed. After 5pm, units of the two sides would camp nearby each other and socialise at a comfortable distance. To this end, Oudone, coming from the more 'prosperous' side, regularly carted

5-10 boxes of Scotch whisky into battle with him which he shared with the PL commanders. At nine the next morning they would officially resume battle – if any of them were awake.

How they managed to come to this sort of arrangement I was to learn the following Friday, August 11, 1967, in the Lane Xang Bar. After four o'clock in the afternoon Vientiane's diplomatic community descended on the bar for the end of the week Friday drinks. There to one's amazement in the 'neutral capital' the 'diplomatic' representatives from the local embassies and offices of the UN, the US, Britain, Australia, France, China, North Vietnam, South Vietnam, Laos, Cambodia, the Pathet Lao, the Vietcong, Canada, Spain, Poland, the Vatican, the ICC (International Control Commission), the Red Cross, and various others inter-mingled in a variety of tongues. Here was a seemingly serious international diplomatic-intelligence clearing and exchange house of one kind or another. Whether it worked or not who would ever know? Estelle and I stood off in a corner exchanging notes and jokes. She'd met them all on many occasions at numerous cocktail parties and elsewhere and gave me introductions to those she claimed were the most knowledgeable, influential and newsworthy.

Among other people of note she led me to was the 40 year old Prince Sisouk Na Champassak, from the deep Laotian south, who was the Minister of Finance and his assistant Tianthone Chantarasay who was later to become ambassador to Australia. Sisouk, another dark charmer, was like Souvanna Phouma married to a French Catholic and was widely regarded as being both more or less incorruptible and the logical successor to Souvanna. He had written a very good book in 1961 titled *Storm Over Laos: A Contemporary History* (Frederick A. Praeger, New York, 1961). He did not use the title Prince as he said there were too many princes already in Laos and it had all become a bit embarrassing. He saw himself as a Western Asian. He did not speak any Lao language but was fluent in both French and English. None of his family spoke Lao. At the end of the year, after the Manila

PI Conference, I suggested to Bob Santamaria that we might invite him to future conferences. Bob never seemed enthusiastic about this – perhaps he felt uneasy at the thought of associating with royalty or of having a prince within his camp. In any case, Sisouk and I were to keep in close contact and were able to help each other in various ways, especially as he was a frequent traveller to Washington and other world capitals and I had excellent contacts, from his point of view, in Saigon though Serong and others.

It was August of the next year, 1968, that I finally met another of the well known Lao generals, Kouprasith Abhay, again through Estelle Holt. He was the Commander of the 5th RLG Military Region which included Vientiane and was reputed to be "the most powerful man in the country". He lived in a villa in the Chinaimo army camp a few kilometres out of town and on one occasion when I turned up at the house I was astounded to find a live crocodile in his front yard. As I was hesitantly escorted by an aide through the front wire gate I was relieved to see that the croc was in his own wired pen. It went with the general's tough image, I thought, and when I was sitting in his huge lounge-dining room waiting for him, I was startled when a magnificent brown long-nosed mountain cat appeared out of nowhere, jumped onto the dining table, condescendingly looked down its nose at me and then just as quickly disappeared. Out the back I could hear all the noises of what was a large aviary which the aide escorted me through pointing to an amazing array of wild birds Kouprasith had somehow obtained.

Eventually, the general ambled into the room in casual gear. Over the next couple of hours and three or four whiskies he gave me a remarkable run down on the political and military events of the previous five or six years. In a good mood he roamed over the complex issues involving the rise of the tripartite neutralist government, the machinations surrounding the eventual overthrow of the right-wing prime minister and former military commander, General Phoumi Nosavan in 1964-65, the rise of General Ouane Rattikone, the commander of Military Region 1 and warlord of northwestern Laos, as Commander of the RLG military and his taking over of the opium trade from the deposed Phoumi. It was all both serious and placed in the context of the war and at times highly comical. We both laughed during his hilarious descriptions of some of things he claimed various people and notably Phoumi got up to. I was to meet Phoumi several months later in the southern Thai beach town of Songkhla where he lived in exile. Phoumi and I would subsequently meet many times, mainly over small Chinese dinners with his pilot Captain Kun Vououraj in Bangkok for no particular purpose, as far as I could see, other than to exchange views and information on what was happening in Laos and the Vietnam War. Then one day he asked if the Americans might support him in another coup against the neutralist government in Vientiane. I said I had no idea and that he should ask the Americans. Everything Kouprasith said about him seemed probably right, while Phoumi never seemed to hold much of a grudge against the mates who had overthrown him. In the long run Phoumi is probably best remembered for having constructed the mini Arc de Triomphe monument in central Vientiane which today is an iconic symbol of the nation. Legend has it that angered at the pressure the Kennedy administration, and notably Averell Harriman, was placing on him to agree to merge his right-wing government into a tripartite neutralist one, Phoumi diverted USAID money earmarked for a new airport to build a monument to himself. When I told him I'd heard this story, the jovial, rotund Phoumi belly laughed saying "they are comedians".

I never did meet General Ouane Rattikone although I saw his tubby figure walk across the lobby of the Lane Xang a few times, for he kept a room and a mistress upstairs somewhere. While Kouprasith and Oudone ran the war, Ouane ran the Laotian opium trade, poppy cultivation being for many years an important economic activity in a region stretching from the Shan State and other parts of northern Burma across northern Thailand and Laos into Vietnam. Opium was smuggled out to China, Vietnam and Thailand for use there and in global markets. Heroin, which was first refined from opium in the early twentieth century in places like China and Iran, did not begin production in this part of the world until the 1960s. By then opium and heroin had become major products financing governments, armies and guerrilla organisations, generals, politicians and thousands of families. When the US and its CIA army set out to support the anti-communist forces in Laos, including those of the mountain Meo tribesmen, during the Vietnam war, the CIA's airline Air America found itself inevitably transporting opium along with Laotian soldiers for Ouane, Oudone and Kouprasith.

Despite the impression given in some movies, the CIA was not itself interested in smuggling opium, as Alfred McCoy explained very well in his book *The Politics of Heroin in Southeast Asia* (Harper & Row, New York, 1972). The CIA, Air America and the US Embassy in Laos tolerated opium smuggling by the locals in the interest of building a strong and effective anti-communist Meo army in Laos. The alternative was to send in US combat troops and four successive US presidents and their advisors opposed that. (At the time there were about 36,000 North Vietnamese Army (NVA) troops in Laos supporting the Pathet Lao and travelling down to South Vietnam via the Ho Chi Minh Trail. There were many more thousand NVA already in South Vietnam their numbers having built up from the moment Hanoi restarted the war in 1962 in an effort to militarily conquer the South. Right from 1962 South Vietnamese, US and Australian soldiers were killing NVA soldiers in NVA uniforms in South Vietnam.)

Like the Cambodian Prince Sirik Matak and many other people, no right-wing or neutralist Laotian general or politician I met ever believed that the United States would lose in Indo-China and allow the communist North Vietnamese and/or Communist China, which had 350,000 troops in North Vietnam releasing NVA troops into South Vietnam, to take over. They just naturally assumed they were on the winning side, historically, politically and ideologically. They said to me in effect "we've been educated in France and we know the truth – and it lies with America". It is ironical and fascinating that Pol Pot and his Khmer Rouge mates in Cambodia not only thought that they were on the winning side historically, but were also educated in France at the same time and in the same universities including the Sorbonne, becoming inveterate, crude Marxist totalitarians who would massacre millions of people especially the educated and self-motivated entrepreneurs and farmers while burning every book in existence.

CALCUTTA, INDIA

Poverty and Intellectuals

On August 12, 1967, I crossed the raging Mekong again in another hair-raising taxi boat ride and took what was commonly called the overnight opium train from Nong Khai to Bangkok. In Bangkok I had another uncomfortable secret meeting with John Myint in General Chat's residence just to assure him that we were continuing to push things along. The next day I flew out to Calcutta no doubt under constant surveillance.

After walking though the poverty stricken streets of Calcutta from the city bus terminal stepping over and around bodies dead or dying on the streets, I checked into the venerable colonial Spencer Hotel where I was upgraded into a suite comprising an entrance hall, a lounge, dining room and two magnificent huge bedrooms with four-poster beds like Raffles in Singapore. I had no interest in reporting on India, but many Indian newspapers and publications were carrying my articles and I had come to talk with them about the future. They had been carrying my articles ever since the Wheat for India Campaign in 1964 which had been a project of the Melbourne University Democratic Labor Party Club (DLP Club) which I had established in 1962 and led as the founding president.

The Wheat for India Campaign asked the Australian government to give a million tons of wheat to democratic India to help feed its starving and poor millions, if necessary diverting it from our sales to communist China. It was a brilliant success, the government reluctantly capitulating to our demands within a few weeks of the launch of what some our greatest opponents said was a stunning national low cost but brilliantly co-ordinated newspaper campaign utilising the national resources of the NCC.

During the Wheat for India Campaign one of its major national sponsors, the 43 year old Bengali agnostic Professor Sibnayaran Ray, the head of the Indian Studies Department at Melbourne University, arranged for a number of Indian newspapers and magazines to carry my articles on the campaign and after that they continued to publish most of what I sent them on all sorts of subjects. These papers included *The Statesman*, *Ananda Bazaz Patrika* and *The Hindustan Standard* all published in Calcutta, *The Hindu* in Madras and *The Times of India* in New Delhi and Bombay. The magazines or journals included *The Radical Humanist* (Calcutta) and *Thought* (New Delhi). *Thought* was a quality intellectual, literary and cultural publication while *The Radical Humanist* was a product of the anti-religious Radical Humanist Society founded by M.N. Roy in 1948. Roy had been a communist activist intellectual and a member of the Soviet Comintern. He was the founder-secretary of the Mexican Communist Party in 1919 and a leading figure in the founding of the Indian Communist Party in 1920. He was a major communist party theorist and operator and had a close association with Lenin, Stalin, Mao, Trotsky and Ho Chi Minh who was also a fully trained and paid Comintern agent.

However, Roy broke with communism and became something like what we once called a democratic socialist. Until he died in February 2008, the strongly anti-communist Sib Ray remained an admirer of Roy. I have to say here that Ray was one of the seminal influences in my youth and my twenties. He widened my horizons and knowledge of the world immensely – as did others, Santamaria, McAuley, Knopfelmacher, Serong, Rodulfo, Colin Clark, John Maynes, Johnny Tan, Harry Tjan (Silalahi), Geoffrey Fairbairn and Bill Cawthorn – to name a few. We led a rich intellectual and cultural life. Sib regularly invited me to his home in East Kew in Melbourne on Saturday evenings in 1964-65 to participate in discussions with his students and others on Rabindranath Tagore, Shakespeare, Milton, philosophy, western classical and Indian music and occasionally Indian and Australian politics and international affairs (but never M.N. Roy!).

But here I was in 1967 and after a couple of hours writing articles and reports, I rang Sushil Bhadra, a Sib Ray friend and senior editor at *The Statesman* whom I had met on a previous visit to India in 1965 and invited him over the hotel. I was in my hotel dining room when the phone rang. It was Sushil. He was outside the hotel somewhere telling me they wouldn't let him in because he was wearing a dhoti – more or less the Indian national dress. They told him he'd have put on a suit if he wanted to come in. I fumed down the stairs and put on a scene a la Russell Crowe. They let him in. He came up to my room, we had a room service meal of grand proportions and when he saw that I had a two litre-sized bottles of Johnny Walker black label on the sideboard, he said he'd bring a "couple of friends" along on Saturday night when we agreed we would share it all. In the meantime, he took me by rickshaw around to all the newspaper offices. Why can't those rickshaw boys win all the marathon races around the world?

On Saturday night he turned up on time. I opened the door and in they came one another in their dhotis, Sushil announcing them with a swinging lilt: Chaterjee, Chaterjee, Chaterjee, Bannerjee, Bannerjee, Gosh; Chaterjee, Chaterjee, Chaterjee, Bannerjee, Bannerjee Gosh. Fifteen of them altogether, each carrying a bottle of, to me, undrinkable Indian whisky. Most of them were members of the Radical Humanist Society. They were all university graduates with two or three of them holding Ph.Ds from Indian or British universities. It turned out their main interests were philosophy and English literature and we spent hours well into the morning discussing Shakespeare and Milton. None of them held a position in academia; they all worked for newspapers, banks or insurance companies occupying lowly positions and often walking 5-8 miles a day to their jobs. There were many millions of other cultured, highly educated people just like them in places like Calcutta so they were happy to get any job they could. By Australian and American standards they all lived in poverty. But they were happy with a free India and their erudition which was something no one could ever take from them.

When I awoke the next morning I found two empty Johnny Walker bottles on the mahogany dining table along with fifteen untouched bottles of the local product. And of course they ate well keeping the room service busy all night so there were dirty plates and many bottles of the local beer everywhere. I quickly packed my bags and walked out the door for a flight to Madras and then a connection to Colombo. Their newspapers were to keep publishing my articles for the next decade or so.

COLOMBO, CEYLON

A Racial Divide and Simmering Conflict

I spent the first five or six days in Sri Lanka, or Ceylon as it was then known, writing articles and reports and catching up on my reading in a very nice room in the wonderful old colonial Galle Face Hotel in central Colombo. Once again I was up-graded into an Indian Ocean view "deluxe suite" and constantly and embarrassingly called "master" and spoken to deferentially, from almost a genuflecting posture, simply because, I thought, I was white and to them English. Damn the English, I thought. Apart from writing, journalists and political advisors have to read a lot. I had to get through constantly not only the local daily newspapers, but gathering bundles of weeklies like *The Economist*, *The Far Eastern Economic Review*, which in those days was a plainly printed, very serious journal of quality economic and political analysis edited by Dick Wilson and later Derek Davies, *Time*, *Newsweek* and *U.S. News and World Report* as well as various quarterlies likes *Foreign Affairs*, *Asian Affairs*, and *Pacific Affairs*, a number of which I wrote for at one time or another. In addition to that there were the books on the region I bought during my travels, read and posted home. They all sit on my bookshelves today and occasionally I consult them as I write this book – along with all of the reports I wrote for Bob Santamaria and other interested parties.

I spent just over two weeks in Ceylon in 1967 learning a lot about its politics and meeting many important and interesting people through friends or contacts of Bob Santamaria like Noel Mendis and Giom Kurukulasuriya who was to become a Pacific Institute regular. Colin Clark's name was also very useful as he had advised Ceylonese governments in the past and was a special friend of former prime minister Dudley Senanayake. But, as with India, I had no enduring interest in reporting on the place.

In the middle of the second week I was there I travelled with Fr. Anthony Fernando, the articulate and generous Oblate provincial, on a slow train from Colombo to picturesque Kandy in the hills where we stayed the night in a rambling convent. This was the same train ride that Michael Ondaatje was to write about with so much bitter humour many years later in his entertaining book *Running in the Family* (Victor Gollanz, London, 1983). In the convent I was staggered to find an unbelievably sharp racial divide between the Sinhalese and Tamil nuns in a Christian community which professed to believe that all people were created equal in the eyes of God. The Sinhalese nuns who welcomed me at the door and ran the place were charming and obviously well educated. But they treated the Tamil nuns like dirt and never personally spoke to them. Communications were conducted through notes and posted orders. The Tamils did all the menial tasks while the Sinhalese were waited upon grandly. For me it was a shocking revelation and I have to say that when "paradise" broke into civil war fifteen years later, in the early eighties, I was saddened but not surprised.

SINGAPORE

Lee's Authoritarian Soulless City State

When I touched down in Singapore from Colombo on a magical BOAC VC10 flight, I headed for The Cockpit Hotel on Oxley Rise which was then my favourite in Singapore on account of its out-the-back private bungalow rooms.

When I first visited Singapore in 1965, it was still a smelly economic backwater, as was Malaysia. There were no industries, no international financial houses and only three hotels on Orchard Road which was lined with stinking black-water canals and few shops. From the airport you drove through smoky rural kampongs or villages to get to your hotel. What changed it all, for both Singapore and Malaysia, was the regional economic activity generated directly and indirectly by the American involvement in the Vietnam War. The American military machine required all sorts of things – access to ports, industrial and mechanical inputs like motor and aircraft spare parts and refrigerants, bases for their active forces and accommodation and entertainment facilities for those spending hundreds of thousands of dollars on Rest and Recreation (R & R). Apart from that, the war bought to Singapore and the region thousands of free spending journalists and Western academics, many of them left wing and ironically hostile to the US war effort, who nevertheless shamelessly exploited the region's poor girls while condemning the US military for doing the same thing. On top of that were countless NGOs, commercial enterprises of numerous kinds trying to make a buck out of the war, and a legion of diplomats and intelligence officers and agents seeking information on the war and its significance for the region and the world.

I regularly ran into journalists from Italy, Germany, Sweden, Holland, France, Latin America and other places. Many of these people required accommodation, food and transportation in Singapore – and Malaysia and Thailand – because most of them chose not to live in South Vietnam. They travelled back and forth. One of the reasons for that was that the whole of South Vietnam was declared to be a war zone by the world's insurance companies and only Lloyd's of London would insure you against war risk and then for a massive premium. I was fortunate that one of my and Bob Santamaria's business associates in Melbourne, a well known multi-millionaire businessman and race horse owner, and many others supported me in this regard so I was able to stay for long periods in South Vietnam. The others included Frank James, Tom Danaher, Bing Molyneux, Sir Michael Chamberlin, Lou Arthur, John Gartner, Matt Cody, Sir Frank Packer and Dick Austin who were helpful in various ways as we built the Pacific Institute. And then, of course, there was my ever supportive and unquestioning father, Frank Mount senior.

Today, Singapore is what they call a modern Asian city. There are still traces of the old entrepot and colonial outpost mainly along the river banks and in the old Chinatown but most of the city is made up of soulless office blocks, malls, supermarkets and hotels. Half of it is underground. You can walk for miles without ever seeing the sky. Lee Kuan Yew and his friends even wanted to tear down Raffles Hotel but were persuaded otherwise by strong international pressure. So they renovated it, but back to the wrong period so that it lost most of its charms and ambiance. While we know there are many wonderful and generous Singaporeans, foreign businessmen living in the city describe the place as "heartless", "antiseptic", "utterly materialistic", "riddled with hypocrisy", and "dominated by an unbelievably greedy, male chauvinist culture." Lee and his mob have crushed the heart out of the place, if it ever had one, while denying everyone except themselves an opinion on just about anything. To criticise them is to risk facing a judge.

In recent years, Kuan Yew has travelled around the region and the world warning against the perils and evils of liberal democracy. Years ago, I saw him once telling a group of bemused Middle East national leaders never to allow themselves be forced into dealing with difficult elected representatives let alone be obliged to form a government from them. He was telling them never to hold elections. I suspected that these smiling Arabs were thinking the same thing I was – that the only person in the room who had come to power through elections was Lee himself! With considerable assistance from the British and their various agencies, Lee, having been educated in England thanks largely to his wealthy parents, returned home to eventually lead the Socialist and trade union based People's Action Party (PAP) to victory over Lim Yew Hock.

Although the communists who broke away from the PAP to form the Barisan Sosialis Party were strong, Lee was expected to develop a vigorous democratic state. Instead, he decided to simply crush the communists and gaol them, developing an authoritarian regime in the process. There might have been some excuse for taking a strong authoritarian approach in the sixties when the Barisan Sosialis was so strong, had unknown connections throughout the region and there was the risk of communist forces coming to power in Indonesia and South Vietnam while insurgencies raged in other parts of the Region of Revolt. But those days passed long ago. Singapore today could have become a shining liberal democracy and a great free wheeling regional centre of art, literature and culture. Instead, all of those things are still mistrusted by the Singapore leadership. Much the same could be said about Malaysia.

On this 1967 visit to Singapore I met for the first time a number of people who were to be important to me over many years. They included Professor George Thomson, who held a position in the Department of Government and Public Administration but was primarily an advisor to Lee with both Singapore and British intelligence connections; Alex Josey, a British journalist who was another advisor to Lee with British Intelligence connections; the razor sharp Tay Seow Huah, the founding director of the Security and Intelligence Division (SID), the Singapore foreign intelligence organisation, at the age of 33; the then Foreign Minister Sinathamby Rajaratnam whom I regularly met while he was minister; and another British journalist, Dennis Bloodworth, who wrote for the *The Observer* in London and was to become an intellectually stimulating companion who loved opera. There were also a number of Australian journalists based in Singapore at the time whose observations and company I valued including Garry Barker, Ian Ward and John Bennetts, who was later to be the head of Australian Joint Intelligence Organisation (JIO) at the time of the Indonesian invasion of East Timor in 1975. Some years later in 1972, I was to meet S. R. Nathan, Tay Seoh Huah's successor as director of SID and thereafter every time I visited Singapore he or his agents were there at the airport to invite me to lunch and I was only too happy to exchange notes with him. He was, for example, exceedingly informative in the months prior to the Indonesian invasion of East Timor, an act he was insistent the Indonesians had to undertake for the sake of the security of the entire region. He understood very well my links to Indonesians like Harry Tjan, Fr. Beek SJ, Subchan, the religious leader of 60 million Muslims in Nadhlatul Ulama (NU), Mochtar Lubis and Ali Moertopo very well, all of whom I will come to later in the book.

During this visit to Singapore, I had a very entertaining and enlightening lunch with George Thomson who chided me gently about Bob Santamaria and *News Weekly* for being "too anti-communist", to which I replied, "Well, OK, but we don't believe in jailing ours". However, he was highly receptive to the ideas involved in the Pacific Community concept which was not surprising as Singapore had for some years been trying to develop forms of regional co-operation and were at that very time engaged with our Indonesian and

Malaysian friends in establishing ASEAN. The Pacific Community was a much grander strategic idea and it certainly appealed to George. I outlined to him our network of regional contacts, their capabilities, the up-coming December Manila conference which would become the Pacific Institute, and how we thought we could develop political leverage within the nations of the region and more broadly in pursuit of common strategic and political objectives.

These objectives included protecting the sea lanes of communication (SLOCS) between the Indian and Pacific Oceans running through the Indonesian waterways and the South China Sea through which ran many of our trade routes and bringing the emerging China into the community of nations, including Japan, so that it did not feel isolated. Thomson responded by saying that he would take it to the others, by which he meant Lee, and was confident they would be more than interested because of the pressures and uncertainties of the Vietnam War. I invited George to the Manila conference, but he was already committed. He said he would like to come to future conferences which he did regularly for over six years. Another subject I discussed with him was the future of the Anglo Malay Defence Agreement (AMDA). I had done quite a bit of work on this with a senior officer in the Australian Defence Department who had been introduced to me in a Canberra watering hole by the academic historian Geoffrey Fairbairn, who was one of the patrons of the Defend Australia Committee (DAC).

KUALA LUMPUR, MALAYSIA

Building ASEAN

In the Malaysian Ministry of Foreign Affairs (Wisma Putra) I found a major division between what we might call the anti-communist regionalists led by the Permanent Secretary or head of the Department, Ghazali Shafie, and the progressives who were subtly anti-American, pro-European and condescendingly anti-Australian. Most of the progressives were Oxford educated, wore fancy cravats and spoke in cultivated British accents. They called themselves "realists". While the Ghazali group and its Indonesian associates like General Ali Moertopo and Jusuf Wanandi were working hard to develop effective regional co-operation and were at that very time setting up ASEAN, these progressives were openly sceptical of the "utility" of these efforts saying they believed in "regional neutrality". While ASEAN was established and gradually consolidated, the influence of these Malaysian progressives grew in Kuala Lumpur especially after Tun Abdul Razak became prime minister succeeding the Tunku Abdul Rahman in 1971. Eventually, they began advocating "regional neutralisation" through the declaration of a Zone of Peace, Freedom and Neutrality (ZOPFAN), the real objective of which was to push the Americans out of the region. In 1976 three of them were arrested, along, sensationally, with the cultured Editor of *The Straits Times*, for being part of a Soviet spy ring. In certain circles, champagne corks popped around the region. (The full story is quite intriguing, but it is not a part of this book).

Over the years, I was to meet many Malaysian politicians in a variety of parties including Dr. Tan Chee Khoon the leader of the Gerakan Party and Lim Kit Siang the leader of the Democratic Action Party (DAP). Both the Gerakan and DAP were predominantly Chinese parties one Christian – social democratic, the other a more traditional, secular social democratic, towards both of which I felt some attraction. Tan Chee Khoon was a medical practitioner. He had been in parliament for many years and was a Methodist. He held his practice deep in the heart of run-down, down-town Chinatown and he invited me to meet him in his office. I trotted along enthusiastically between the stalls and smells of footpath noodle soup and chestnut vendors to find his name on a brass plaque at the door of a four or five story colonial terrace building. I looked up to see washing hanging out over the road and then stepped through the single door up sets of dull grey wooden rickety steps to the second floor where the Chinese receptionist behind a chest high desk counter said, "You Mista Mao?" With what I imagine were raised eyebrows, I replied, "Yes". "Take Seat", she said.

Thirty minutes later Mr. Mao was shown into Dr. Tan's surgery. Tan was sitting head-down behind his desk when I walked in. His balding head looked up through dark, heavy horned rim glasses. "Mr. Mount, you are an Australian journalist?" he asked in excellent English. "Yes". "How is Sir Donald Bradman doing these days?" I was taken aback. Here was a cricket fanatic, a Chinese Socialist cricket fanatic or tragic in one of the poorest areas of Kuala Lumpur who thought I might know Bradman. While we went on then and over future years to swap many cricket stories, from memory I never discovered how he came to be so interested. It could have been something to do with his maverick personality. I liked and admired the man and we enjoyed each other's company. However, we never clicked politically. I felt he was a very good man, committed to fine principles of social justice, but one who lacked feeling and political judgement – and he had little interest in regional or foreign affairs.

Lim Kit Siang the leader of the DAP and his social democratic colleagues were a bit more on my wave length. I attended a number of their functions in the late sixties, including a memorable barbecue in Port Klang. Like Gerakan, the DAP was rather insular with little interest, at least then, in regional and international affairs. All of these opposition parties and their connections were useful for information on the local political scene. But, for my purposes, not only did they have little regional interest and no regional connections of any note, none of their leaders pulled any weight with the government in Kuala Lumpur. So I concentrated on people in the government and foreign affairs and intelligence communities – and of course the military involved in the low level counter-insurgency on the Thai border.

3
Round the Region Again

As I prepared to go round the region again to most, but not all countries, I was pretty happy. I had opened the idea of regional co-operation to people who hadn't thought much about it before and to those who had, I hoped I was bringing a geo-strategically wider and more multi-dimensional vision of it than that which was then leading Southeast Asia towards ASEAN. In my second tour I was looking forward to seeing how far this had taken root. I wasn't too optimistic because nothing happens fast in Asia. As someone once said, if you want to work in Asia you need to be very, very patient and have a good sense of humour. But I was sure we were on the right, long term track. The other thing that pleased me was that I felt I had spotted a few long term potential participants in our own small regional organisation which was to become known as the Pacific Institute. They included Prince Sisouk Na Champassak, Professor George Thomson, Senator Leck Vanich Angkhul, Jack de Silva, Ngo Khac Tinh and Truong Cong Cuu none of whom at this stage were personally known to Bob Santamaria. Add to them Ted Serong and his friends, Bishop Thuan and his friends, and the Indonesians Bob told me were coming to the Manila conference, and things looked promising.

MANILA

Progress or more Manana?

When I checked into the Filipinas Hotel on Padre Faura I found a message for me from the Jesuit historian Horatio de la Costa saying he had organised a meeting of friends at the provincial's rooms on the 29th – more than a week away – and was anxious that I should attend. What could this be about, I wondered? I tried to ring him back immediately, but in those days the telephone system in the Philippines – like most other counties in Asia – was appalling. One could dial endlessly to no effect. So bad was it that some high level executives, both Filipino and foreign, regularly took dawn flights to Hong Kong because it was easier to make international calls back into the Philippines and to almost anywhere in the country than it was to make the same calls within the country itself. In the end, I took a taxi to the provincial's office and left a message there saying I'd be at the meeting.

I then decided to move out of the Filipinas because it was too expensive for me. I walked up the road to the Solidaridad Bookshop run by a gritty intellectual I'd first met in 1965, Francisco Sionil 'Frankie' Jose. Sionil was a novelist and poet and edited *Solidarity* magazine, the best literary-intellectual journal ever published in the Philippines then or now. A great raconteur and womaniser who loved the British flag, he and I had some great conversations over the years. He took me up the road and booked me into the Luneta Hotel at a very generous tariff. The old-styled Spanish Luneta was owned and run by a very conservative Catholic family, so much so that the hostelry did not have a bar or serve alcohol anywhere on the premises. When I gently complained about this oversight, they directed me to a bar across a narrow laneway just outside the front door. That evening, I descended about twenty steps down into a dimly lit bar. As I walked through the door, there was the bar itself and stools on the left and the band playing beyond dining and other tables far to the right. I sat at the bar behind which was an enormous mirror through which I could see the band playing. With a beer at hand I could work out a five-piece jazz combo including a piano accordion, a drummer and a guitarist. They were very good and I was tapping away with the music.

At the next music break, they came up to the bar. One after another they pulled pistols out of their belts and placed them gently along the bar beside me. This is what you might call a mild culture shock. In those days, before Marcos declared martial law in 1972, every Filipino carried a weapon. If you got on a domestic flight, the first thing the smiling stewardess asked at the door was "would you like to check your weapon in, sir?" And there before you was a rack of checked-in, loaded pistols on a wall. The same thing occurred in restaurants all over the country.

The day after checking into the Luneta, I telephoned Christopher Clark, the son of the famous economist Colin Clark who had been one of the fathers of national income accounting, creating what we now call the Gross National Product (GNP). Chris was working for the newly established Asian Development Bank (ADB) which had, and still has, its headquarters in Manila, then not far from the Luneta. Chris was a pleasant fellow but an overly scrupulous and slightly unstable one and was giving the ADB management a hard time over the large expense accounts given to its officers and what he called their decisions to live in "elite walled suburbs" rather than "with the people". For his part, Chris had housed himself and his family in a rundown terrace in the old suburb of Santa Ana where basic facilities like water were not always readily at hand. We discussed many subjects relating to aid and local politics and at the end of our lunch at a little Swiss restaurant he invited me stay at his place for a few nights. I told him I'd come across on the next Saturday morning – a couple of days away. In the interim I got to work writing and making a number of appointments for the following week with various politicians, trade union leaders, academics, journalists and diplomats.

When I arrived at Chris' place on the Saturday morning, I found he wasn't there and that his elegant wife, Cecilia, was in a distraught state, mainly over Chris' mental condition and general instability induced by his being naturally a very stressful and scrupulous person and one cast into a rough and tumble and often corrupt milieu. Chris had gone to the office and I set about trying to console her over cups of coffee. We chatted about family matters and the idiosyncracies of living in Asia and this seemed to lift her spirits a bit. She then told me that Chris' parents were also worried about his health and that Colin was flying in that evening from London and that he too would be staying in the house for the next few days. I suggested that perhaps it would be best if I moved on, but she insisted I stay.

Colin, whom I'd previously met in Melbourne had been a friend of John Maynard Keynes and had resigned as one of Labour Prime Minster Ramsay MacDonald's economic advisors when asked to write a protectionist policy for him. He had also at one stage been an advisor to the Ceylonese Prime Minister Dudley Senanayake as well as to a number of Southeast Asian cabinet ministers. He had also been a long time friend of Bob Santamaria's and in 1952 was briefly an advisor to Vince Gair, later a DLP senator, when he was Premier of Queensland. So he had been around a bit. Apart from his abilities as an economist, econometrician and statistician, he was one of the world's leading demographers and an expert in 1960s third world developmental economics. Keynes reputedly called him "a bit of a genius" and quoted him approvingly in *The General Theory of Employment, Interest and Money* (Ch. 8) when Clark was only in his late twenties.

Some of his peers thought he should have been nominated for the Nobel prize in economics because of his work on national income, but it wasn't to be. Being a keen economics graduate myself, having got through to the masters preliminary stage at the University of Melbourne before Bob Santamaria offered me the job of roaming around Asia, and having been secretary of the Melbourne University Commerce Society helping to produce and edit, along with Peter Samuel, its cutting-edge intellectual journal *Boom and Bust* in the early sixties, I looked forward to meeting Colin again. The jewel in Colin's own prodigious output, his book *Conditions of Economic Progress*, (published by MacMillan, London, in three revised editions in 1940, 1951 and 1957), has long been recognised as a classic text lifting Clark from the level of a great statistician and econometrician to that of one of the twentieth century's great general economic theorists. It is hardly possible to rate an economist any higher than that, but it should also be noted that late in his career he was invited by the World Bank, along with a number of "pioneers" of developmental economics, to contribute a chapter on his own career to a book it was publishing. This put him on a par, at least, with, among others, Sir Arthur Lewis, Gunnar Myrdal and W.W. Rostow.

Colin stayed for three or four days during which we had some of the most seminal conversations as far as I was concerned. While Chris went off to work and Cecilia went shopping, Colin and I sat around the kitchen table drinking endless cups of coffee and cans of San Miguel beer as we discussed economic and political issues. During these conversations, and others later in Australia and Asia in and around meetings of Peace with Freedom (PWF) and the Pacific Institute, Colin was to cause in me a new way of thinking about economics. I can't describe it precisely, but it's been with me ever since. And it's been reliable. At Oxford University and during his days with MacDonald, he worked with, apart from Keynes, many of the great British, and largely Oxford, economists and economic historians of the time including G.D.H. Cole, Lionel Robbins, Hugh Dalton, R.H. Tawney, Sir Roy Harrod, Sir John Hicks, Lord Beveridge and A.C. Pigou, with whom he co-wrote a book in 1936 called *The Economic Position of Great Britain*. He talked often about these people, their ideas and prejudices. As I had studied these economists and historians during my course I found it all quite fascinating and it was through the insights that arose during these conversations that I learned so much. One of the things he taught me, for example, was that one should judge the progress of a developing country's own economy on its capacity to import, not export. This was another thing that held me in good stead over the years.

However, my major interest was to talk to Colin about regional Southeast Asian economic and other forms of co-operation. Initially, he was sceptical to say the least. After all, it was still the region of revolt, as far as academia was concerned. However, after the Manila Pacific Institute conference the next November and during subsequent conversations with him in Melbourne around Peace with Freedom seminars, he began to understand our Pacific Community strategic vision and to see things geo-politically and globally whereas beforehand he had only looked at nations individually. Both in the gradual formulation of what became known as the 1970 Pacific Institute Resolution and in private discussions with regional co-operation policy makers in Asia and in Canberra he was to have a significant influence – for example with Sir John Crawford of the Australian National University with whom he had co-authored a book in 1938, *The National Income of Australia* (MacMillan, London), and who influenced considerably a number of Australian prime ministers, foreign ministers, bureaucrats and academics in matters of regional economic co-operation and Asian economics generally. (Crawford and his ANU associates greatly assisted Indonesia in the early Soeharto years).

A bit like myself, Colin was a loner, although an endearing and eccentric one. At the time of this visit to Manila he was the Director of the Institute of Agricultural Economics at Oxford University, a position he held from 1953 to 1969. In that capacity, I took him out to meet Jeremias Montemayor, the leader of the Federation of Free Farmers (FFF), that is peasant farmers, who was also a friend of Bob Santamaria's and in whose house I had stayed in 1965 and 1966. The FFF had branches throughout the country and Montemayor was truly one of the most outstanding men I ever met – although I warn you there have been quite a few of them. Montemayor, the son of a wealthy family, and a very brilliant lawyer, had dedicated his life to helping the humble Filipino peasant. (See Jeremias U. Montemayor,

Ours to Share, An Approach to Philippine Social Problems, Rex Publishing, Manila, 1966.) I had already travelled many parts of the country seeing him at work and staying with him in village communities. He was delighted to meet Colin and told me he looked forward to the great economist's observations. But when Clark declared Montemayor's central idea, that of giving Filipino peasants ownership of the land they tilled for their absentee landlords, a disaster on the grounds that modern agricultural technology demanded large scale, intensive corporate holdings, he was almost shot on the spot. Clark told Montemayor that most of the peasants should move into urban jobs where they and their families could be fed by the increased food production of modern agriculture. I was highly amused since years beforehand Clark himself in Australia had raised his own family for some time in Australia on a small 'subsistence' farm with chicks and ducks and had suggested controversially that all Australians should do the same!

Chris and Cecilia had made friends with one of their neighbours, a young journalist who was making a name for himself, one Maximo Soliven. They suggested I walk around the corner and knock on the massive gates to his thoroughly rundown old Spanish colonial villa. This I did and it led to one of my best friendships in Asia and to an urbane, highly intelligent bundle of energy and ideas who was to become one of the region's best and most courageous journalists and battlers for freedom and democracy. He was a graduate of the Jesuit Ateneo de Manila University and at this initial meeting he generously gave me a scintillating and often amusing three hour survey of Philippine politics interspersed with explorations into the history of dozens of pistols and swords, ancient and modern, that adorned his walls.

Early the next evening, I arrived at the Jesuit provincial's residence which was only a kilometre or so up Herran Street from Max's villa. I was met by de la Costa, who in a cool barong tagalog, escorted me into a grand room with a large oval mahogany conference table below a slow fan around which stood or sat about 15 casually dressed men, most of whom I had met a number of times before. Among them were senators Raul Manglapus, Manuel Manahan and Manuel Pelaez, all of whom had been cabinet ministers, two of them foreign affairs ministers, Jerry Montemayor alongside three of his FFF offsiders, including Charlie Avila, trade unionist Johnny Tan and one his FFW offsiders, and a number of Jesuits including Fr. Pacifico Ortiz, the Rector of Ateneo de Manila University, Fr. Francisco Araneta, the Dean of the Ateneo Law School, and like de la Costa an inveterate political activist, Fr. Vicente San Juan, the Director of the Institute of Social Order (ISO), and Fr. Bonningue of the Asian Bureau.

Manglapus was the leader of the Christian democratic Progressive Party of the Philippines (PPP) and also the chairman of the Philippine Christian Social Movement (CSM) and he had brought along Luis Amado Lagdameo, the leader of the Young CSM. In addition to them, de la Costa had invited Charlie Albert, the head of NISA, the Philippine National Intelligence Security Authority. Not a bad group really and all of whom I was to have a lot to do with in the future.

De la Costa pointed to the carver chair at the head of the table and said "You're the chairman of the meeting, Frank. You're here to tell us what to do." "Oh, hell", I thought, because I preferred to play from behind and I said to de la Costa that that was not my position. I was perfectly aware that the first university in the Philippines, the University of Santo Tomas, had been established in 1611, so who was I or any other Australian to tell them what they might do? However, I was obliged to take the chair and – not for the last time in these sorts of circumstances – I would simply talk about what we did in Australia, which they all recognised as a great liberal democracy. I outlined to them what one might call a short course in Australian civics and the rule of law before becoming more political about communist influence in the body politic mainly through its infiltration of the trade union movement, the Australian Labor Party and various 'peace' organisations and how I saw that in a regional and global strategic context. This was well received but they insisted: what should we do? My response was that they – the social and Christian democrats I was addressing – had to take a long view and adopt at least a ten year strategy to take effective political power in the Philippines either directly or indirectly. To that end they needed to build a movement, their own sort of movement, in support of democratic institutions and political parties across the board and against communist totalitarian forces including the Philippine Communist Party (CPP), its guerrilla New People's Army NPA) and its various fronts as they came along – which in time would include the grand umbrella National Democratic Front (NDF), which was gradually developed during the late sixties and early seventies to be formally founded in April 1973 and its various constituents culminating in BAYAN (Bagong Alansang Makabayan or New Nationalist Alliance) which held its foundation convention in May 1985. I said they should look at their movement as being like the hub of a wheel of political influence with spokes going off into trade unions, peasant farmer associations, political parties, NGOs of varying kinds, student organisations, commercial organisations, and various individuals all aimed at building better liberal democratic institutions and influencing the policies of the national government. (I realised that in a country like the Philippines this was a bit like dealing with the icing on a stale cake). I suggested that the various constituent grass roots organisations should utilise the parish, educational and other resources of the Catholic Church as this was an overwhelmingly Catholic country. They should endeavour to get the Church to support these organisations and encourage its lay people to get involved in them. However, I strongly warned against the clergy themselves getting involved actively in any of these bodies, a position I held in respect of the National Civic Council in Australia and Catholic Action in the world generally.

We discussed and debated all of these matters for quite some time –

but over the next twenty years I was to learn that most of those sitting around the table, with the exceptions of Tan and Montemayor, were very good at debating matters but next to useless at doing anything. However, this night their major problem was not with the idea of the inclusive national movement I suggested – indeed they thought that was good and for all I know they might have thought of it before – but with the concept of a ten year, or longer, strategy to gain effective direct or indirect national political power. They said they couldn't wait that long. I've always thought that very strange coming from a mainly Jesuitical group. Since then, I've sometimes thought that maybe some of these Jesuits and their mates in other orders didn't really want to change much because, despite *Rerum Novarum* and the other social encyclicals they kept quoting, at the end of the day many of them came from the establishment.

Immediately after this meeting at Jesuit headquarters, the 49 year old Manglapus, the pin-up crew cut boy of American diplomats with an intriguing, cultivated "trans-Atlantic" accent, who seemed never to age and who was the leader of the Progressive Party of the Philippines (PPP) which argued the case for Philippine peasant land reform if not revolution, invited me to join him on a trip downtown. We jumped into his bright new red MG convertible and zoomed down Roxas (then Dewey) Boulevard to a noisy jazz joint where he joined a band and played very acceptably on drums and piano late into the morning while I chatted with the girls. I can't remember how the night ended, but I can remember thinking that it's going to take a lot longer than ten years to change things. (Apart from becoming President Cory Aquino's foreign affairs minister years later, Raul wrote a fine historical play and a book on original democracy in developing counties, starting with Mesopotamia in Iraq centuries ago, which I have quoted many times in issues of *Asia Pacific Report*).

I have no intention in this book of going into the details of Philippine party politics over the years of my experience with it for it was like a dog's breakfast in noodle soup where nothing had any value and politicians slid in the swill between parties and factions whenever convenient. Few politicians were ever to be believed and at the end of the day it was all run by the dominant provincial families. However, it is, perhaps, worthwhile making a few points about the rise and fall of President Ferdinand Marcos because there are a number of things that are rarely understood about him and, while we all know he was from childhood a crook, he was one of the largest figures in Philippine history. I should say I met him a number of times in the seventies and while I found him engaging and extremely intelligent, this never blinded me to his flaws and failings which contributed so much to his deserved ultimate overthrow.

The first thing that is rarely understood about him is that he was not born a Catholic, but an Anglipayan, a member of the Anglipay sect that broke away from the Catholic Church around 1902 on account, among other things, of the appalling way Spanish friars treated the local Philippine clergy. While today it is associated with Anglicanism generally, it was named after one its founders, Gregorio Anglipay, who lived at the time in Ilocos Norte where Marcos and his adoptive father, Mariano Marcos, were born. In later life Marcos made a political conversion to Catholicism, the religion of his wife Imelda and the vast majority of Filipinos. How real this was only he could tell us and he didn't. (The same of course applied with Indonesia's President Soeharto who was born a Javanese mystic Kebatinan and became officially a Muslim wearing a black peci).

Secondly, the region of the world Marcos grew up in, western Luzon from Ilocos Norte in the north to Cavite in the south abutting Manila, was run by warlords and gangsters involved in illegal activities on a massive scale. They smuggled cars, white goods, boats, women, cigarettes, booze and guns from Hong Kong, Taiwan and other parts of north-eastern Asia into the Philippines and then further south into Indonesia, while protection rackets ran riot. The warlords had their formidable private armies and there was no law as the police and judiciary were well bought. This is the environment in which the young Marcos and his cousin and close friend, the later General Fabian Ver, grew up. It is amazing that he wasn't a greater crook than he was. It is also amazing that such a background could produce such a brilliant intellectual with such an incredible mind whose memory capacity was almost unbelievable. He topped every university law exam showing an amazing ability to remember facts. He simply had one of those memory minds. He did so well in one examination they thought he had to be cheating. So they re-tested him under control conditions and he did even better! Given this, why he ever needed to lie about his military awards is something for the historians and psychologists to ponder.

Another little known fact is that he is the only Filipino president to have been elected in the face of concerted opposition from the United States and the CIA. They backed the incumbent Diosdado Macapagal, the father of the recent president Gloria Macapagal-Arroyo. Marcos refused to be bought by the Americans, although he had accepted their support for his team in earlier congressional elections, and for a long time the CIA hated him for it. This is all revealed in a book by the then CIA Station Chief, Joseph Smith (see Joseph Smith, *Portrait of a Cold Warrior*, Ballantine Books, New York, 1976). Perhaps Marcos baulked at being personally bought by the Americans because his adoptive father, Mariano, reputedly had been drawn and quartered in 1945 by American led guerrillas on the grounds that he was a pro-Japanese war criminal (see Sterling Seagrave, *The Marcos Dynasty*, Fawcett Columbine, New York, 1988). However, policy-wise he remained consistently pro-American and a strong supporter of the continued presence of US bases in Subic Bay and Clark Field. He believed they were strategically necessary given the communist New People's Army (NPA) insurgency in his own country, the rise of Japan as a regional power, the gradual emergence of China, the wars in Indo-China and the general uncertainties of the region.

While I recognised in Marcos a fellow political animal, he was, like a lot of conservatives, not a subtle ideological one. By this I mean that while he was strongly anti-communist, he had never been of or near the left and failed to understand the differences between, say, social democrats, democratic socialists and Marxists and the varieties within each of those categories. He had no idea what liberation theology was about and couldn't understand why the qualification 'radical' might be applied to parts of it. The same things could be said of Soeharto, Nguyen Van Thieu and other Asian conservative leaders, political and military, who thought that when confronted by a communist insurgency or political challenge it was best to jail or take out everyone on the left in case they missed a key figure. (I was briefly tempted to add Lee Kuan Yew to this list, but originally coming from the left he, at least at one time, understood the distinction between a social democrat and a democratic socialist. In his case he simply jailed or suppressed everyone who opposed himself and his family). It was often hard going wrestling with these people trying to explain to them that the social democrats they were jailing were actually anti-communists and the communists' greatest enemies. In the Philippines the man who arrested, gaoled and tortured hundreds of young social and Christian democrats, some of them friends of mine, never to be heard of again, was Marcos' malleable police chief and another cousin, General Fidel Ramos, who was later to become a 'pragmatic democratic' president of the republic following President Cory Aquino. To this day, he has never apologised for any of his Marcos era barbarity. To hear him being touted today as a "statesman" is both ludicrous and appalling.

It is also not widely known that after declaring Martial Law on September 21, 1972, Marcos reached out to the Catholic Church to cooperatively build a "new democratic society" and defeat the communist and radical Muslim insurgencies that were wracking the nation. Cardinal Jaime Sin and other church leaders, among them Jesuits, rebuffed him, despite the fact that Communist Party infiltration of church institutions through its exploitation of radical and moderate liberation theology was damaging the Church. According to De la Costa, who was by then a former Jesuit provincial, they knocked Marcos back because he "wasn't one of us". At the same time most of them appreciated Marcos' efforts, if not his methods, to bring about badly needed reform. They were pleased to see the tens of thousands of weapons handed in after the Martial Law declaration and notably the thousands dumped five foot deep for hundreds of metres along EDSA by ordinary Filipinos hoping the nation was about to turn to reform itself.

After the Church knocked him back – and one can only speculate on what might have happened had there been a Marcos/Church alliance to gradually build a new political structure and movement in the country – he gradually developed another political base centred on the military and a group of new oligarchs. He also established what he called The New Society Movement (KBL) utilising members of his family, some of the new oligarchs and elements of the military, the bureaucracy and the Nationalista Party in an attempt to build a political vehicle along the lines of Golkar in Indonesia. At the same time Army Chief General Fabian Ver and Police Chief General Fidel Ramos ruthlessly crushed the political Left including not only communist activists but the social and Christian democrats as well. As the latter were backed by Jesuit and other Church forces, and there were murky overlaps between them all, Marcos ran into increasing official Church opposition. In the long run, however, there was never any way that the Marcos family and its allies were going to outlast the Catholic Church in The Philippines. Marcos was head and shoulders above any other Philippine politician or public figure I've ever known or read about, but even he had to age and as he did so in increasingly poor health due to lupus and a kidney transplant, he gradually lost his touch and eventually slid into senility. He should have retired around 1977-78. But he overestimated his own importance to the nation, could see no satisfactory successor and thought he could just go on and perhaps cultivate one of his children to succeed him somehow. But it all gradually faded and totally disappeared with the assassination of Benigno 'Ninoy' Aquino at Manila International Airport in August 1983. Marcos was overthrown following the presidential election in January 1986 which he said he'd won. But the opposition and street demonstrators claimed he'd cheated and that Cory Aquino had won and that this was proved by the unofficial "fast", private and independent Namfrel (National Movement for Free Elections) count. The demonstrations gradually grew until thousands massed in a confrontation with the military on EDSA Boulevard on February 26 and Marcos and his wife were flown out of the country by the US. In a final demonstration of his innate political nous Marcos knew the game was up and had refused to allow General Ver to order an attack on the massing crowd which included thousands of nuns. Ramos had already scuttled ship. (For more on this subject read Mark R. Thompson, *The Anti-Marcos Struggle: Personalistic Rule and Democratic Transition in the Philippines*, New Day Publishers, Manila, 1996 and Sandra Burton, *Impossible Dream: The Marcoses, The Aquinos, and the Unfinished Revolution*, Warner Books, New York, 1989).

An interesting, ironical titbit in all of this is that a long-time associate of mine and one of the key organisers of the anti-Marcos push who was very close to Aquino, to the rebellious Reform the Armed Forces Movement (RAM) soldiers associated with Juan Ponce Enrile whom Marcos had unwisely alienated and to the April 6 Liberation Movement (A6LM), confided to me that Marcos had in fact won the election fair and square. He explained that the Church-backed "independent" Namfrel "fast count" – as against the official government Comelec (Commission on Elections) 'slow and therefore fixed by Marcos count' – had been conducted by wives of RAM officers utilising a bank of phoney computers and that it was thoroughly fraudulent. He described the computers as "a joke". Marcos, he said, had won easily.

After Aquino's assassination on August 21, 1983, my social democratic friends decided on a course of action. They would form a tactical alliance with the communist left through which they hoped to destroy both Marcos and the communist left. They went into alliance with the people who then ran the major Communist Party/NDF/NPA political fronts and deliberately became members of a new communist-controlled front which formally emerged in 1985 as a "united" front called BAYAN (Bagong Alyansang Makabayan or New Nationalist Alliance). At the founding convention of BAYAN in May 1985 an intense and rowdy conflict broke out between the Maoist CPP operatives and the largely Jesuit-trained social democrats (Socdems) over the issue of whether they should pursue an electoral or a revolutionary path to get rid of Marcos. This had been provoked by the Socdems, some of whom queried the revolutionary credentials of some of the Marxists and Maoists. After the CPP-controlled delegates loudly and publicly denounced elections in favour of revolutionary struggle and the party ordered its delegates to take control and assert "central command" of BAYAN, the social democrats walked out and formed BANDILA (Bansang Nagkaisa sa Diwa at Layunin or A Nation United in Thought and Purpose) which they envisaged becoming a national movement to guide and co-ordinate their activities in various fields. The idea was the sort of movement, in fact, that I had been suggesting to them for sixteen years. They launched it formally in July 1985. I was living in Melbourne at the time and while I couldn't get to Manila until late that year, my Jesuit and Filipino trade union friends kept me fully informed of what was happening. When Marcos announced in November 1985 the snap presidential election to be held in January 1986, BAYAN, wedged by its conference declarations and acting under directions from the

CPP politburo, opted to boycott it because they said elections alone couldn't defeat Marcos.

This, in effect, spelt the end of effective communist influence in the Philippines and you can put it down to subtle Jesuitical influences in the background. It was to be another three years before the Soviet Union collapsed which in turn led to the collapse of at least radical liberation theology which nevertheless kept rattling away for a while in the Philippines, various South American countries and parts of Australia. It was a remarkable Jesuit success. I could mention many of the people involved – theologians, philosophers, poets and others – but they wish to remain anonymous. I was hoping that BANDILA would become the saviour of The Philippines. But unfortunately it didn't last. Like most things in The Philippines, it was gradually undermined by ambition, avarice and organisational inertia.

Forty years ago, The Philippines was the most prosperous nation in Southeast Asia with a democracy the envy of the region. Its potential to influence, and indeed lead, the whole of Southeast Asia was impressive. Today, it has fallen behind most of those it once led including Thailand, Taiwan, Malaysia, Singapore and Indonesia. Unless things change it will continue to relatively decline. At the heart of its problems is the structure of the Philippine polity which is dominated by an oligarchy of inward-looking family dynasties and provincial warlords. They are mostly warm and welcoming people, but their concern at all levels of politics is solely to promote their own venal interests. There are no policy differences between them, only family quarrels. Few outsiders have been able to challenge the power of these often obscenely rich dynasties and as a consequence the nation is ossifying. In this Catholic country, some energetic reformers have looked to the Catholic Church in the past thinking it might want to challenge the system, if only in the interests of uplifting its own poor who run into the millions. Unfortunately they found that the Church establishment and its bishops are either part of the dynasties or allied with them one way or another. Indeed, some observers see the Church establishment as one of the main protectors of the system.

What the nation needs is a strong, visionary leader capable of launching a program to change The Philippines from a plutocracy to some kind of social democracy. This would not require a direct war on the oligarchs, but a long term indirect strategy in partnership with those political, religious, trade union, academic, student, business and other elements in society who want to move the country in this direction and could help it do so. At one time, it was hoped that President Gloria Macapagal-Arroyo might be that person for, whatever her failings, she understood all of this. By comparison, I suspect that the new president Benigno Aquino III, understands little.

Probably one of the first things that should be done is to change the Constitution in order to (1) introduce a national federal parliamentary system to replace the current US style congressional system and (2) attract greater foreign direct investment (FDI) and open up the economy generally. Proponents of constitutional change, or Charter Change (Cha Cha) as it is known, argue that a federal parliamentary system with proportional representation will serve the national interest rather than family dynastic interests by decentralising power and giving rise to stronger, more independent and more policy-oriented political parties.

It is said that Cha Cha is necessary if the country is to open up economically, encouraging more FDI, lower tariffs and trade liberalisation generally. Another problem is that the current Constitution bans majority foreign equity in "strategic sectors" such as mining and resources, publishing, media, transport and energy and all foreign investment in areas where the Philippines is deemed to have a "competitive advantage". This is crazy constitutionally and economically. Constitutionally because in the immediate frenzied post-Marcos years, the Constitutional Convention wrote detailed policy rather than general principles into the Constitution across many areas; economically, because the Philippines is a mining and resource rich country and a maritime nation of thousands of islands which depends for its growth and development on international trade. Very few Filipinos seem to understand this. Protectionism for such a trading nation is a disaster. It has also hindered its industrial development. But for anti-American protectionism over the past forty five years, the Philippines might have become the 'Detroit' of Asia, assembling and producing American and other cars for the region with all of the jobs, subsidiary industries and exports that would have gone with that. Instead, free wheeling Thailand has become that hub.

This narrow xenophobic protectionism has been the result of demands from both the greedy right-wing dynasties and oligarchs on the one hand and on the other those on the left of Philippine politics, Marxist and liberal democratic, who have campaigned over the years against Western capitalism and multinationals in the name of Philippine 'nationalism'. Is this why you find the children of oligarchs in left wing politics? In the end, all the Left has achieved is to aid the oppressive oligarch cause and seriously limit the country's economic growth thereby condemning the nation's millions of increasingly urbanised poor to endless misery. Never mind that many of the right and left wing middle and upper class leaders of this so-called 'nationalist' cause own property in the US and send their children to be educated in the US and/or work for the very multinational corporations they denounce in the Philippines. Some of them even hold American passports while many of them end up working for oligarch conglomerates in the Philippines because there is simply nowhere else to go.

SAIGON AGAIN

More on Serong, Phoenix and the Nhan-Xa Party

There weren't too many smiles at Tan Son Nhat airport as screaming Phantoms took off two abreast, but Ted Serong and a chap called Clyde Bauer were there to greet me. Ted in an immaculate long-sleeved white shirt, shook my hand, gave me an envelope he said would "bring me up to date on what was happening" and then turned on his heel and walked off. The tall, heavily-built Bauer picked up my pieces of luggage as if they were match sticks and said "Follow me".

Clyde explained as we drove to Ted's PFF/Phoenix apartment block that while he had lived in Vietnam for nearly ten years as the head of Civil Air Transport (CAT) which had a public, commercial office downtown, he was also the head of the CIA's Air America operations throughout Indo-China. He said that he and other people in the CIA, USAID, State Department, Defense Intelligence Organisation (DIO) and other US bodies in Indo-China and Southeast Asia generally had been instructed to give me every assistance I needed or requested – logistical, weapons, people, communications – whatever. He said that whenever I was "in country", that is in South Vietnam, there would always be an aircraft with a pilot at Tan Son Nhat sitting there at my disposal to take me anywhere in the world. Clyde was a wonderful chap, but I asked why all of this? He just shrugged his shoulders and said "Melbourne and Ted seem to like you". We got to chatting about the war. Nearing the apartment he denounced the "madman" Robert McNamara and his "helicopter/napalm/kill ratio/bombing war" in the strongest language imaginable.

On each of the following three days I had long lunches with Ted and then breakfast with him on the fourth. Apart from many other things it was clear to us that as an essential complement to Phoenix and its associated pacification-rural development programs we needed to build national liberal, social democratic organisations and political parties. In this war, we hoped they would be two sides of the same winning coin so to speak. This was to be the beginning of the Nhan-Xa Party.

This war, the Second Indo-China War, was a particularly nasty complex affair because the Vietnamese had been in continuous conflict for more than 40 years before it started. Most of Vietnam, and certainly South Vietnam, had been run for decades, indeed centuries, by local and regional religious, sect and gangster warlords and their armies. On top of this 'traditional scenario' came French colonialism and then in the 1920s the revolutionary, ideological force of communism led by intellectual agitators supported and financed by the Soviet Comintern and the Communist Party of China (CPP) which promised to bring the educated and the bourgeoisie independence and the poor and the "proletariat" land and prosperity. Into the maelstrom following the French defeat in 1954, when Saigon and other cities were run by gangster mobs like the Binh Xuyen, came the Americans in a bid not only to "save" South Vietnam from communism, but the whole of Southeast Asia in an epic three-way contest between the West, the Soviet Union and China for control of the Indonesian waterways between the Indian and Pacific Oceans. My basic point here is that South Vietnam was a thoroughly traumatised society riven with daily violence where many issues were settled with the gun long before the Americans and even the French arrived. Indeed, this applied throughout most of Southeast Asia well into the sixties.

In the mid- to late-1960s the Americans and their allies in Vietnam faced the problem of how to counter and destroy what we called the Vietcong civilian/military infrastructure (VCI) which enabled the North Vietnamese to prosecute their war against the south. While the much older and at times prickly Ted Serong and I had a somewhat love/hate relationship over the years, especially when I lived just around the corner from him in Saigon for three years in the early seventies, we had many discussions about the VCI and how to tackle it well before he established Phoenix in 1967-68. He knew that in Australia I had quite a bit of experience building political organisation through national bodies like the Defend Australia Committee (DAC), the Wheat for India Campaign and the Democratic Labor Party. He also knew through Bob Santamaria that at university I had set up my own DLP Club and that, in league with the ever intriguing Dr. Frank Knopfelmacher, I'd in effect taken over the ALP Club and set up other political clubs while having our opponents defeated in Students Representative Council (SRC) elections and sacked from the student newspaper *Farrago*. Almost every time Bob met Ted, according to Ted, Bob spoke about my abilities in these areas. Ted had no political experience of any kind whatsoever so I was able to bring something useful to his thinking that went to the heart of the counter-insurgency effort. Revolutionary guerrilla warfare or revolutionary insurgency, which was what we were facing, is armed political warfare involving soldiers, political cadres and political organisation. In this case it was a totalitarian armed political movement, the Vietcong, backed and controlled by the North Vietnamese, and supported by China and the Soviet Union. It had to be met both militarily and politically.

Briefly and idealistically, our approach to the political aspect of the counter-insurgency effort was on the one hand to identify and destroy the VCI and on the other hand to replace it with liberal democratic organisations, notably the Nhan-Xa Party which we hoped would have an existence of its own in any event. Ted would concentrate on attacking the VCI for that would require a lot of support from the US military-intelligence-aid complex while I'd concentrate on helping to build the Nhan-Xa which would be a coalition of a number of existing political forces and parties like the VNQDD (Vietnam Kuomintang), the Dai Viet (Greater Vietnam) and others centred in many provinces around the resources of the Catholic Church and other religious organisations like the Cao Dai and the Hoa Hao.

The VCI was made up of full time VC guerrillas many of whom were also trained political cadres and local Vietnamese civilians who worked during the day and became soldiers or political and propaganda cadre and assassins at night. They both supported and were supported by regular North Vietnamese Army (NVA) soldiers who were in South Vietnam in their thousands from the start of the war in 1962 and by 1967 numbered tens of thousands. The distinction between civilians and combatants in this sort of warfare has always been difficult with women and children performing key guerrilla roles, many of them assassins and terrorists. Apart from the war, the lawless conditions that prevailed, especially in the pitch dark of night, saw countless family, personal and other feuds settled in the most violent, horrific manner. A Conradian *Heart of Darkness* type situation of horror and torture prevailed. Most of Vietnam had been at war since the 1920s and VC/NVA atrocities, among others, were truly horrendous and frequent.

The Phoenix Program had two clear equal objectives: Firstly, to destroy the VCI by identifying and killing, that is assassinating, its key cadres at both high and low levels and, secondly, collect intelligence on the VCI and NVA movements which Serong facilitated through his establishment of the District Intelligence Operations Co-ordination Centres (DIOCC'S). Supported by the Police Field Force, Provincial Reconnaissance Units (PRUs), elements of the ARVN's Popular and Regional Forces, the Census, Grievance and Revolutionary Development Cadre Program and other agencies, Phoenix did extremely well both before, but especially after the 1968 Tet Offensive which was a massive defeat for the communists resulting in vast damage to the VC and its VCI over the ensuring months. In ordering the VC to surface and launch the Tet Offensive, Hanoi and the VC expected the population to rise up against the Thieu regime. Hanoi thought that the Thieu regime would fall and that the NVA would then come over the top of the VC and take power in Saigon – as happened seven years later. But the population rose up not against Thieu but against the VC and the NVA, as Paul Ham makes clear in his book.

Ham says that for a time, Phoenix was extremely effective, by 1970 breaking the Viet Cong Infrastructure (VCI) and its logistical system. After the war, North Vietnamese leaders convinced the historian Stanley Karnow that Phoenix caused them extraordinary damage, the loss of thousands of cadres forcing hundreds of NVA and VC troops to withdraw into Cambodia. At the time, Serong told me and others on a number of occasions that while Phoenix targeted the VC leadership, excesses had and were occurring because some overzealous Phoenix operatives wanted to "make sure we won". For example he said, they killed too many teachers and postmen because some of them were, at night, part of the VCI. Serong said he knew from the outset that excesses would occur if only through people settling old scores as this had been happening for decades. As I mentioned earlier, these activities took place within an almost totally lawless, darkened, horror-filled environment. I heard Ted say more than once: "We are in a gutter war and in a gutter war you have to be prepared to get down in the gutter."

The CIA knew from very early on that Phoenix was being effective. A September 1968 edition of the CIA's Directorate of Intelligence's secret *Weekly Summary* reported the following:

> In the first seven months of 1968, more than 7300 of the Communist infrastructure in South Vietnam are reported to have been neutralized by allied operations ... US officials hope to neutralize a total of 12000 members of the Viet Cong Infrastructure (VCI) during 1968. This goal will probably be reached and may even be surpassed ...
>
> Over the past several years, an improvement was noted in the effectiveness of the government's anti-VCI operations. In some areas of the country ... intelligence operations against the VCI prior to and during the enemy's Tet offensive succeeded in restricting the enemy's military action. Moreover, during Tet, a number of additional important communist cadres surfaced and were apprehended. In some cases, these people provided leads which enabled the government intelligence services to extend the

roll-up to other members of the VCI. In no area, however, have the VCI and its subordinate networks been completely neutralized.

(This CIA document has been declassified and is accessible on the CIA website as MORI Document ID:> 11814:11814).

One of Serong's counter-insurgency ideals, which he repeated to me often was to convert as many enemy guerrillas and cadres as possible to his side rather than kill them. That, he said, was always his first aim because they were usually worth converting. While reality usually intervened, it was nevertheless true that during the US/South Vietnamese Pacification programs thousands of VC surrendered to the Saigon regime or simply returned to their native villages (Karnow, p. 603) many of them converting and aiding the non-communist cause in various ways. Serong set up the South Vietnamese-run Chieu Hoi (Open Arms) program to facilitate this. The South Vietnamese forces suffered thousands of deserters, but few defectors.

As a result of the Pacification programs, of which Phoenix, the Provincial Reconnaissance Units (PRUs), PFF and other projects were parts, and Vietnamisation, the VC/NVA complex was seriously weakened in the years following its decisive hammering during the 1968 Tet Offensive which was scandalously and in large part deliberately misreported in the Western media as a US/South Vietnamese defeat. By 1971, morale was a massive problem for the VC/NVA. They were on the ropes. This led Ted Serong and myself, and no doubt others, to believe in mid-1971 that the communists could no longer win the war, even if it went on for some time. We both made a number of public statements to this effect. For example, I told a branch of the Young Liberals in Melbourne that "the Vietnam War was 'over' and that the North Vietnamese would be unable seriously to threaten South Vietnam for another six to eight years" (*Moorabbin News*, June 9, 1971).

After 1975, Ted and I were often ribbed for these comments, but we were right given the circumstances. This was proven when

Hanoi launched its massive Easter 1972 Offensive when a number of NVA divisions crossed the borders of South Vietnam to launch co-ordinated attacks against northern and central Highlands cities and towns. These divisions were repulsed and smashed by the much maligned South Vietnamese Army (ARVN) supported only by the US and South Vietnamese air forces and the US Navy. All US and allied ground forces, including Australian, had been withdrawn by early 1972. (It is one of the great Australian Labor Party (ALP) myths that its leader Gough Whitlam withdrew Australia's combat forces from South Vietnam when he didn't become prime minister until November 1972).

One of the few people who was not surprised by the ARVN performance was my Australian photojournalist friend and associate, Neil Davis, who had specialised in covering the ARVN for years and who was immortalised in the very fictional character of Mike Langford in Christopher Koch's novel, *Highways to a War* (William Heinemann, Melbourne, 1995). The ARVN's performance not only strengthened our optimism about South Vietnam's future, but led to some interesting diplomatic adjustments. Like us, the Soviet Union thought that South Vietnam would survive and couldn't imagine the US would let it fail given the possible regional and global strategic consequences. Consequently, it began sending special emissaries to non-communist and anti-communist governments around the region, including South Vietnam, in order to shore up its regional position vis-a-vis communist China. When Henry Kissinger eventually finalised the Paris Peace Accords in January 1973, we said it was a seriously flawed agreement but good enough to allow South Vietnam to survive.

But that was before Watergate and its consequences which none of us could have predicted. By the end of 1973 we had become pessimistic while the NVA rebuilt its divisions and expanded the Ho Chi Minh Trails with very little disruption. In April 1974, I wrote an assessment of the situation for Bob Santamaria and his associates in Melbourne and Canberra, a copy of which I gave to Serong for his then associates in Saigon, London and Washington titled *Vietnam Prognosis, April 1974 to Mid 1975: Eight Scenarios* (See Chapter 11 and Frank Mount Papers). It was decidedly pessimistic saying that South Vietnam's future depended, among other things, on continued US aid. In the end, all of that gradually disappeared as Watergate paralysed Washington and its government and military bureaucracies and a vindictive Congress cut off all aid allowing the NVA to overrun South Vietnam with little or no resistance (see Chapter 12 on The Fall of Saigon). (For regularly updated detailed assessments of military, political and economic developments in Vietnam including Saigon political intrigue over the years, see my Reports to B.A. Santamaria and our correspondence 1970-75. These also contained some of Ted Serong's assessments and much more. These are on my files in the Frank Mount Papers and I believe they can also be found in *The Santamaria Papers*, National Library of Victoria).

As the 1967-75 military scenarios unfolded I was working diligently to help build the Nhan-Xa Party throughout the country in the hope of creating a liberal democratic political entity to run the political party side of the pacification program and in the future rule the country after the war. I had no illusions about any aspects of it, but I was there to give it a go. Having read Graham Greene's *The Quiet American*, Eugene Burdick and William J. Lederer's *The Ugly American* and seen Marlon Brando's 1963 movie of the latter, I thought I had some ideas of what not to do – although I was still only 26 years of age and many mistakes were to follow. In early October 1967, Truong Cong Cuu, the then Chairman of the Nhan-Xa took me to meet the party's leaders, many of whom were former members or associates of Ngo Dinh Diem's Can Lao Party which had been run by his brother Ngo Dinh Nhu and had been loosely based on the personalist philosophy of the French Catholic thinker Emmanuel Mounier. Some Western journalists and academics had absurdly and mischievously portrayed this as the propagation of a Diem personality cult whereas in fact it was almost the opposite.

Cuu introduced me to a number of people who were to become both friends and political colleagues of mine, notably the Paris-educated democrat Ha Nhu Chi, who had spent two years in gaol following Diem's assassination in 1963, and Ngo Khac Tinh, a dapper down-to-earth Confucian cousin of the Catholic President Thieu with a wicked sense of humour who was later to become Minister of Information and Acting Foreign Minister in Thieu governments. Tinh and I had some great intellectual and entertaining times together.

While Can Lao remnants formed the core of the Nhan-Xa it was never going to be anything substantial if not a coalition of a number of national and regional political, ethnic and religious forces including elements of the VNQDD, Hoa Hao, Dai Viet, Cao Dai, Hmong and others. This is what we set out to build from the start. It would also not have got off the ground without the support of Thieu himself who saw it from the outset as a liberal democratic coalition or alliance party that could take power in South Vietnam following the war. Thieu told his province chiefs and others to back the party and give it freedom to move – for what that was worth given the fluidity of life and the arbitrary 'rule' of warlords and police chiefs in the countryside.

Over the years, I visited Nhan-Xa branches and addressed meetings in almost every province in the country talking not only with Can Lao hardcore but with leaders of the various local ethnic and religious groups as well. In this I relied on interpreters and could only hope that they were not relaying the opposite of what I was saying. Of course I never for one moment attempted to tell them what they should be doing. What I spoke to them about – and always briefly – was what we did in respect of liberal democratic organisation in

Australia and in some other countries like The Philippines; that it took time to build such organisation and that they were in the forefront of the fight in Indo-China against global communist totalitarianism and in support of freedom and prosperity for Vietnam. I was never sure how anything I said went down or was accepted, but everyone seemed to smile, even I suspect the VC in the audiences and they were no doubt there.

I travelled around the country to these countless Nhan-Xa meetings and other engagements on Air America light aircraft, Air Vietnam DC3s, US and ARVN helicopters and in aging black Peugeots, Police Field Force white and green jeeps and South Vietnamese Navy riverine patrol craft when in the Mekong Delta which was quite often. Wherever I went I met with up the local CIA, USAID, DIO (US Defence Intelligence Organisation) and other American officials for briefings on what was happening locally – courtesy of Ted and Clyde Bauer. Among them was the CIA station chief in the Cu Chi and Ben Cat areas north of Saigon, Bob Walkinsaw, whose previous post had been that of Labor Attache at the US Consulate in Melbourne. I, of course, knew him from Melbourne where he had provided help to the DAC and the MU DLP and ALP Clubs. I remember the conversations we had in a wonderful Vietnamese restaurant in a rubber plantation in Cu Chi where he reminisced about his friendships with Bob Hawke, Jim Cairns, Mike Young, Clyde Cameron and many others, some of whom he claimed had stayed in the homes of CIA station chiefs when visiting places like Singapore. This was interesting news to me and I tucked it away for further reference.

The eminence gris of the Nhan-Xa, although never a member of the party himself, was Bishop and later Cardinal Nguyen Van Thuan who was a nephew of Ngo Dinh Diem. Thuan was not a politician and never tried to interfere in the party's day-to-day affairs. However, he did take a keen interest in the overall strategic direction of the party and in its leadership, matters in which he expressed opinions which always carried some weight. He recognised the need for strong anti-communist political organisation and encouraged Catholic lay people and others like his Confucianist friend Ngo Khac Tinh to build it. He and Tinh were instrumental in persuading President Thieu to support the party. Thieu and Tinh were cousins and had grown up together in Phan Rang, a coastal town in Central Vietnam.

While Thieu ensured that the party was adequately financed and that resources, such as transport, accommodation and conferencing facilities, were made available to it, Thuan also provided material support where necessary. Bob Santamaria raised money in Australia for Thuan which at various times I passed on to him. I understood that most of this was for a seminary he was building in Nha Trang for this was truly his major concern, although I assumed he used some of it to assist his Nhan-Xa associates. My understanding was that most of the money had come from Australian businessmen and a few bishops who had raised it from some of their wealthier parishioners. It wasn't until historian Patrick Morgan was working on his book *B.A. Santamaria: Your Most Obedient Servant* in 2006 that I realised that some of the bishops' money had come from Church funds I would not have approved of. However, this was just a part of it. Bob received money from many people for a variety of projects in South Vietnam and elsewhere. I myself passed on cheques to help orphanages, refugee settlements, hospitals, leprosariums and other institutions including one associated with Rosemary Taylor.

Between 1967 and 1970 the Nhan-Xa grew quite impressively and its members did well in elections under either the party's own name or those of its coalition partners. By early 1970 it was the strongest of all parties in the provinces, according to my informants in and outside of the party. I have no serious reason to doubt this. It had great influence within the government and had many assets in the cabinet. Quite independently of Ted Serong and myself, the CIA's Directorate of

Intelligence reported the following in its officially classified secret *Weekly Summary* for 12 September 1969:

> Some critics of President Thieu's new cabinet selection have pointed out that Prime Minister Khiem and Foreign Minister Tran Van Lam, as well as the ministers of information, economy, finance and legislative liaison have been Can Lao members or sympathisers. General "Big" Minh, for one, has privately suggested that renewed Can Lao influence could lead to a tragic clash between Catholics and Buddhists. One prominent friend of the government, Senator Dang Van Sung, is worried that Can Lao leaders are trying to revive their old youth organisation, possibly with Thieu's blessing. Apprehension is likely to increase over reports that the new information minister (Ngo Khac Tinh) has appointed some 20 cadre from the Nhan-Xa Party, a neo-Can Lao group, to key subordinate positions.
>
> President Thieu presumably considered this risk when he made his cabinet selections. He apparently concluded that the need for better administrative performance, particularly in the information and economic fields, and thus for men of experience and talent, outweighed the dangers of lingering anti-Can Lao feeling and the desirability of bringing in more popular faces.
>
> Meanwhile there are indications that some of the leaders in the government-sponsored National Social Democratic Front (NSDF) who did not receive positions in the cabinet are considering withdrawing from the front.
>
> (This *Weekly Summary* has now been de-classified and, at least until recently, was available on the CIA website as *Mori Document* ID: > 28912:28912).

At this time, not only did the Nhan-Xa have great influence over the government's policy and tactics in many areas, including peace negotiations, but it was in a position to place its people within both the administration in Saigon and South Vietnamese embassies and other assets around the world. While the Americans had a good appreciation of this, the same cannot be said of the Australian government, its diplomats, intelligence officers and generals. This can be seen, for example, in the statement of the now celebrated former Australian general, Peter Cosgrove, that not only was the Vietnam War futile and mistaken, but that during his tour of duty there (from mid-1969 to mid-1970) he never saw any sign of democratic development in Vietnam (quoted by Stephen Morris in *The Australian*, August 2, 2002). Yet with their various flags flying in the breeze the Nhan-Xa, VNQDD and other democratic parties, national trade unions and participatory bodies of many kinds, including Western opera and literature societies, held many national conferences in the coastal resort of Vung Tau, just a few kilometres up the road from his barracks. There were over thirty registered political parties in South Vietnam some of which traced their clandestine origins to the 1920s. Many of them were anti-Thieu and some of them were socialist. Cosgrove couldn't have got out too much among the people and his local and village intelligence must have been lousy. It makes one wonder what sort of counter-insurgency he and his senior officers thought they were engaged in. Judging from the Vietnam chapter of his autobiography it seems that he never ever met any South Vietnamese during his tour whether military or civilian (see General Peter Cosgrove, *My Story*, Harper Collins, Sydney, 2006, Ch. 4).

However, as the Nhan-Xa grew stronger, in-fighting developed and in mid-1972 it split. My letters and reports to Bob Santamaria cover this in detail (as they did many other South Vietnamese political and military developments over the years, including Thieu's defeat of Nguyen Cao Ky in 1967, the internecine conflict that plagued South Vietnam in 1974, and the internal problems within the VC/NVA complex in the seventies which I had infiltrated to great effect). The Nhan-Xa split between what we might call the traditionalist Can Lao section of the party led by Cuu which looked to the past and the modernist section led by Ngo Khac Tinh who, backed by

Thieu, looked to the future and Asian regionalism along the lines of the Pacific Institute. The Nhan-Xa gradually lost strength and in December 1972 Thieu and Tinh's modernists formed the liberal social democratic Dang Dan Chu (Democratic or Dan Chu Party). In early 1973, the Nhan-Xa went out of existence and Cuu's Can Lao group formed the Dang Tu Do or Freedom Party which was still the strongest of any democratic political party in the provinces, all of which had been seriously disrupted by the NVA's 1972 Easter Offensive.

However, with Thieu's backing, the Dan Chu rapidly grew in strength and was the only party at the end of the year with the qualifications to register under new rules for the August senate elections. The Tu Do party failed to meet the registration requirements and went out of existence. However, in late 1973 and 1974 the Dan Chu succumbed to the usual internecine in-fighting which was largely generated by a conflict between the Party's leader Nguyen Van Ngan and Thieu's Chief of Staff, Hoang Duc Nha, who was another cousin of Thieu's. Ngo Khac Tinh, then Minister for Information and the Foreign Minister Tran Van Lam, both members of the Pacific Institute, were also involved in this. By early 1974, I was dealing with all of these people on an almost daily basis. The heavy-handed Nha won this fight, but in June 1974 Thieu tired of it all and declared that no soldier, public servant or public official at any level was allowed to join any political party effectively snookering the Dan Chu which had been his own creation. (For details on the machinations involved in this see my reports and letters and especially my confidential letter to Bob Santamaria of March 4, 1974, concerning the intrigue and conflict between Thieu, Khiem, Nha, Nga, Dang Van Quang, Pham Van Dong, Tran Van Don and others in the Frank Mount Papers).

By this stage – mid 1974 – Thieu was an increasingly demoralised man on account of what was happening in the US and this partly explains his actions. This was not helped when Ted Serong returned from a trip to Europe and the US in late June. He said to me on the way back from the airport that Washington was paralysed from Watergate, that Vietnam was forgotten and that US aid to Vietnam would continue to fall. He didn't say anything else. But PI member Professor Nguyen Van Chau, a close associate of Bishop Thuan's, reported to me that he told Thuan, and presumably Thieu whom he saw often: "The US does not care what happens to Vietnam; US aid will decline sharply; the present fighting in Vietnam will slowly escalate into a major offensive throughout the country; that by the end of 1974 or early 1975 North Vietnam will control all of South Vietnam down to at least Qhi Nhon and probably Vung Tau; by mid-1975 to end 1975 they will control the entire country; that you and I will not be sitting here talking to each other" (quoted from my Letter to Santamaria, June 27, 1974).

Of course this is exactly what did happen, so once again Ted was spot on and once again no one listened. Ted did not at the time express this opinion directly to me, because he had read my April Prognosis document, as had Thieu, which while not so dogmatic, didn't exclude the possibility of what Ted had said. The irony is that had the South Vietnamese adopted the withdrawal/consolidation strategy he proposed to Thieu and his generals to meet the situation he predicted the scenario he outlined might not have come about because of both local factors and international, superpower interests.

Ted became increasingly depressed and began coming around to my house every two or three days for a drink, in between my dropping in on him. Prior to this I'd regularly come by his house during the week and then on Saturdays and Sundays to swim in his pool and listen to the Australian football. However, by mid-1974 his supposed 'mistress', and personal agent or spy in the US Defense Attache's Office (DAO), had taken over the house for at least the weekends to entertain her toy boys, usually blond-headed American and German soldiers. Unfortunately, he kept becoming more morose and pessimistic and one day I found him in his office above his garage on Phan Dinh Phung looking at a Galliano bottle in the middle of his desk filled with rainbow layers of different coloured liqueurs. I was amazed. He kept me waiting and waiting as he looked at it and then said: "It has taken me hours to put this together, to build this delicate thing. This is Vietnam." He then slowly lifted the bottle and gently shook it. The brilliant colours blended into a dull grey. "That's the Paris agreement", he said.

Serong, Thieu and other South Vietnamese were not the only people demoralised. So too were the NVA in South Vietnam and the remnants of the VC. I had sent the Pacific Institute's Vu Quy Ky and a couple of his associates on an extended two-three week tour of the Mekong Delta to determine the situation there and specifically the strength of the NVA/VC (see my letter to Santamaria, July 11,1974). Ky's reports were brilliant and eventually read by foreign offices and intelligence services around the globe. Unknown to him, I had also run, through a number of cut-outs, a source or agent into COSVN headquarters. COSVN was Hanoi's mobile HQ in the lower half of South Vietnam and the acronym stood for Central Office in South Vietnam. This mobile HQ was generally located north west of Saigon on the South Vietnamese-Cambodian border in the Parrot's Beak region. It moved locations within both South Vietnam and Cambodia, depending on circumstances. It had a number of sub-branches covering different aspects of the war such as operations, intelligence and logistics all of which moved independently of each other.

COSVN never controlled the whole war in South Vietnam, only in the bottom third of the country which was the old Cochin China known to the Americans in this war as IV Corps. Some people, including many journalists, doubted COSVN existed, but there is no doubt that it did. I can fairly claim to be the only Westerner to run a long term, sustainable and reliable source within COSVN over a couple of years. Among the products of that operation were many pre-off-the-press copies of COSVN Directives to NVA/VC forces in the field. Original copies remain on my files. My COSVN source confirmed much of what Ky was saying, including that communist guerrillas across the Mekong Delta were overwhelmingly North Vietnamese with very few southerners amongst them. The local people could easily tell this from their accents and they were extremely unpopular on account of their cruelty. Most of them were NVA regulars disguised as guerrillas. They were thoroughly demoralised because once again they were being told that the war would go on for many years after only a couple of months earlier being told during the Easter Offensive that ultimate victory was at hand. They had been let down similarly following the 1968 Tet Offensive and before that following the 1963 Diem assassination. They longed for their families, but instead they were being found throughout the country chained to their weapons, armour and artillery.

The Soviet Union, for its part, thought that South Vietnam was now safe; that the North could not defeat it; that US support for the south, even if declining, ensured that. Accordingly, Moscow started sending special envoys across south and southeast Asia to shore up diplomatic links with all the governments of the region, including the non- and anti-communist ones. This included South Vietnam and Cambodia and Russian diplomats and intelligence officers unofficially visited both Saigon and Phnom Penh. However, Moscow failed to appreciate the true nature and temperament of the US Congress and the paralysis that Watergate had brought to the US civil and military bureaucratic machines. Meanwhile, as is evident from the Serong quote above, we in Saigon were under no such illusions about US support. And it went back some time. In a letter from Saigon to Santamaria of July 3, 1974, I wrote: "There is considerable concern over the future levels of US economic and military aid there being general agreement that should this decline seriously the present air of optimism would quickly turn to pessimism. In other words ... the future of South Vietnam still rests with the US Congress". Then, on August 27, 1974, I wrote: "As mentioned previously, the future of this place now largely depends on US Congressional decisions regarding economic and military assistance. And things don't look too good on that front. We have just had one of 'Scoop' Jackson's advisors through here who, arriving from the seat of Watergate, ... grandly stated that US aid decisions would be easier if the Americans and the Congress could have some guarantees against corruption in Vietnam!" (See Mount-Santamaria Correspondence, the Frank Mount Papers).

As we know, the US Congress gradually cut off all economic, military, humanitarian, educational, financial and other forms of aid to South Vietnam by April 1975 and the country slowly and totally collapsed – as would any of a couple dozen countries around the world today if the same thing were to happen to them. As this occurred, the Soviet Union raced to deliver weapons and supplies to North Vietnam so as to ensure that the inevitable North Vietnamese victory would be a pro-Soviet one and not a pro-China one. This reached the point where at any time in March-April 1975, there were about fifteen Soviet ships off-loading supplies in Haiphong harbour and no US support ships anywhere in South Vietnam, while the Chinese sent what they could over the border and down the Ho Chi Minh Trail.

It is fascinating that long before the signing of the Paris Agreement in January 1973, the Chinese leadership in Beijing was fearful of this sort of pro-Soviet development. In early 1972 when General Alexander Haig visited China in preparation for President Nixon's February visit, Zhou Enlai gave him some strong advice: don't lose in Vietnam. Haig was so dumb he didn't understand this. So Chou explained to him something that Washington should have always understood – that the last thing China wanted was a Soviet client on its southern border (Alexander M. Haig, Jr., *Inner Circles, How America Changed The World: A Memoir*, Warner Books, New York, 1992, pp. 133-134).

When Saigon fell in 1975, China immediately stepped up its support for Pol Pot's Khmer Rouge in Cambodia as a balance against further Soviet influence. This led to wars between Cambodia and Vietnam then, after Vietnam's invasion of Cambodia in 1979 and its takeover of the government, to a civil war between the Khmer Rouge and Vietnam's Cambodian proxy government, a conflict that dissipated away, not surprisingly, after the decay and collapse of the Soviet Union in 1989 when China no longer had a reason to support the Khmer Rouge. (Claims that this war was brought to an end by Australian Foreign Minister, Gareth Evans, are ludicrous as were embarrassing statements at a Melbourne seminar in the early nineties, attended by me and many Cambodian students that Australia's General John Sanderson was the "greatest leader Cambodia has ever known").

Before returning to our pivotal 1967 tour around the region, it might be worth considering two questions I've been asked over the years about the Vietnam War. The first is often prefaced by the assertion that the war was futile followed by the question, what were we fighting for? The second is could we have won it? – often accompanied by claims that it was an "unwinnable" war. Over the years I have dealt with both of these issues in editions of *Asia Pacific Report*. Apart from the obvious point that we fought it to save South Vietnam from the communist totalitarian rule that prevailed in the north and therefore give it a chance of developing into a liberal democracy, I explained in APR47 (September 19, 2002):

> This war was just one part of a three way regional conflict between the USSR, China and the US and its Free World allies for control of Southeast Asia and in particular the Indonesian waterways running between the Indian and Pacific Oceans which carry nearly all of the trade and oil between Europe, the Middle East and East Asia and most of Australia's trade. At the time of the commitment to Vietnam in 1962-64, the Indonesian Communist Party (PKI) was threatening to take over Indonesia, Soekarno was

trying to undermine Malaysia, and there were wars being fought against communist revolutionary guerrilla movements in Malaysia, Thailand, and the Philippines as well as Laos and Cambodia.

While we ultimately lost the war in Vietnam and the rest of Indo-China for a variety of reasons having to do primarily with Watergate, US military and bureaucratic incompetence and 'fatigue' and the fact that America's primary focus was on Europe and not Asia, we won the much greater battle for Southeast Asia. The Vietnam War gave us ten years or so in which to defeat the PKI, end the Malayan Emergency, negotiate the Five Power Defence Arrangements (FPDA), build ASEAN and develop liberal democratic movements throughout the region.

As to whether the war could have been won, I have already argued that it was won by 1971 and then lost as a result primarily of Watergate. Without Watergate, South Vietnam would have held despite all the other factors including the horrendous strategic and tactical errors made in the field by the US which never understood counter-insurgency and simply substituted firepower for strategic thought. However, it could have been won long before that, indeed at almost any time from Hanoi's launching of the war in 1962. This could have been achieved, for example, by cutting the Ho Chi Minh Trail at an appropriate point across Laos. Ted Serong was a member of a delegation that took this to the US leadership in Washington on at least two occasions. On one of those occasions Serong argued it to the US National Security Committee chaired by a gum chewing Robert Kennedy.

Following the war, North Vietnamese leaders acknowledged the truth of the case. In 1995, Colonel Bui Tin, a former member of the General Staff of the North Vietnamese Army who received the unconditional surrender of South Vietnam on April 30, 1975, and was later an editor of the *People's Daily*, said during a long interview, "If Johnson had granted General Westmoreland's request to enter Laos and block the Ho Chi Minh Trail, Hanoi could not have won the war" (*Wall Street Journal*, August 3, 1995). So why wouldn't Washington agree to it? Serong told me the man who stopped it was Averell Harriman, the senior diplomat and Presidential advisor who Serong otherwise saw, naively in my view, as one of his strongest supporters in Washington. (I'd never trusted Harriman on ideological/Soviet issues given his record since World War II). Harriman had negotiated the 1962 Agreements on Laos providing for Laotian neutrality which America, the Soviet Union, France and other foreign powers including North Vietnam promised not to violate. Of course North Vietnam and Russia took no notice of it otherwise there would have been no Ho Chi Minh Trail. But Harriman would not allow the US to respond and also ignore it because, he said, that would upset his Russian friends and they might react in Europe or Turkey. Harriman had been US Ambassador to the Soviet Union between 1943 and 1946. As was mentioned earlier, the US still looked primarily to Europe and rarely to Asia and this skewed their whole Vietnam perspective and approach to the war. Before 1965, few Americans had ever heard of Vietnam, Cambodia or Laos.

* * *

The day before I left Saigon for Bangkok I dropped by to see Ted Serong at his home and then headed for the Continental Palace Hotel terrace for dinner. I was sipping on a local 33 biere and reading, head down, one of the local newspapers – probably the *Saigon Daily News* which carried some of my articles – when for some reason I looked up. There sitting opposite me was the lovely Kate Webb (see photo). She was staring at me with a wry grin and said "Hello" in that incredibly low and light husky, sexy voice of hers. She just knocked my socks off. I had known her at Melbourne University where as an eighteen year old assistant editor of the student newspaper, *Farrago,* she had published my first ever newspaper article in April 1961 titled "Crisis in Australian International Policy". I'd met her the year before and had immediately fallen in love with her. Many other men had already done so and would continue to do so, for apart from her beauty, she was a very quiet, self-effacing and seemingly vulnerable girl at risk in a wild world and therefore in need of masculine protection.

Nothing could have been further from the truth. Behind that delightful, delicate, elfin screen and smart intellect was a courageous tough as nails professional as she would show on the battlefields of Vietnam and Cambodia, through the 1968 Tet Offensive and during the ordeal of her capture by the VC/NVA in Cambodia in April 1971. She described this ordeal in her amazing book *On the Other Side: 23 Days with the Viet Cong* (Quadrangle Books, New York, 1972), which heavily influenced, to say the least, the latter parts of Koch's award winning *Highways to a War*. This experience damaged her health and along with being a chain smoker and a solid drinker, probably contributed to her early death at 64 in 2007. Having started her journalism with the *Daily Mirror* in Sydney, where I also knew her, she was working for United Press International (UPI) in Saigon and now she was with me.

Over the next few years we were to become what Hollywood once called "just good friends". We dined and then talked, drank and smoked into the night, she on her chain Marlboro cigarettes and me on my trusty old Petersen pipe. We canvassed various aspects of the war including questions relating to what it was all about. She was a brilliant philosophy graduate and so approached life and the war from a different perspective to me. She called herself an agnostic, a professional journalist, a war correspondent and a "de Bouvier feminist" by which she meant, as she explained, that she wanted to be treated like any male war correspondent in the field and to control her own fate. She did both of these things right through her life. She was open if not sympathetic to my politics and even to my Catholic religious position. Her father, Professor Leicester Webb, had written a very good book *Communism and Democracy in*

Australia (F.W. Cheshire, Melbourne 1964) so she understood where I came from and she had seen for herself the results of communist atrocities in the field. Before we knew it, curfew was upon us and we scurried off to her apartment near the Majestic Hotel on the Saigon River. Early the next morning, I got a little clapped-out blue and yellow Renault taxi to the Dakao apartment, gathered up my things and headed for the airport.

BANGKOK AGAIN

In the Shadows of War

The first thing I did after arriving in Bangkok on October 12 was to have lunch on the Erawan Hotel terrace with three old Asia hands who were to teach me a lot and open many doors for me over the years: Bill Klausner, the local head of the Asia Foundation who had lived in Thailand for years and was known for his CIA contacts; George Tanham, an American academic whose speciality was counter-insurgency; and Dick Noone another British counter-insurgency expert who was working in the Bangkok headquarters of the Southeast Asia Treaty Organisation (SEATO) for whose quarterly journal, *Spectrum*, I was to write many articles. Others who used to add to the atmosphere of the Erawan Table were Keith Hyland, a scion of a Melbourne frozen foods and feather processing family and famous as both an inveterate playboy and the Thai duck feather king who produced the fluffy stuff for NASSA clothing, and Sir Robert Thompson.

The aristocratic Thompson was an outstanding British counter-insurgency expert with an extremely impressive record. From 1957 to 1961 he had been Deputy Secretary and then Secretary for Defence in the Federation of Malaya during the Malayan Emergency against Chin Peng's communist guerrillas. Dick Noone had worked as an assistant to him there. Then from 1961 to 1965 Thompson had been the Head of the British Advisory Mission (BRIAM) in South Vietnam and later in the sixties a special advisor to the American government where he was close to Kissinger. He had also written a couple of classic books and texts on counter-insurgency and Vietnam. I should have mentioned him earlier when talking about Serong and Pacification, including Phoenix, for Thompson took part in some of the conversations I had with Serong as to the best ways of approaching the war. Serong and Thompson didn't always see eye to eye and there were some tense times as they were both proud men and in some respects were competing for influence and support in Washington. A major area of agreement, however, had centred on the strategic hamlet program. This was something Thompson had brought from Malaya where it had been most effective in tackling a Chinese insurgency in a majority Malay-Indian society. At first, the cultured, calm and urbane cigar smoking Thompson had thought that it would win the Vietnam War for them. But Serong was never optimistic. He described the concept as "faultless" and agreed that theoretically it could have brought victory, but pointed out that in Malaya there was a British administration and a British judicial system that ensured to a considerable extent that the rule of law prevailed. No such situation existed in Vietnam.

The Strategic Hamlets Program in South Vietnam not only got "over-extended" as both Serong and Thompson put it, it was ultimately destroyed by an inept and corrupt Vietnamese administrative, military and judicial system and a US that didn't understand anything about counter-revolutionary political guerrilla warfare. Among many other things, the Americans refused to get down on the ground and conduct village foot patrols and relied on Robert McNamara's bombing, napalm, Agent Orange and helicopter madnesses that killed thousands of innocent civilians, alienated people and destroyed any hope of an intelligent counter-insurgency approach. We railed against it at the time. Serong and Rodulfo explained to me repeatedly that one of the essentials of CI was foot patrolling partly aimed at bringing the insurgent to you in order to confront him on your terms with superior weapons and techniques. Unless you have the proper procedure for that, they said, you can march for years through enemy territory unmolested leaving his forces intact for deployment elsewhere.

I appreciated this and no doubt commented that the same was true in ideologically contested political party and other forms of politics. The Americans did the opposite in Vietnam. For example, they cleared the roadsides of trees and scrub, using Agent Orange, bulldozers and other means, pushing the enemy back a hundred yards into the jungle. From there, VC/NVA guerrillas and main forces could fire under little presuure at noisy US trucks, convoys and other vehicles roaring up the road. Australian foot patrols would have brought the guerrillas to the roadside scrub and engaged them in there with superior counter-guerrilla weapons and techniques, including ironically, simple shotguns.

When Sir Robert Thompson died in 1992, Serong wrote a very fine obituary, describing him as a genius, a great man and a gentleman (*News Weekly*, June 20, 1992). All students and practitioners of strategy, counter-insurgency and especially counter-revolutionary guerrilla warfare should read Thompson. Despite Serong's high opinion of Thompson, he claimed on more than one occasion, that he, himself, was the greatest practitioner of counter-guerrilla insurgency the world had ever seen. While he and I had over the years what might be called a wonderful, gritty, love-hate relationship, due in part to a combination of our age differences and his at times insufferable arrogance, I believe that in this boast he was right. However, when the war escalated into an essentially main force war in the late sixties, which it had to do, because revolutionary guerrillas don't win these kinds of wars on their own, as General Vo Nguyen Giap and Mao

Tse Tung well understood, Serong again came into his own because he was also a fine conventional soldier.

***

A couple of days later I travelled by train from Bangkok to the busy and ugly town of Haadyai in the deep Muslim South and from there by taxi to the languid and pretty coastal resort of Songkhla on the Gulf of Siam. I lay on the beaches alone. The deep south was suffering from a widespread Muslim insurgency against Buddhist Thai rule and endemic banditry. This taxi ride remains one of my most vivid memories. There I was sitting and sweating profusely in the back seat of an old totally clapped-out windowless black Buick with my various pieces of luggage when half a dozen dark-looking fellows in various coloured singlets emerged from the jungle by the roadside each of them carrying a huge bow with arrows on their shoulders. This was one of those "What am I doing here?" moments. The driver tensed up and accelerated a little while I reached into my shoulder bag for an umbrella which contained a few extra features provided by one of Clyde Bauer's friends in Bangkok. As they strolled across the road in front of us we were forced to slow and just as we feared the worst, they casually kept on going into the jungle on the other side of the road. The shower in the Samila Hotel and the subsequent gin tonic never went down so well.

It was in Songkhla that I first met Phoumi Nosavan in his beachside villa. But Phoumi aside, I had a busy three days with meetings with the local governor, vice-governor and various district officers, as well as a series of pre-arranged briefings on local conditions from Ted Lambert, a US Advisor to the Thai Border Patrol Police (BPP), Colonel Ron Merrick of US Special Forces Intelligence and Bob Morse of Stanford University who was another friend of Clyde Bauer. All of these briefings were followed by long discussions and chilli hot lunches. On the last day I was taken by a conservative Thai

Muslim Senator, the wonderful Leck Vanich Angkhul, whom I had earlier met in Bangkok, and who had flown down from Bangkok for the occasion to meet some of the leaders of the Pattani United Liberation Organisation (PULO), the major guerrilla force fighting the Thai armed forces. In a heavily armed three jeep convoy we travelled for hours into the jungle to meet a group of six rifle-bearing guerrilla leaders in a concrete farm house. Leck acted as my interpreter and introduced me. Since none of their names meant anything to me – and I had read a lot in detail about the insurgency – I assumed they were either aliases or these chaps weren't the top leaders. The meeting was simply an introductory affair and we did not discuss anything of substance. It had been suggested and arranged by Leck with the idea that I would maintain contact with these people and gradually build up a relationship. We had another pleasant long lunch and returned to Songkhla. I was to meet him with some of these fellows a few times in later years, but we never got anywhere. Were they for real? As I read a lot about them today, their claims and demands seem as ephemeral as they did forty-five years ago.

BACK TO MALAYSIA

From Songkhla, I flew across the border and its cloud-topped mountains to Penang in Malaysia. From Penang Island, I took a ferry to Butterworth on the mainland where I had a briefing from an Australian Air Force Intelligence Officer at the RAAF Base before catching a train to Kuala Lumpur. He also handed me a bundle of mail from Bob, Ted and other friends sent by the inter-country military network. In KL I rang Paul Tai mainly to encourage him to come to Manila PI conference in November. He took me along to the headquarters of the Malaysian Chinese Association (MCA) of which he was an active member and introduced me to some of the party's leaders. I then headed for yet another briefing, this time from an old contact, C.C. Too, the Head of the Psychological Warfare

Department in the Prime Minister's Office. He was a tubby, bubbly very talkative aging Chinese playboy who spoke in staccato sentences punctuated with words like "funny buggers" and shocking expletives and who drove a sexy little red MG. But he knew his stuff and gave me a rundown on how he saw things on and over the Malaysian-Thai border. He also had some revealing things to say about the corrupt activities of some the local politicians. He explained that one of the common local practices involved corrupt bank loans to cabinet ministers. A cabinet minister would go to a state bank whose senior executives had been appointed by the government and ask for a loan – let's say of two million dollars – to set up a business. The banker would agree to the loan and at a very low and generous interest rate. He would further explain to the minister – or usually it was simply just understood – that the minister need never repay the loan, just the interest. For this arrangement, the minister would then arrange that a personal 'commission' be paid to the banker of, let's say, five hundred thousand dollars.

Everyone was happy and of course the more loans ministers required for their businesses, many of which failed after a short period, the happier everybody was. Before I left, Too said he was accompanying the prime minister, the Tunku Abdul Rahman, to Kuching in Sarawak, East Malaysia, for the national convention of the ruling Alliance at the end of the week – 4 days away – and that I would be welcome at the meeting. As I was going in that direction to Manila, I said I'd try to be there and immediately started changing my flights and bookings. I wanted to be in Manila by November 1 to help organise the Pacific Institute Conference opening on the 10th and so I had some time up my sleeve. I decided to spend three days in Singapore reading and writing in a languid, spacious bungalow by the ground floor swimming pool of the old Raffles Hotel and then fly to Manila via Kuching and Jesselton, the capital of Sabah in East Malaysia, which were on the flight path to Manila.

SINGAPORE

I did a lot of writing in Singapore. To send my articles to Bob at *News Weekly* and to other newspapers and publications around Asia, the US and Europe I often used the telex facilities at UPI offices around the region because Kate Webb worked for UPI and was able to make special arrangements for me.

For weeks Bob had been telling me to get to Manila early to organise the conference because he had no faith in the Filipinos doing it satisfactorily as they had already changed the location and dates a number of times. He said he trusted my organisational ability because he knew how well my father organised things. My father was a prominent caterer in Melbourne in the fifties and sixties and did nearly all of Melbourne's major government, royal and Olympic Games functions. His greatest effort, perhaps, was to cater for a one sitting five course dinner for 5,020 guests at the Duke of Gloucester Ball held in the Royal Exhibition Buildings in Melbourne in 1953. I think Bob would have attended or known about this function and he would have been impressed.

BORNEO

More War threats

When I arrived at the Borneo Hotel in Kuching, Sarawak, after a mid-morning MSA de Havilland Comet flight from Singapore, C.C. Too was waiting for me. The flight was a bit scary because immediately after take-off the cabin filled up with condensation from the ceiling which became so dense I could hardly see the seat in front of me. That the Comet had had an early history of falling out of the sky, didn't help the atmosphere. However, the effervescent Too, mumbling about some "silly buggers", soothed the nerves and took me off to meet the the Tunku and a bunch of cabinet ministers over lunch at the Alliance convention, all of which was useful. He had also arranged a meeting for me the next day with the Chief Minister Datuk Penghuli Tawi Sli who turned out to be a former Anglican pastor with an avid interest in Australian politics. The following day Too took me on a tour of some nearby Land Dayak villages. I had encountered both Land Dayaks and Sea Dayaks (Ibans) in my readings on the region, but had never met one. The Land Dayaks were famous for their wonderful and comfortable bamboo longhouse-villages built on stilts above the jungle floor and for their long tradition of being enthusiastic about head-hunting, the trophies from which they liked to display on bamboo sticks and walls around the villages and in what they called head houses. I thought this was a barbaric practice until I visited the Savage Club in Melbourne and found it alive and well among the Yarraside establishment. I was assured that today's civilised Dayaks, although still accustomed to sometimes wearing native gear, had mostly given away the practice many decades ago. While they were originally all animists, today they are overwhelmingly Christian and mainly Catholic. The British colonial bureaucrats, I was told, handled the problems of tribal head-hunting and the stacking of skulls in head houses under the category of "recalcitrant activities". But all this aside, it was a wonderful society and the longhouses were works of remarkable, cool ingenuity. That was now long ago. I haven't been back for many decades and fear it has all been spoilt and lost by late twentieth century tourism.

After the longhouse tour, Too invited me to an early dinner with a former colonial officer, journalist and now diplomat named Ivor Kraal who had recently completed a tour as Vice-Consul in the Malaysian Embassy in Manila. Kraal was a dark, handsome, long haired and bespectacled Eurasian character in his early forties of seemingly great colonial, political and sexual experience, who had spent a lot of his time sailing the world and was therefore a subject of fascination for me, the young 26 year old straight out of insular East Coburg. Kraal's paternal ancestors had come to Asia with Dutch East India Company in the late eighteenth century and they had lived in the region ever since. He described them with great eloquence. He was like someone out of a Somerset Maugham novel, full of intelligent ideas about a host of topics with the conversation continuing over a few hours and into the obligatory British large glasses of port. But one thing he was thoroughly expert about was the Philippine claim to the North Borneo Malaysian state of Sabah, which at the time the Filipinos were threatening to go to war over – a part of Milton Osborne's Region of Revolt. Kraal, both politically and legally, dismissed the claim as fanciful based as it was on the claims of some ancient Sulu sultanate. But some of Marcos' gung ho "nationalist" boys in Manila wanted to pursue it even if it meant war with Malaysia, Singapore and Indonesia. Eventually cool heads prevailed. Kraal knew just about anyone of any consequence in Malaysia and what they were up to – or so he said. For many years he was a very good and reliable source of information for me.

When I arrived in Jesselton (today known as Kota Kinabalu), the capital of Sabah, I was a happy lad and skipped off to a pre-arranged appointment – again courtesy of C.C. Too – with someone who was to become a good and faithful friend – Dato Donald Stephens. Stephens, as head of the United National Kadazan Organisation (UNKO) had played a major role in negotiating the independence of Sabah and the creation of Malaysia along with Tun Mustapha of the United Sabah National Organisation (USNO) and the Tunku Abdul Rahman, the Prime Minister of Malaya. He then became Sabah's first Chief Minister between 1963 and 1964. He relinquished this post in 1964 to step on to a larger stage to become the first federal cabinet minister from Sabah in the role of Minister for Sabah Affairs under the Prime Minister's Department. When I met him he was the head of a new Kadazan political party called UPKO. He welcomed me warmly probably because he had an Australian father and a Kadazan mother. To look at this tubby 45 year old, you would have thought he had just stepped out of a Carlton pub and he had an ebullient personality to go with it.

The Kadazans are the clear majority ethic grouping in Sabah and the vast majority of them are Christians, mainly Catholic. Stephens was then a Catholic. When he took up the position of Malaysian High Commissioner to Australia in 1968, I met him many times in Canberra and other places and I was able to introduce him to many people including academics, politicians and bureaucrats. Stephens, of course, gave me introductions across Malaysia and none more interesting than to his own Kadazan protégé Peter Mojuntin. Mojuntin, who was two years older than myself was at that time the youngest person ever elected to a Malaysian parliament at the age of 24 in 1963. Peter and I hit it off immediately. With an Elvis Presley hair style and swagger, he was a dashing, extremely intelligent, Machiavellian, warm, woman-loving politician. Despite his being a Kadazan Catholic in a largely Muslim nation I saw in him considerable political potential. I thought he could be anything. Over the years he invited me to many political rallies organised by the various political parties and organisations he belonged to and I have memories of him holding rallies of thousands of supporters spellbound through his oratory. In return, I invited both him and Stephens to attend the Pacific Institute annual conferences in 1974 and 1975 which they were unable to do for various domestic reasons and again for 1976 which, as it turned out, was to be the last of the conferences.

In 1971 Stephens converted to Islam, the religion of his wife, and in 1973 he was appointed State Governor of Sabah by the King of Malaysia, the Sultan of Kedah. He resigned from this post in 1975 to re-enter politics. That year he, Mojuntin, Datuk Seri Harris Salleh, the bright leader of the Kadayan people of Labuan, and others formed a new multi-racial party called the United Malaysian People's Organisation or Berjaya. It easily won the April 1976 state election defeating Tun Mustapha's USNO and Stephens again became Sabah

Chief Minister while Mojuntin and Harris were given senior cabinet positions. Apart from the 1976 PI Conference, I was looking forward to many things, some even in the foreign policy and defence areas, when disaster struck. On June 6, 1976, Stephens, Mojuntin and several cabinet ministers were killed when their Australian-made Nomad aircraft crashed on approach to the Kota Kinabalu airport on a flight from Labuan. At first foul play was suspected, but it was later revealed that the Nomad had design faults, that others had crashed and that the aircraft might have been overloaded in any case. Stephens and Mojuntin are today remembered as Kadazan heroes. Both have had their biographies written including one titled, *Peter J. Mojuntin, the golden son of the Kadazan*, by Bernard Sta Maria, published by Melaka, 1978.

From Jesselton I flew up to Manila on November 1, 1967, to help organise the Pacific Institute Conference. I was feeling good about its prospects. I was confident that de la Costa, Johnny Tan, Raul Manglapus, Jerry Montemayor, Charlie Avila and Fr. Ortiz would be there and I was fairly sure they would bring along a couple of others I'd invited following de la Costa's September meeting namely, Charlie Albert, the Head of the National Intelligence Security Authority (NISA) and Senator Manuel Pelaez, a former Secretary of Foreign Affairs under President Macapagal. I was also sure that the reliable Max Soliven and Colin Clark would be there and that they'd add zest to our deliberations. On top of that I was more than hopeful we'd have Ngo Khac Tinh, Truong Cong Cuu and Bishop Thuan from South Vietnam, Fr. Beek and Lim Bian Kie (Jusuf Wanandi) from Indonesia as I'd been told that Bob Santamaria's office had already sent them, and others, airline tickets. Of course this didn't always guarantee that they'd turn up as we'd known from past experience in Australia and elsewhere. We also understood that this was to be very much an embryonic meeting and our expectations were modest: but it wasn't going to be a bad start to a long term program. What other kinds are there in Southeast Asia?

However, before heading to Manila and the conference, I need to diverge and focus on Indonesia, a nation which in many respects was the one with which I was most involved with over the years. I don't know why I didn't visit Indonesia on this long 1967 tour of the region, my first substantial visit there being in 1968. Perhaps in 1967 the people I wanted to talk with most weren't there at the times that fitted in with my round the region itinerary. I had, of course, been to Indonesia before in early and late 1966 as a holidaying university student but while valuable, these were fleeting visits. Secondly, I need to focus there now because some of the most important and influential people in the Pacific Institute came from Indonesia and before talking about the conferences it is important to put them into perspective. The Indonesia I am talking about is a big story stretching from at least the PKI coup attempt in 1965 and the subsequent fall of Soekarno through the rise of Soeharto and the New Order, the rise of the Soeharto family and its eventual attempts to hijack the nation while cultivating radical Muslims, to the overthrow of Soeharto in 1998 and throughout it all the gradual rise of liberal democratic institutions. For most of this I was never far away and from beginning to end it has involved in significant ways Indonesians and others either in or associated directly or indirectly with the Pacific Institute including Harry Tjan Silalahi, Jusuf Wanandi, Dr. Soedjati Djiwandono, General Ali Moertopo, General Benny Moerdani, General Soedjono Hoemardani and the remarkable Dutch Jesuit Fr. Beek.

4
Indonesia, 1968

While Indonesia might be the most populous Muslim country in the world, it is not a Muslim majority country. It is according to official government statistics, but it is not in fact. This is the most important single fact about the nation for both domestic political and regional/global geo-political and strategic reasons. Let me explain it this way. All Indonesians must carry an ID card and on that card they must nominate themselves as belonging to one of six religious groups namely Islam, Catholicism, Christianity, Buddhism, Hinduism or Confucianism. They cannot say they are agnostic, atheist or belong to one of the many traditional animist beliefs that attract millions. So countless millions of Javanese mystics and animists, for example, when faced with the ID card say they are Muslims because that is the most convenient thing for them to do. They are seen by most people to belong, at best, to the abangans, that is, nominal Muslims as against the Santri or practising Muslims. But in fact they are not Muslim in any sense at all. To further illustrate the point, when Indonesia took over East Timor in 1975 only about 10-20 per cent of the population was officially Catholic, according to the Portuguese colonial records of the time. Within a few years of the introduction of the Indonesian ID card, 95% said they were Catholic, partly because Catholic religious orders run most of the schools.

A reasonable estimate is that practising Muslims constitute about 45% of the total Indonesian population. Some Muslims I know put it much lower than that even in what are generally regarded as strongly Muslim regions. The number of radical Muslims likely to support al Qa'ida, Jemaah Islamiah, Abu Bakar Bashir or some of the radical political parties is put at between 5 and 7% which is still a considerable number of people in a population of 237 million. Most Indonesians adhere to one or other of the many mystic and animist beliefs, if anything at all.

A second background fact about Indonesia that should be appreciated is a geo-political one: it sits on the strategic waterways running between the Indian and Pacific Oceans. Through these waterways, such as the Malacca, Lombok, Makassar and Sunda Straits run all of the regional Sea Lanes of Communication (SLOCs) which carry most of the oil supplies for Japan, China, South Korea, Indo-China, Taiwan and The Philippines. They also carry a very high percentage of the trade between Asia and Europe and most of Australia's trade which amounts to about a quarter of its consumption. If we extend our vision from Indonesia across Papua New Guinea to include the SLOCs running through the Pacific island nations of the Solomon Islands and Vanuatu that would cover most of the trade between Australia and the United States. These SLOCs are the central strategic, geo-political factor in Southeast Asia and constitute the point or place where the interests of all the nations of the region from India across China to Japan and down to Australia converge. They are of global strategic importance and it can be argued that it was these SLOCs that the Vietnam War was ultimately all about, at least for Russia, China and the Western allies. It is in everybody's interest that they be kept open, free from the domination of any one power or combination of powers. That is, or should be, the principal aim of bi-lateral and multi-lateral political, defence, security and intelligence co-operation in the region. It is the basic purpose of both ASEAN and APEC. It also explains the extensive military co-operation between the US, Japan and Australia, the only Pacific nations, so far, to possess strategic naval power. Acting in alliance they protect the SLOCs and Australia is currently developing a navy that will be better able to contribute to this task. It should also be noted that the French Navy in the Pacific is not a disinterested party in this.

Because of Indonesia's strategic importance, who controls its government and the nature of its international alignments are matters of major interest to other nations in the region and around the world. They were of considerable interest to the Pacific Institute.

Another geo-political point worth throwing into the mix here is that despite occasional misunderstandings and diplomatic irritations, Australia and Indonesia are natural allies which can be briefly explained by saying that they both the face the north strategically.

Arriving in Jakarta

When I arrived in steamy grey equatorial Jakarta for the first time as a professional journalist on August 30, 1968, it was already just a tick under three years since the attempted PKI coup in September 1965 which led to the overthrow of President Soekarno. I had, of course, been to Jakarta briefly twice before, the first time in January 1966 as a student tourist on my way back from a Liberal International Youth Conference in New Delhi and later in December 1966 on a tour of the region with two ALP Club student political activists and writers, Bob Browning and John Horwood. On this second trip we had met briefly on the streets and elsewhere with some of the Indonesian student activists in organisations like KAMI demanding the resignation of Soekarno and a new socio-political order. Many of these activists, I was later to discover, had been trained by Father Beek.

Why it took me so long to get to Indonesia for a substantial, professional visit I don't know. Perhaps I was fixated on the Vietnam War and rescuing John Myint. But I never stopped reading broadly and in depth about what was happening in Indonesia and Fr. Beek kept sending me, and of course Bob Santamaria, fascinating reports on what was happening through friendly Jesuit channels, much of which Santamaria passed on to Australian intelligence who reciprocated whenever and wherever they could. As Patrick Morgan points out in one of his books concerning Santamaria, Beek warned Santamaria in the early 1960s of an approaching coup in Jakarta (Patrick Morgan, *B.A. Santamaria, Selected Letters*, p. 545).

A good place to start the story of my engagement with Indonesia over the years, if it is all to be put in perspective, is the attempted PKI coup of September 1965 and the eventual removal of President Soekarno. Now, even 46 years later, it can be said that if you do not understand the nature of the forces and issues that led to the demise of the PKI and the overthrow of Soekarno, you cannot fully understand Indonesia today for many, but not all, of those same forces and issues continue today. Some Australians might understand this better if I say that you cannot fully understand Australian politics today if you know nothing of the 1954 ALP split.

After many years leaning back in a variety of chairs talking to Indonesian friends military, civilian and religious, including Muslim leaders like Zainuri Echsan Subchan and Abdurrahman Wahid and others like Beek, about what happened concerning the PKI attempted coup, and having observed what has happened since, I have drawn a few tentative conclusions.

The first is that the secular nationalist generals, including abangans and moderate Muslims, decided at least two years before 1965 that Soekarno had to go. Through his indulgences and incompetence he had destroyed the economy with inflation running at 1000%, and was encouraging both the extremist Muslims and communists through his supposedly inclusive NASAKOM (Nationalism, Religion and Communism) policy. He was bringing the radical and strict Muslims and the one million strong Indonesian Communist Party (PKI) to the brink of power; giving them both a chance of seizing power, and then, perhaps, of destroying the other in one of the greatest bloodbaths of all time. Both were minorities in the nation and with potentially devastating international linkages, one to the Middle East and other to Moscow. Had either of them grabbed power and screwed the place down, they would have been very hard to remove.

The PKI would have brought the nuclear armed Russian navy with its SLBMs to every port in Indonesia while the Muslims would have seen the nation overrun by Wahhabism, ruled by Abu Bakar Bashir, and probably with the Russian navy to defend them to boot. Where would this have left Australia? My friends and the Pacific Institute understood all of this at the time. Most Australians, including most military and intelligence chiefs and politicians in both the ALP and Liberals, understood little or none of it.

The secular nationalists who plotted against Soekarno, the PKI and the radical Muslims were led by, among others, generals Sarwo Edhie, Ali Moertopo, Kemal Idris, Achmad Yani, Soedjano Hoemardani and Soeharto and some key civilians, among them Muslim, Christian, Chinese and abangan political and business figures including socialists and social democrats. And, of course, Father Beek. I knew a number of these people and discussed these issues with them including Moertopo, Beek, and Hoemardani.

I don't wish to get into the nitty gritty or a detailed description of what happened on the day the PKI struck because nobody really knows. Even those totally involved at the time including Moertopo, Beek and I'm sure most on all sides, including the PKI, would not have been sure of what was happening around them. The PKI putsch was a politico-military operation and therefore it was guaranteed that little would go to plan. Something would change things, maybe everything, something as simple as the weather or an alarm clock not going off or generals Soeharto and Abdul Haris Nasution not getting out of the right side of the bed.

However what we can say, from what I understand, is that the secular nationalists set out to provoke the PKI into going for a coup. They knew that the PKI and its leader Dipa Nusantara Aidit, wanted to go, but they also knew that the PKI, despite its many assets in the military, was under-prepared, as Aidit knew himself. However, the PKI was led to believe that if it didn't go, the Muslims who had many more assets in the military would attempt to seize the day. There were, of course, spies in every camp. In the end the PKI went for it and the rest is history or at least it can be read about in many books.

It is important to put the subsequent horrific and to many people unbelievable bloodbath into perspective. This was not simply a matter of the military sooling on people to kill communists. There were of course soldiers doing that sort of thing, but most of the killings were either the work of Muslims, including moderate Muslims and Muslim soldiers, killing hated communists (and the PKI officially numbered many millions), or people of all kinds, abangans and animists included, settling past grievances. Hundreds of thousands, if not millions of people, were chopped to pieces and thrown into rivers and streams. The Indonesians are Malays and amok is a Malay word. We were to see Malays run amok again a few years later in Kuala Lumpur, although fortunately not to the same unconstrained extent. When Abdurrahman Wahid, the moderate social democratic Muslim cleric and former leader of Nadhlatul Ulama (NU), the largest Muslim organisation in Indonesia with about 60 million adherents, became president of Indonesia in 1999, one of his first acts was to apologise to the nation for the atrocities of 1965. Later on in his presidency, he also tried to get Indonesia to recognise Israel.

Having smashed the PKI, the secular nationalists set out to push Soekarno aside and then neutralise the Muslims politically. Soeharto was prevailed upon by some of the other generals including Moertopo to step in and take the leading role with a view to replacing Soekarno. They backed Soeharto, their senior officer, not only because he was the only senior general still with a current operational role, the others having been executed by the PKI, but because he already controlled Jakarta as a result of being the Commander of Kostrad (Strategic Reserve) which was based in Jakarta alongside the presidential palace. Furthermore, and perhaps most importantly, a number of them, and notably Moertopo, had risen through the ranks with Soeharto as members of the Diponegoro division. Apart from Moertopo, they included generals Ahmad Yani, Yoga Sugama, Sarwo Edhie Wibowo and Soedjono Hoemardani.

Apparently as a young officer in 1956 Moertopo had played a significant role, along with Yoga Sugama, in organising and manipulating forces to get the then Lt. Colonel Soeharto appointed Commander of the Diponegoro division. Moertopo was rewarded by being appointed Territorial Assistant to Soeharto, Yoga became Intelligence Assistant while Hoemardani was placed in charge of finance, an important role as Indonesian military units and divisions had to raise most of their own money through business operations because governments couldn't raise the taxes to finance them.

When in the early sixties Soeharto became Operations Assistant to the Army Chief of Staff, General A. H. Nasution, and Commander of the Strategic Reserve, then known as Caduad, Moertopo became Intelligence Assistant to the Caduad Chief of Staff. He was also made head of the Army's Special Operations (OPSUS) which was set up secretly in 1961 by the army and, among other things, soon became the Army's primary means of undermining and hopefully terminating Soekarno's Confrontation of Malaysia (Konfrontasi) by conducting secret talks with the Malaysians and British to end the conflict. To this end, Moertopo posted his most brilliant young intelligence protégé, the then Major Benny Moerdani, to Bangkok in February 1965 under civilian cover as a Garuda Airlines marketing officer. Some have suggested that another reason for this posting was the PKI situation. The theory is that the army leadership knew that a showdown with the PKI and Soekarno was coming and that since the young Moerdani idolised Soekarno who treated him like a son, the best thing to do was to post him outside the country. Whatever, it all worked out well.

After the crushing of the PKI following the September 1965 coup attempt, Soeharto was reluctant to push himself forward as Soekarno's successor because he did not see himself to be a politician and had had no civic political or governmental experience. However, Moertopo and his friends insisted and it is no exaggeration to say that they put him into power and that it was their support on and off the streets that gradually consolidated him in the presidency by March 1966 (Supersemar). Moertopo was not only a soldier but a brilliant innate politician and intelligence operative from the start of his military career. Personally, I saw him not so much as a soldier but a politician in uniform and I came to know him well. Soeharto recognised his capabilities, gave him the most senior jobs, but eventually came to fear him. As the head of OPSUS – and some said he was OPSUS – he could do just about anything; actually at that time just about anywhere in Southeast Asia since military leaders running military dictatorships directly or indirectly throughout most of the region recognised the regional leadership of the Indonesians (that's another fascinating story understood by few other journalists, academics or Western intelligence officers I have known).

In the process of consolidating Soeharto into power, the secular nationalist officers set about neutralising the political power and potential influence of the radical and strict Muslims. The Chief of Staff of the Armed Forces (ABRI) and Minister Coordinator for Security and Defence, General Nasution, who was the logical man to take over after Soekarno, was a strict Muslim. He wasn't a radical in any way, but he was regarded as someone who was politically naïve and might be used by the radicals and therefore promote them into positions of influence. It was seen as essential that he be removed from office so as to eliminate him as a possible successor to Soekarno. This was achieved on February 21, 1966, when Soekarno, under pressure from the secular nationalist generals, dismissed him as both ABRI Chief of Staff and Defence Minister. This did a lot of damage to Soekarno because many people quite rightly saw Nasution to be an anti-communist, moderate Muslim patriot. In truth, Nasution almost certainly saw the political writing on the wall, knew he couldn't beat

Soeharto and even if he could, didn't have it in him to take him on.

Once secure in office, Soeharto set out to reform Indonesia economically and politically for the nation was an unstable basket case with hyperinflation running at an annual rate of many thousands per cent and with uncertain political forces on the loose. Soeharto set up an advisory panel of four generals to help him guide the nation. This was called ASPRI (Presidential Assistants) and comprised, as they were at the time, Maj. Gen. Suryo, Brig. Gen. Ali Moertopo, Brig. Gen. Soedjono Hoemardani and Colonel Widya Latif. Moertopo was far and away the most important of these officers and this position gave him constant, almost daily access to Soeharto. He was also appointed in 1967 Deputy Head of the National Intelligence Co-ordinating Agency (BAKIN) which was headed by his old comrade Yoga Sugama. While Moertopo was the Deputy Head it is generally acknowledged that on account of his temperament, charisma and developed intelligence sources, he actually ran BAKIN while the more relaxed, but highly intelligent, Sugama oversaw things from his armchair. In addition to these posts, Moertopo was still OPSUS which gave him almost carte blanche to do anything he liked. He was clearly the most powerful man in the country next to Soeharto.

While Soeharto and Moertopo were positioning themselves to reform the nation politically, about which I will say more shortly, they were doing the same thing in respect of the economy. Soeharto appointed some extremely capable economic and financial ministers who became known as the Berkeley Mafia as many of them were graduates of the University of California at Berkeley in the United States. Among them were Dr. Sumitro Djojohadikusomo, Radius Prawiro, Ali Wardhana and Emil Salim. In addition to that, they proved themselves open and receptive to international advice which was more than just a response to the enormous amounts of foreign aid that was pushed into the country through organisations such the International Governmental Group on Indonesia (IGGI). Some of the most influential foreign economic advisors were Australians led by Sir John Crawford, Heinz Ardnt, Peter McCawley and Peter Drysdale, among others. These people turned the Indonesian economy around over ten to twelve years so that by the early eighties Soeharto was being hailed as the "Father of Development". Standards of living, while generally low, were slowly rising across the nation. It was an extraordinary success story.

During this same period Moertopo was reforming the nation politically, while keeping a check on Islamist radicals. In this effort it is important to understand the role of Fr. Beek. Two of his protégés, both brilliant Chinese student activists who had organised student protests on the streets in 1965-66 became personal assistants to Moertopo and Hoemardani. They were the Lim brothers, Lim Bian Kie and Lim Bian Koen, today known respectively as Jusuf Wanandi and Sofyan Wanandi. Another brilliant young Chinese activist and intellectual and Beek protege stood off to the side and played a sort of overall father figure role. That was sauve and softly spoken Harry Tjan (born Tjan Tjoen Hok in 1934) who had been a trade union leader and secretary of the Partai Katolik or Catholic Party (and who was later to run rings around Australia's puffed-up diplomat and Ambassador Dick Woolcott over East Timor).

Out of a small office on Gunung Sahari in central Jakarta, which he called "The Bureau", Beek produced papers and ran a network of cadres and informants throughout Java and beyond. These cadres he trained himself through extended courses usually held at a convent at Klender which was then on the eastern outskirts of the city. I spent many days there in the late sixties giving lectures on various subjects. The actual training of these cadres, who over time ran into many hundreds, if not thousands, I will talk about later (See Part II, Chapter 2). It suffices to say here that they were required to brief Beek weekly, forwarding to him information and intelligence on what was happening in their areas. They were asked to report on the activities of local political and religious organisations, governmental bodies and military and police forces which usually dominated everything. Appropriate parts of this information were passed on to Moertopo though Jusuf Wanandi and to Hoemardani though Sofyan Wanandi. It contributed greatly towards Moertopo establishing his authority within the military and the Indonesian Intelligence community. So good was the intelligence that some other generals thought Moertopo must be running his own private secret, perhaps CIA- trained, network within the military.

From the start, Beek's motivation in training his people was the defence of the small Catholic and other Christian communities in Indonesia against the short term threat of a Communist Party (PKI) takeover and the longer term threat of a radical Islamist government allied with and financed by the worst in the Middle East. In the meantime, he could use it to promote his colleagues and allies, some of whom, like Moertopo, he had never met in the sixties. While Beek was an anti-communist and a political conservative, who ridiculed my suggestions that we could open up the country for liberal democracy, he was a theological liberal like most Dutch Jesuits and greatly tolerant of those who succumbed to the temptations of the flesh, which very clearly didn't include his ascetic, monastic self. However, his love of Bols Genever (Dutch gin) might have helped kill him in the end. Over the years I brought him many opaque 'stone' bottles of the stuff along with many, many thousands of dollars from Santamaria and his friends.

In the early seventies, Beek had difficulties with some of the local district authorities and police where he lived. The police came under pressure from local strict Muslim interests to act against the strange foreign priest whom they suspected of all sorts of things. There was nothing unusual about this as many Christians had similar problems. However, Beek told me that after he was arrested on one occasion and his bureau raided, Ali Moertopo decided to protect him and his files by providing him with an office and an apartment within a new civilian research body which he would create for the purpose with appropriate security. The defiantly independent Beek rejected the offer. Moertopo however went ahead and established what became known as the Indonesian Centre for Strategic and International Studies (CSIS). This was officially opened on September 1, 1971, with Ali himself and Soedjono Hoemardani as Honorary Chairmen. The Board of Directors included key executive officers Jusuf Wanandi, Harry Tjan Silalahi, Hadi Soesastro and J. Soedjati Djiwandono as well as Daoed Joesoef as its Chairman. The CSIS was to become the most influential political and foreign policy think tank in the nation and one of its most important political foreign operational bodies. It also became a driving civilian force building Golkar, mainly through the agency of the unbelievably energetic Jusuf Wanandi, and played a major regional role in building ASEAN and therefore APEC, for the latter could never have been possible without ASEAN.

Moertopo's political reforms in the early to mid-seventies revolved around building a political electoral machine for Soeharto, which would become known as Golkar, while "rationalising" and amalgamating the many opposition parties into two main groups which could be called Islamic and Nationalist with the aim of gradually taking, as far as possible, extreme religious forces and extreme ideology out of politics. He was another visionary and set about using his extraordinary powers to do these things. Golkar was built out of a representative non-political social organisation called the Functional Groups (Sekber Golkar). Ali had it supported by and its branches built by military territorial units throughout the country directed and co-ordinated by SOSPOL, the socio-political unit of the Armed Forces (ABRI). Its civilian superstructure based in Jakarta, but supporting the military-backed branches throughout the country, was organised by Jusuf Wanandi – and he did it brilliantly. Golkar would never have become what it did without the crusty Wanandi. He was rough and he was tough but he got things done in a society where that was rare. I saw him operating up close many times. It wasn't always nice for he sometimes rubbed people the wrong way with his bluntness and bluster, but all Indonesians should thank him today for their democracy – which he, too, told me could never come about.

For years Golkar was never a political party as understood in the West, but a machine cracked up at election time by ABRI to get Soeharto the vote, when Jusuf Wanandi would come into play. I used to visit occasionally the national secretary of the party and his offsiders and ask them what they were doing. Almost invariably the answer was "nothing". I would ask, "Aren't you out there organising and building new branches?" The answer was a shrug of the shoulders from some people who were later to become cabinet ministers. It more or less remained this way until the 1980s when the Soeharto family decided to try to take it over for themselves – like everything else in the country.

In the early seventies Ali amalgamated all the opposition Muslim parties – almost at the point of a gun – into the PPP (People's Progressive Party) and all the other opposition parties which included the PNI (Partai Nasional Indonesia) and the PSI (Partai Sosialis Indonesia) into the PDI (Indonesian Democratic Party). The non-Muslim religious parties including the Partai Katolik and Parkindo, the Protestant party, went out of existence. There was a lot of trauma involved here and Ali was not popular because he was doing hard, ruthless things – and sometimes I was able to tag along. To be very brief, we ended up with Golkar, the PPP and the PDI and Indonesia was slowly on its way to democracy even though most of them did not realise it.

In 1974 Ali's power and influence, exercised through OPSUS, ASPRI and BAKIN, was challenged by General Soemitro, the head of Kopkamtib, the national security organisation which possessed draconian powers to arrest almost anyone it liked. The tubby and flamboyant Soemitro sought to destroy the equally charismatic Ali and put himself in a position to succeed Soeharto. It was great theatre. As far as I could see, and once again I just happened to be in Jakarta at the time, Soemitro represented nothing more than himself and his mates but was able to exploit student grievances over continuing corruption and the sidelining of Muslim influence, and xenophobic, nationalist sentiment over the opening up of the economy to foreign investment, particularly from Japan and America. He chose to launch his attack through public demonstrations on the occasion of the visit to Jakarta of the then Japanese Prime Minister Kakuei Tanaka in what became known as the Malari Affair. There were riots across Jakarta and other parts of Indonesia. To cut a long story short, Soeharto sacked Soemitro when he came to understand what was happening. But he also cut down Moertopo by abolishing ASPRI, through which Ali had had Soeharto's daily ear, and OPSUS. This was the first indication of Soeharto cutting down the people who had put him into power as his family began growing up around him. He was later, disgracefully, to say in a 1988 autobiography (*Soeharto, My Thoughts, Words and Deeds*, as told to G. Dwipayana and Ramadhan K.H., Citra Lamtoro Gung Persada, Jakarta, 1988), that these people had done nothing for him or the nation. But these people – the ABRI secular nationalists – would overthrow him in 1998. It's a long story and I'll come back to it, but it might be said in hindsight that it began immediately after Malari in 1974 when Ali Moertopo recalled Benny Moerdani to Jakarta from Seoul, South Korea, and posted him to major intelligence positions. From these positions he would assume eventually Ali's role as the political leader of the secular nationalist military forces following Ali's sudden death at the age of sixty in 1984 as he lay on a couch in his CSIS office. In the end, it was Moerdani more than anybody else who removed a senile Soeharto and his outrageously grasping, corrupt family from power in 1998.

My first professional visit to Indonesia in August-September 1968, which is where we started this section on Indonesia, took much the same shape as those that followed during my regular tours of the region over the next seven or eight years. I'd lob into Jakarta, make contact with Beek and go to see him either in his Bureau in downtown Jakarta or his training school at Klender. I'd also get together separately and sometimes collectively with some of my other PI associates including Harry Tjan Silalahi, Jusuf Wanandi and Soedjati Djiwandono, all of the CSIS, to discuss recent events and exchange ideas on a range on national and international subjects and operations. Then I'd do the rounds of local politicians across the political and religious spectrums as well as local journalists, academics and cabinet ministers. Over the years I came to meet many fascinating people. I interviewed the very serious and erudite but politically powerless Adam Malik, the Foreign Minister, many times including on one occasion for Dutch television. Then there were the Muslim leaders, the liberal Subchan and Abdurrahman Wahid who at different times led the 60 million strong Nahdlatul Ulama and the more radical Mohammad Natsir as well as Johnny Naro, the garrulous leader of the Muslim PPP who was a belly laugh a minute between serious and insightful political observations. Then there were the many journalists among them Mochtar Lubis, Rosihan Anwar, Goenawan Mohammad and P.K. Ojong who published my articles in *Harian Kompas* as I mention below.

Most of these meetings, at least initially, were set up for me by Harry Tjan. Apart from Ali Moertopo and Benny Moerdani I met many other military officers. I can also clearly remember visiting BAKIN headquarters in company with Jusuf Wannadi to meet a range of people including its official boss, General Yoga Sugama. Briefly put, I had easy access to many parts of the Indonesian administration and I made the best of it I could.

I also regularly visited the offices of the largest circulation newspaper in Indonesia then and now, *Harian Kompas*, which was and still is a Catholic publication then edited by the short, articulate Jacob

Oetama and the more proper tall Chinese gentleman P.K. Ojong, both of whom were to become friends and philosophical, theological sparing partners of mine for a while. They published, translating into Bahasa Indonesia language, almost every article I wrote, including for many years my sixteen-page, 7000 word, end-of-the-year reviews on Southeast Asia for *News Weekly* (which were also carried by many other newspapers around the region from India to Japan).

Following these meetings around Jakarta, I often set off on a tour around Java visiting many places including the cities and towns of Semarang, Magelang, Surabaya, Jogjajakarta, Bandung and Bogor privately meeting the many contacts I had been given in Jakarta. In those days it was impossible to telephone anyone almost anywhere in the country, let alone outside Jakarta, as, indeed, was the case throughout Asia. One just went along and knocked on doors. I was given many contacts by Beek so, he said, I could both learn from his cadres and Jesuit colleagues and impart a few political ideas along the way. But I had just as many contacts among Muslim leaders and politicians across the spectrum and among military officers. Not only did I visit these Javanese towns and cities, I walked around them, as I did throughout the region. Indeed, the necessity to walk around cities to visit informants in an era of no air-conditioned taxis whose drivers spoke no English made Southeast Asian journalism a young man's game. As one grew older it gradually became more difficult to do the footwork. Today, many of these impediments have disappeared, yet the quality of the reportage from the region has dramatically fallen away. Where is the equivalent today of the *Far Eastern Economic Review* of forty years ago?

Travelling by train, bus, taxi, foot and bedja, I had some extraordinary times and experiences, many of them on the roads, eating local stall food and meeting some memorable local people. I recall an extraordinary midnight bedja ride through totally unlit streets of Semarang in Central Java. The scrungy driver could have cut my throat or taken me anywhere he liked. He didn't seem to understand the name and address of the Jesuit House I showed him in the darkness. Yet after a tense one hour ride through countless back streets we arrived at the gate. At the time I thought the risks were necessary to get me from the darkened and lonely train station to where I was staying. In hindsight I can only wonder at some of the things we found ourselves involved in to get the Pacific Institute and associated projects under way.

1. Relaxing at the Oriental Hotel, Bangkok, 1967

2. From left: myself, Senator Tran Van Lam, later South Vietnam Foreign Minister and Chief Negotiator at the Paris Talks, and Bob Santamaria at the Cercle Sportif, Saigon, 1968.

3. From left, Ted Serong at the Vietnamese Police Field Force (PFF) Training Centre, Trai Mat, with Larry Arritola, an American advisor to the PFF and John Morley, Station Chief of the British Secret Intelligence Service (SIS) or MI6 in South Vietnam, circa 1967. (Serong Collection).

4. From left, Bob Browning, Australian writer, Patrick Pohla, PFF Advisor, John Horwood, Australian writer, myself and Col. Monty Rodulfo, PFF Advisor and MI6 officer, inspecting a PFF outpost in 1967.

5. Myself and Bob Santamaria meeting President Thieu of South Vietnam at the Independence Palace, Saigon, December, 1972.

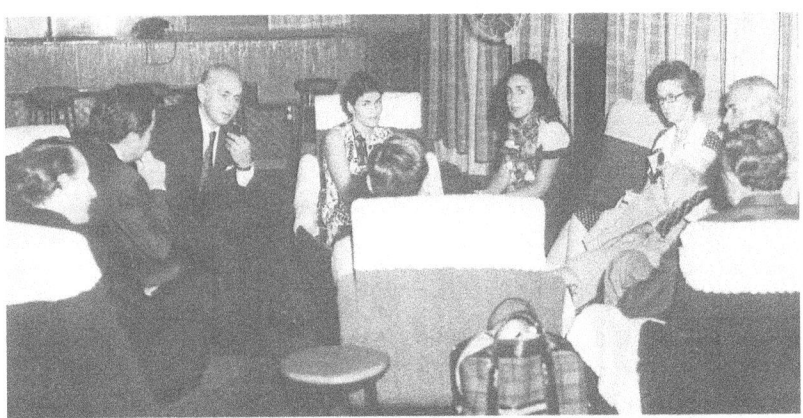

6. Round from left, myself, an unidentified Vietnamese official, Bob Santamaria, Eileen Mount, Anne Santamaria, Helen Santamaria, Ted Serong, Fr. W.G. Smith and the back of the head of another Vietnamese official in the VIP Lounge, Tan Son Nhat airport, on the arrival of Santamaria and his party, Saigon, 1972.

7, 8, 9. Bishop (later Cardinal) Nguyen Van Thuan in Hue, 1967, shortly after his consecration as a bishop. Is now a Vatican subject for beatification. British-Australian economist, Colin Clark and Pacific Institute member. Keynes called him "a bit of a genius" (News agency photo) and the cigar-chewing Sir Robert Thompson, British counter-insurgency expert – another sort of a genius. (News agency photo)

10. The fledgling Phoenix Program office in 1967, ground floor behind car. My Serong-supplied PFF apartment was on the 2nd floor.

11. Ngo Khac Tinh, 3rd from left, National Secretary of the Nhan-Xa Party, visiting the party's An Giang province Committee, Mekong Delta, 1969, and photographed by me.

12. Addressing a large and emotional Nhan-Xa Party gathering at the Cercle Sportif, Hue, South Vietnam, shortly after the Tet Offensive, 1968. The Nhan-Xa National President, Dr. Truong Cong Cuu, looks on.

13. With tribal chief officials of the Nhan-Xa Party Central Committee, Tuyen Doc province, Central South Vietnam, 1970.

14, 15. Kate Webb, South Vietnam, 1969, and Lt. Gen. Ali Moertopo, Intelligence officer, Personal Assistant to President Soeharto and 1962-74 Head, Indonesian Army's Special Operations (OPSUS). Photo circa 1978.

5

The Pacific Institute Conference, 1967

At the time of the first Pacific Institute annual conference in Manila in early November 1967, ASEAN was just getting under way, thanks mainly to our Indonesian friends and their Malaysian associates led by Ghazali Shafie.

As I mentioned earlier, I travelled up from Jesselton in Sabah on the first of November to help organise the conference due to start on the tenth. Bob was worried that the Filipinos would muck it all up, although he, himself, was one of the worst organised people I'd ever met, one who couldn't even read an airline schedule. Initially, the conference was to be held in Manila and then in the mountain resort of Baguio. That fell through so then it was to be here, there and then somewhere else. I went to de la Costa and we got it settled – it would be held in conference facilities at Ateneo de Manila University and we'd stay in attached student dormitories as it was a term holiday period. We were to sleep and meet in rooms that were monastic, but the surrounds were majestic with purple bougainvillea flowering everywhere. In the Jesuit dining room the conversations were always stimulating and the local San Miguel beer and Filipino-Chinese food more than acceptable.

To be true, this conference was to be a modest one, but we knew where we were going. It is not easy and it takes time to diplomatically and indirectly persuade Asians to change track or think differently. Since the early sixties we had pushed the idea of a Pacific Community and greater regional co-operation and democratisation in many organisations and publications in Australia and these were our overall, long term objectives. Within this strategic framework our short term or tactical objectives were ideally to get consensus among delegates on policies and ideas in the economic, political, military and social fields and then have them return home to pressure their respective governments to adopt these policies. My job, at least theoretically, was to then go around the region encouraging them to do precisely that. I remember Bill Cawthorn thinking this was a brilliant stratagem.

I cannot remember everyone who attended this inaugural conference nor everyone who attended the later ones either. Officially, minutes were supposed to be kept, but it was obvious to all that they weren't since I was the Executive Secretary and I made it obvious that I wasn't recording anything, at least not during the sessions. This was because we wanted delegates to open up and speak confidentially which many of them did because no one was taking notes. After the conference we never distributed Minutes because that would have looked silly. Instead we passed resolutions, indeed, rather uniquely, one great resolution built up and refined over a number of years from 1968 to 1972 involving some of the best minds around the region. (For a full copy of it, called The 1970 Pacific Institute Resolution, see the the PI Files, Frank Mount Papers).

The 1967 delegates included Bob Santamaria, Bill Smith SJ, Dr. Colin Clark and myself from Australia; Bishop Thuan and the Nhan-Xa Party leaders Truong Cong Cuu and Ngo Khac Tinh, from South Vietnam; Giom Kurukulasuyia from Ceylon; Paul Tai from Malaysia who was an academic politically active in the Malaysian Chinese Association (MCA) and whom I'd met a number of times in KL; Fr. Beek and Jusuf Wanandi (Lim Bian Kie) from Indonesia; and, as could be expected, many Filipinos including Johnny Tan, Jerry Montemayor, Senator Raul Manglapus, Horacio De La Costs SJ, Max Soliven, Sionil Jose, Charlie Avila, Senator Manuel Manahan, Charlie Albert, the head of NISA (the Philippine National Intelligence

Security Authority) and Norberto Gonzales a Muslim-associated Chrisian democrat who many years later became President Gloria Macapagal-Arroyo's Secretary of Defense and before that head of Intelligence. Ted Serong in Saigon and Harry Tjan in Jakarta and George Thomson in Singapore were not to join us until the following year, but they then attended nearly every subsequent year.

Apart from getting our regional agenda under way, the most memorable thing about the conference was that I actually got to meet Beek for the first time. He arrived a few days before the conference started and we hit it off from the moment we met in the university's lush grounds. He was one of those proud, larger then life characters who loved people and theological and political ideas as well as gin and cigars. But having been a tortured Japanese prisoner of war he had his feet on the ground and one sensed a deep inner humility and an awareness of the limits of any one man. We were to become solid friends until his untimely death at the age of 66 in 1983. But in that time we were able to do a lot of things. This conference was notable for two resolutions. The first one declared:

> That we agree to set up a body which in principle shall be an operational body, but which shall begin on the basis of an exchange of information and move as rapidly as possible to the formulation of policies on specific issues, on the basis of which national centres will seek to influence the policies of their respective countries. (see Frank Mount Papers)

The second resolution decided on the name of the organisation. Various possibilities were thrown around. Bob wanted Pacific Community, then Asia Pacific Community (thereby pre-empting the recent Australian prime minister, Kevin Rudd, and his advisor Richard Woolcott by forty years). Other suggestions included The Asia Association, The Asia Group, Asian Strategic Studies Association, the Pacific Association and the Indo-Pacific Community, it being obvious to many at the table that in the long run democratic India would have a significant role to play in the sort of strategic regional cooperation we envisaged. However, some of the Southeast Asians strongly objected to Indian involvement, presumably because they thought it would dominate. I have to say it was myself who suggested the Pacific Institute and it immediately resonated. (I was most upset when many years later Bob sold the name, without my knowledge and while I was still Executive Secretary of it, to some of his retired Intelligence mates at the Melbourne Club).

After the conference, I had arranged for Bob to meet with the famed Philippine Communist guerrilla leader Luis Taruc, who was in jail at Camp Crame, and with a number of Filipino cabinet ministers, including the Foreign Secretary Carlos P. Romulo. Following this, Bob, Fr. Smith, Colin Clark, Jerry Montemayor, Charlie Avila and myself travelled out to rural peasant villages a few hours drive from Manila to visit FFF groups mainly so that Bob could get a sense of the life of peasant tenant farmers and their problems. It was noticeable that Bob wasn't greatly attracted to the peasant life.

At the 1968 Conference we were able to put some bones on our major resolution, but I will come back to that later. After the 1967 conference I had to return to Australia where I was still politically active and had significant responsibilities in that regard – and all of this while committed to writing regular articles for newspapers and magazines around the region and the world and giving them as objective a picture of what was actually happening in Asia as I could. I was still National Secretary of the Defend Australia Committee (DAC), a member of the Victorian State Executive of the Democratic Labor Party (DLP) and one of the main movers in the university based group Peace with Freedom (PWF). In these capacities I was still appearing every now and then on national television programs like the ABC's *Four Corners,* giving speeches around the nation on the Vietnam War and Asian affairs and writing speeches for DLP and Liberal Party politicians and trade union officials.

6
Back to Melbourne

Terry Tobin

According to my diaries, one of the first things I did on returning to Australia after six months on the road – Bob Santamaria claimed my travels rivalled those of Marco Polo – was to have dinner with an old student mate, Terry Tobin, on November 26. Terry is today a renowned QC in Sydney and played a significant role in the Wilfred Burchett court case in 1974 (see Part Two). But back in 1967 we were just friends interested in the world and the Vietnam War and I remember telling him about my travels and the various things I was up to in a very general way, emphasising to him that we were trying to build regional co-operation and liberal democratic organisations in the region. Like many others at the time, including academic Owen Harries and diplomat Dick Woolcott, he thought democracy was impossible in Asia and certainly in places like Indonesia, Taiwan, Thailand and South Korea. A few years later he married one of Bob Santamaria's daughters, Bernadette, who, forty years later, was to be one of the driving forces behind the publication of a selection of Bob's letters and documents, edited by Patrick Morgan of Monash University, which among other things revealed to the world Bob's role in the creation of the Pacific Institute and his support for democratic organisations in Asia like the Nhan-Xa Party in South Vietnam.

Peter Frankel

A couple of days later I lunched with Peter Frankel, the National Chairman of the Defend Australia Committee (DAC) at the RACV

Club in Melbourne. He wanted to talk about the DAC, be brought up to date on Vietnam and had organised for me to speak at a number of functions. Peter was both a largely built and larger than life character and altogether a remarkable fellow on many counts, including an eye for tall, elegant women whom he entertained often. Always erect and sprightly behind his horn-rimmed glasses, he did things with style. He was a bit like Dick Hughes, but then again, totally different. Peter was a wealthy, highly skilled international trader who had come to Australia in 1963 from Brazil where he had been the World President of the Junior Chamber of Commerce. He was born in Berlin in 1921 and educated in Vienna from where his family escaped nazism and communism by fleeing to the UK and later Brazil. He spoke six languages fluently including Spanish, French, German, and English. While he was not an intellectual, he was cool and rational about everything including his strong anti-communism. The NCC's Gerald Mercer once described John Maynes as being "a sort of practical visionary". Frankel was much the same. We were very lucky to have him in the DAC where he gave solid personal and financial support to almost everything we did including the holding of dozens of meetings around the country during the so-called Vietnam debates. One of the things that surprised me was how well he got on with Frank Knopfelmacher, the often acerbic and brilliant Czech Jewish intellectual who was one of our main performers and who had escaped from Vienna and the totalitarians in similar circumstances.

Early the next year, Peter who was for ten years a member of the Victorian Executive Council of the Liberal Party, arranged for me to brief a number of federal Liberal parliamentarians on Vietnam including a number of junior cabinet ministers in the national Liberal government including Andrew Peacock, Philip Lynch, John Jess and Kevin Cairns, as well as Sir Wilfred Kent Hughes. Most of these meetings took place before dinner at his Toorak home. I mention this because at that time we were in the midst of the raging Vietnam

War debates in which the left and the anti-war mob in general, led by Dr. Jim Cairns, a Labor Party MHR, argued that the war was a South Vietnamese civil war. They said there were no North Vietnamese soldiers in South Vietnam and no Communist Chinese soldiers in North Vietnam supporting the war. We had tremendous debates with the left over this as we insisted that not only were there North Vietnamese soldiers supporting the South Vietnamese National Liberation Front (Vietcong) but that the North Vietnamese had unilaterally and deliberately restarted the war in 1962.

In all of these debates the ruling senior Liberal party cabinet ministers said nothing. While we argued and struggled in defence of their policy decisions, they said nothing. We now know publicly from Paul Ham's book that right from the start – that is, 1962 – Australian soldiers in Vietnam, initially those in Serong's AATTV, were regularly killing North Vietnamese soldiers in uniform. (See Paul Ham, *Vietnam: The Australian War*). Australian senior cabinet ministers, from the prime minister down to the foreign and defence ministers at least, knew that this was the case. Yet while American government publications, handed out to us for distribution in Australia, documented in great detail the case under the heading "Aggression from the North", Australian government ministers said nothing. They just spoke about the war against the VC, never mentioning the NVA. Not one of them ever telephoned Bob Santamaria, Peter Frankel, me or anyone in the DLP and said, "We've got the evidence to defeat the left in the debate". These were the same Liberals who won government for more than a decade on DLP preferences and were constantly ringing the NCC and DLP for advice on how to win the next time. Given the effort and pain we put into those Vietnam debates words desert me as to how to describe the Liberal Party ministerial leadership. Am I still angry? You bet.

In case it is thought that the DAC was solely a Liberal Party-DLP oriented body it should be said that we had some interesting support and involvement from people in the ALP. Apart from many members of the Melbourne University ALP Club, including at the time Ray Evans, Patrick Morgan, Brian White, Paddy O'Brien and Vincent Buckley two of the DAC's initial national sponsors were Capt. Sam Benson, a Victorian Labor Party member of the Federal Parliament and Laurie Short, the courageous anti-communist National Secretary of the Federated Ironworkers' Association who accepted my invitation to join the DAC after a lunch in Sydney. In July 1966 the powerful left wing, pro-communist faction of the ALP succeeded in having the party declare the DAC to be a "proscribed organisation" on account of it being close to the DLP and NCC. The party demanded that Benson and Short resign from the DAC. Benson refused and was expelled from the party. Short took the view that his membership of the New South Wales Labor Party was more important than his membership of the DAC given his position within the Labor movement and the political circumstances of the time. We agreed with that view and he left the DAC amicably and continued as an effective associate.

None of this affected Peter Frankel much and he continued to give the DAC great support and me very useful contacts all over Asia, a consequence of his days as the World President of the Junior Chamber of Commerce, some of whom contributed to building the influence of the Pacific Institute. One of them was the Thai Muslim Senator Leck Vanich Angkhul.

Vincent Buckley

Ten days after lunching with Frankel, I had an appointment on December 6 with the quiet, gentlemanly poet Vincent Buckley in room 202 of the Old Arts Building at Melbourne University after which we proceeded to a long lunch on Lygon Street a few blocks away in the heart of Carlton. It was the only occasion I ever spent an extended period alone with Vin and I remember it well. I only wished

I understood him better. At times, I was a bit like Fr. Jerry Golden the Jesuit rector of Newman College, who, according to Buckley's biographer, said he could spend hours listening to Vin speaking on account of the wonderful cadence of his voice "even though he didn't understand a word he was saying" (John McLaren, *Journey Without Arrival: The Life and Writing of Vincent Buckley*, Australian Scholarly Publishing, 2009, p. 58) Vin wanted to talk about Vietnam and Asia and what I was trying to do there and this is what occupied most of our three hours together. He just sat on the other side of the table and, in between questions, nodded at most of what I said.

I had known Vin for many years around the university and in the context of the Melbourne University Newman Society of which I was not a member. The Newman Society was looked upon as being anti-Santamaria and therefore anti-DLP for various esoteric theological and I suspect familial reasons. Many of its adherents and hangers-on were members of the Melbourne University ALP Club and some of them of the local Carlton ALP branch, including Vin himself at least at one stage. However, back in 1964, when I invited Vin to be a sponsor of the Wheat for India Campaign he accepted immediately even though he knew that it was a national project of the Melbourne University DLP Club. In truth, Vin in my experience was always strongly anti-communist, and while he said he objected to some of Santamaria's methods and tactics, he was sympathetic to the DLP. I don't know why, or can't remember why, I never invited him to be a DAC sponsor, but I'm sure he would have accepted.

Some of those in the Newman Society or associated with it saw themselves as 'liberal' Catholics who said they disliked organisation in principal and all institutions and saw themselves involved in religion and politics as individual actors or influences – "carriers of ideas" as one of them put it to me. At heart they were anarchists and disliked Santamaria's kind of 'social order' organisation. However, they would have been nothing without the Newman Society which was housed in Newman College, funded by the archdiocese, and blessed by its founder and their theological/political nemesis (or so they thought), Archbishop Daniel Mannix, who also provided them with their much-loved chaplain, Fr. Golden SJ. Moreover, without the Melbourne University ALP Club which was largely kept alive and certainly out of the hands of the extreme left by me, they would have had no political outlet. They also believed that religion and politics should be kept apart and, taking a morally superior stance, attacked Santamaria and Mannix, his mentor, for mixing the two, while they, as unorganised individuals of course, dabbled in both as Newman Society apostles. How many angels and cherubs can dance on the head of a pin? In those days when I might see Buckley and Santamaria within a few hours of each other there was, on account of Vin's angelic little hands and Bob's cherubic lips and chubby, praying-hands-together poses, and the general demeanour of both, a somewhat Raphaelesque atmosphere about the place.

I remember wild Friday night ALP Club and Newman Society parties around Carlton after six o'clock hotel closing in the early sixties in places like Paddy Morgan's house on Pigdon Street. At three in the morning we'd be thumping the floor in some sort of Irish dancing to Tommy Makin and the Clancy Brothers. Among many things I can remember is Vin Buckley putting an arm around my shoulders as we swung around the room, kissing me behind the ear and whispering mischievously, "I'm really a Grouper, Frank". To which I replied, "For God's sake, Vin, don't tell anyone!" At a few of these and other parties, we were sometimes joined by another musically inclined, woman-loving poet, James McAuley, the founding editor of *Quadrant*.

Harold Holt's Funeral – Crashing the Party

The next interesting thing that happened in my life, and of more direct relevance to what I was doing in Southeast Asia, was the sudden disappearance of Prime Minister Harold Holt in the pounding surf and undertow of Cheviot Beach at Portsea south of Melbourne on Sunday, December 17, 1967. There is little, indeed no doubt, that Harold simply drowned and his body was eaten by crabs and sea lice, even though I wrote an un-published, and I hope both an entertaining and revealing, espionage novel centred on, and speculating about this and other events.

I had known Harold Holt for some years. We first met when, as Treasurer, he was invited to deliver a public Liberal Club lunchtime address at Melbourne University in 1961. After such meetings, it was customary for the speaker to proceed to the Student Union coffee shop for discussions with any interested students. I was one of those students and met him this way on three or four occasions over the years. In 1964 and early 1965, I also met him in his parliamentary office in Melbourne a number of times. I cannot remember whether I ever went there to meet him specifically, or whether it occurred when I was visiting other federal parliamentarians who held offices in the same building, including Sir Wilfred Kent Hughes and the DLP Senator Frank McManus, both sponsors of the DAC. In any event, we discussed at various times many things including Southeast Asia in which he had a keen interest, unlike Prime Minister Sir Robert Menzies who regularly flew over it on his way to London. He knew of my interest in the region not only from these conversations but from his reading of my articles in *News Weekly* and elsewhere and his communications with Bob Santamaria and some of our mutual associates. I can remember personally giving him copies of everything Bob, I and others had ever written or published on the idea of a Pacific Community.

When he succeeded Menzies as Prime Minister in January 1966 one of the first things he did was to embark on a tour of Southeast Asia visiting as many capitals as he could thereby opening Australia to the region. Of course there were many people in government and the public service involved in the region, but they now had a prime minister, and not just a foreign minister, supporting them in a way that had never happened before. Throughout 1966-67 Holt continued to receive articles and reports from Bob and myself and was constantly brought up to date on what we were doing in the region through a mutual friend who regularly met Harold either in his Yarraside Toorak home or sitting on the beach at Portsea. When Harold disappeared, I had not long finished lunch around the family dining table at my parents' home in Nicholson Street, East Coburg. We were astounded as we watched it all on television and it was not long before I was getting telephone calls from people like journalist Peter Samuel in Canberra and Richard Krygier of the Australian Association for Cultural Freedom in Sydney as to what I knew about it. The next day Asian embassies in Canberra were calling and politicians, diplomats and journalists around the region as well.

Within a day or so it was announced that there would be a funeral service for Harold on the following Friday, December 22, at St Paul's Cathedral in central Melbourne, and that following that there would be a reception cum wake at Government House a short distance away. This was partly because it was already known that US President Lyndon Johnson was coming for the funeral along with prime ministers, presidents and foreign ministers from around Asia and beyond. We were about to be swamped by Asians, thanks to Harold. Immediately, I decided to get official press accreditation for both events as I knew there would be a lot of people there I'd like to meet and perhaps interview on the side. On the day, I decided to skip the cathedral ceremony and headed late for the reception. I decided to wear a suit because I knew those I wished to interview, outside of the reception as they arrived and departed, would be similarly dressed. I drove up to the majestic gates of Government House in my trusty 1964 Falcon and was casually passed through the gates to the car park. I wandered down the track and found the journalistic cabal with TV trucks and cameras and the venerable Eric Pierce in a splendid pin stripe suit waiting for the eminent visitors to appear from the reception. I stood around for half an hour or so before deciding to walk through the gardens and around the House. I got to the front of the building, walked past a nonchalant security guard, saw the massive front doors open and then nothing between me and the reception. So I strolled in. Amazing. Here I was crashing Harold's wake with as little security for all these world leaders as there was for Harold himself a week earlier at Portsea.

I casually gathered some canapés and a glass of good Coonawarra red and started to circle the room. I could see many friends or at least contacts I'd made on my trips around Southeast Asia – and some interesting people I'd never met before. Lee Kuan Yew and Malcolm Fraser were standing together like the twin towers and I introduced myself to both of them. They seemed a little puzzled. Then I spotted Prince Sisouk Na Champassak and Tianthone Chantarasay from Laos and I moved off to more familiar territory, welcoming them to Melbourne. Soon I also ran into the foreign ministers on my contact list, all of whom I had interviewed for *News Weekly* and Dutch Television – Thanat Khoman from Thailand, Adam Malik from Indonesia, Tran Van Do from South Vietnam and Narciso Ramos from The Philippines. I could see President Lyndon Johnson and British PM Harold Wilson in the smoky distance across the room but they were surrounded by Australian ministers and bureaucrats and it looked like a formidable wall to me.

When I wandered off for another red and more canapés, I noticed some Australian faces looking at me aghast – no doubt at least intrigued as to what I was doing there and how I had been allowed in to the place. I spotted some American friends chuckling to themselves. The next day Bob Santamaria got telephone calls from his friends Brigadier Sir Charles Spry, the head of The Australian Security Intelligence Organisation (ASIO), and General Bill Cawthorn, the head of ASIS, and others asking what the hell I was doing there and whether he had sent me to crash the party. In the end, it eventually all blew over. But what a row! The security boys were upset, but the intelligence mob thought it was a hoot and gave me full marks. While, of course, it was an accident on my part, my major regret is that I didn't shake the hand of an American President when I had an easy chance.

A footnote to this story is that early in the New Year during the Christmas holidays, the second week of January 1968 to be precise, the Liberal Party met to elect a new leader and therefore Prime Minister to succeed the caretaker PM who was the Deputy Prime Minister at the time of Holt's death, Sir John McEwen, the leader of the minority Country Party in the ruling coalition government. I was in the editorial office of *News Weekly* on the morning of Monday, 8th, working on some articles and waiting for the paper's wonderful editor, Ted Madden, to turn up to finalise some matters we had been discussing. In the end, he never arrived that day. He was probably on Port Phillip Bay sailing around somewhere as he was an obsessive and founding member of the Port Phillip Coast Guard Auxiliary and often wore his 'naval' gear and cap into the office. I was totally alone in the building, an old red brick Edwardian house in Riversdale Road, Hawthorn, when the phone rang on Ted's desk. The holidaying central telephonist had switched all incoming calls to him because only he was expected to be in over the Christmas break. Bob Santamaria was lying on the beach at Mornington enjoying the midday sun. I answered the call. It was the distinctive and familiar East European voice of Richard Krygier from the Australian Association for Cultural Freedom, now known publicly to have been financed at that time by the CIA. In his hard guttural consonants, he asked for Bob. I told him he wasn't around. He said "you must" and he repeated, "you must", pass on to Bob the message that Senator John Gorton has to be the next prime minister. I said thanks for the message. But while he was a prominent member of the cabinet, I didn't like or trust Gorton, who didn't like Asia, and given those on offer I preferred Paul Hasluck, the Minister for External Affairs and a former Minister of Defence, who was keen to advance Australia's involvement in Southeast Asia. So I immediately decided I wouldn't pass it on. This was politics after all.

Shortly afterwards a similar call came in from an eminent Sydney journalist, then others from cabinet ministers and various Liberal Party power brokers. I was impressed with how many highly placed people thought that Bob might be able to sway the day and decide the next prime minister of Australia. In the end, Gorton was elected on January 10, narrowly defeating Hasluck, but proved to be an abject failure, eventually voluntarily stepping down in March 1971. Whether Hasluck, who had some weaknesses, would ever have done any better politically, no one can ever know, but he was a statesman and a far more stable and mature person who knew the world and his own limitations. He retired from politics to become Governor General.

I had already begun planning that my next long, 5-6 month trip around Southeast Asia would not begin until mid year – in the event the end of May – so that I could fullfil my responsibilities concerning the DLP, DAC and PWF and begin winding them down. A part of my January for many years – going back to university days – was to spend a week or two in Canberra attending political science and international affairs conferences, visiting Asian embassies to pick their brains and make possibly useful contacts, and simply sit around chatting with old friends like Australian National University (ANU) historian Geoffrey Fairbairn, journalists Peter Samuel and Peter Kelly and John Barich, a senior member of the Prime Minister's department. I was in the midst of the 1968 visit between January 26 and February 4 when the Tet Offensive exploded in South Vietnam on January 30/31. I knew that tensions had been building and that the North Vietnamese were planning an offensive, but it still came as a shock. I was staying in a student hostel at the time and headed off to lunch with Geoffrey Fairbairn and a group of highly placed bureaucrats to discuss it all. (I say a lot more about the Tet Offensive later).

Easter with McAuley

In the first half of 1968 the most memorable thing, along with Tet and the brief to Liberal cabinet ministers, was an invitation during a Peace With Freedom gathering from the 50 year old James McAuley to spend Easter with him and his family in Hobart. This remains to this day one of those wonderful experiences in life. I arrived in Hobart on Thursday, April 11, shortly after midday to be met at the airport by the craggy-faced McAuley who was not only one of Australia's greatest poets, but its greatest convert to Catholicism and the only poet, as far as I know, to play a leading organisational role in a state-wide political organisation, the Tasmanian NCC. He was also internationally famous for the Ern Malley literary hoax. We, of course, immediately headed off to one his favourite pubs where we engaged in a couple of hours of political discussion and elevated gossip.

That evening I sat in the lounge of his home reading while he worked in his office or wherever and the family quietly shuffled around the house. Two of his teenage children, Katherine and Philip, seemed to keep moving in and out of the place and to be away for long intervals. The other three weren't around. The next day, Good Friday, we rose late, ate lightly and again sat around the house until the afternoon Good Friday ceremonies at 3 o'clock for which Jim, his wife Norma and I headed off to the local Gothic church. We returned and sat around again. I began wondering what this was all about. I was getting bored. What's going through this man's mind? He's fifty, I'm 27 what's happening here? Is he trying to set me up with his nineteen year old daughter? If so, he hasn't introduced us. I hoped he might start playing the piano for I had heard him before and knew he had a great touch and feel for the music. I knew he had once been called Honky Tonky Jim or something like that because of his love of jazz and his ragtime pianissimo around the wild haunts of Sydney in his younger days. I can't remember whether he told me on this visit or another or elsewhere that he had once faced a momentous career choice. Having been classicly trained, he had had to decide whether he wanted to be, or aim to be, a concert pianist – and he was that good – or a poet. He decided on that latter – more freedom he said. This almost floored me because months earlier in Saigon Ted Serong had told me something similar. He and I were sitting in the Dakao apartment with low-flying Phantoms screaming overhead, with Carling Black Labels in hand, and a small, snowy TV going in the corner when the famous pianist Arthur Rubinstein came on Armed Forces TV seated at a grand piano in tails and bow tie playing a Chopin sonata. Ted looked at the screen and said: "Frank, there but for the grace of God go I." At the time I thought he must have been a classical pianist. But many years later I learned he was a violinist. I never heard him play, so I don't know how good he was. But he obviously had a high opinion of his potential. Were there any other similarities between the poet and the soldier? Yes, at least one. They both thought they could be good at party politics or any sort of politics, and they were both hopelessly wrong.

The next day, late in the morning, Easter Saturday, Jim and I headed off in his car for the countryside and what was a sunny, pre-Autumnal Huon Valley and its rolling, hilly apple orchards. At my request, he recited poetry and I just listened. I still have him on a 45rpm vinyl recording reciting in his precise voice much the same poetry including "In The Huon Valley" with its wonderful and politically evocative last verse:

> Something is gathered in,
> Worth the lifting and stacking
> Apples roll through the graders
> The sheds are noisy with packing.

When we got out into the orchards he pulled up at a scenic spot and came to the point of the whole invitation: Would I run Peace with Freedom as its national director or secretary? There was plenty of money available he said. The answer was no. I explained to him that I was gradually running down my involvements in Australia with the DLP (that I was not really a Party man, but rather a loner), the Defend Australia Committee and other things in favour of my Asian activities. This led on to a vague discussion in a pub somewhere about nationalism and internationalism. We eventually agreed that while he was a patriotic nationalist, I was just a just a somehow rootless, unaccountable internationalist. When we eventually got back to the house we took a couple of hours' nap before the Easter Vigil which was scheduled to start at the church at 9 o'clock that evening.

The little Gothic church was overcrowded and Philip and I sat at the back with the choir and the accompanying ensemble. McAuley played the organ while the ensemble and choir were conducted by Norma. From memory, the ensemble was made up of a drummer, a bassist, a flautist, a trombonist and a couple of others. Some of these musicians had come from the local Anglican church and the Salvation Army. Most of the music and hymns had been written by McAuley himself and his musical collaborator Richard Connolly. McAuley had arranged the program so that the music gradually and quietly built up through the ceremony to a loud glorious drum rolling choir-backed crescendo as the priest declared in exalted tones: "Christ is risen, Christ is risen", for this lay at the essence of Christianity. If Christ hadn't risen, it is all a falsehood. We walked back to the house for what I anticipated would be a good night's rest, but, instead, a truly magnificent midnight roast beef dinner was being laid out to celebrate the Risen Christ with lashings of good Hunter River red. We were joined by the priest, all of the musicians and others and the music and the wine went on until daylight. Christ might have risen, but I was sinking.

Not surprisingly, the next day we awoke late and had a light lunch of leftovers. Jim and I then set out in his car again and in late afternoon we called on Archbishop Guilford Young. They were obviously on very good terms because he called him, respectfully, "Gilly". The horn-rimmed archbishop and Jim discussed local issues for an hour or so before he turned his long patrician face to me and asked rather condescendingly, "And what are you about Frank?" I said, "Southeast Asia". He said Bob Santamaria wants to Christianise Asia. I said that was news to me. He said you will never Christianise Asia or build anything like the Movement there. I replied that I had no desire to do anything like that. He said what do you want to do then? I said I wanted to help stop communism principally by building regional co-operation and democratic institutions wherever possible. He laughed and said that was more impossible than Christianising the place, adding, "those people – Muslims and Chinese – don't want or understand democracy and they will always fight among themselves."

Blueness

Two years later on March 8, 1970, following a two day Peace with Freedom conference at the Lygon Inn in Carlton, I drove McAuley, Geoffrey Fairbairn and Colin Clark to Essendon airport late on that Sunday afternoon. Fairbairn and Clark flew off to Canberra, but McAuley had missed his flight to Hobart. He couldn't get another for more than three hours, so we adjourned to the bar. In an ebullient mood at first, cracking some of his wicked jokes, he soon sank into his cups. For some reason he seemed to want to unburden his soul to me and it became increasingly painful. I really didn't want to know but he went on and on, almost incomprehensibly at times. I was flattered of course that he would take me into his deep confidences and discuss his personal and family problems and demons with me. But I still didn't want to know. Although I can't remember the details, I know there was nothing scandalous in anything he said for I would have remembered. I later discovered the same mood and despair in much of his poetry. I loved the man and this saddened me. I took him to the plane and then somehow drove home.

Looking back, apart from anything others have said, I can see a Frank Sinatra-like deep blueness in McAuley, in his words, poetry and being. Bruce Springsteen has said that Sinatra had a "voice filled with bad attitude, life, beauty, excitement, a nasty sense of freedom, sex, and a sad knowledge of the ways of the world…while his music became synonymous with a black tie, the good life, the best booze, women, sophistication, his blues voice was always the sound of hard luck, and men late at night with their last ten dollars in their pockets, trying to figure a way out." (Springsteen at Sinatra's 80th Birthday celebration). This is redolent not only of McAuley, but also of Vincent Buckley and even Ted Serong. And there is another similarity between McAuley, Buckley and Sinatra. Like Buckley and McAuley's best poems, Sinatra's best songs were not only pleasant to hear, but stimulated both the intellect and the emotions. To paraphrase and expand upon a Tony Bennett comment on Sinatra, they all communicated strongly and intimately, an art that should ensure that they all stand the test of time and, who knows, perhaps the centuries. (Tony Bennett, in the liner notes to his album *Perfectly Frank*, 1962, and in his autobiography *The Good Life*, Pocket Books, New York, 1998).

There is no doubt that McAuley was beset by his devils – that is those things he saw or imagined in the world as evils and which he believed he must fight and wrestle with and that he battled with depression. However, that is very different from saying, as Cassandra Pybus did, that he believed himself to be "possessed by the devil" (see her review of Michael Ackland's book, *Damaged Men: The Precarious Lives of James McAuley and Harold Stewart*, in *The Australian*, March 10, 2002). The mention of Pybus leads me to also say that in all the time I spent with McAuley I never saw the slightest sign that he possessed any kind of homosexual proclivity.

7

On My Bike Again

Angry Days

Hundreds of thousands of students and workers were still demonstrating and striking in Paris and other cities across Europe and elsewhere when I boarded a Qantas flight in Melbourne for Manila on May 31, 1968. They'd been going on for months in one the greatest outbreaks of essentially anarchist discontent the world had ever seen. They wanted to overthrow governments, institutions and most of the Western social order. They were against everything. They thought they were original revolutionaries. But in fact they were just a part of a general movement of change at the time – having been preceded by among other things a rather conservative Vatican II four or five years earlier – and long before that by Marlon Brando who, in the 1953 film *The Wild One* as a black leather jacketed bikie leader taking over and terrorising a conservative town, said he was against everything. Running parallel, sort of, with the European anarchists were the anti-Vietnam War protests, especially in the US. It was a difficult, but exciting, time and they were all angry. And so was I – with the way America was fighting the Vietnam War for I knew the future of Southeast Asia and the whole Asia Pacific region rested on the way it went.

This trip through the region would take me to The Philippines (May 31-June 17), Taiwan (June 17-22), Hong Kong (June 22-29), South Vietnam (June 29-July 15), Thailand (July15-August 3), Laos (August 3-August 10), back to Thailand (August 10-18), Malaysia (August

18-25), Singapore (August 25-30), Indonesia (August 30-September 14), then back to Manila for two days, Saigon for two days, Bangkok another two, down to Singapore and back to Melbourne on September 21. I was then back in Hong Kong for the annual Pacific Institute conference between October 26 and 29 after which I again visited Saigon, Cambodia and Bangkok. In all these places I did the usual rounds for the usual purposes. What was most valuable of all in many respects was my visit to Saigon and tour of South Vietnam four months after the Tet Offensive. But before I got there I was happy to find in Manila that Charlie Avila and some of his student friends had set up new political party in Mindanao called Kamayaan which, apparently, was the closest they could get in Tagalog to national civic council or movement. The idea of the party was to give students experience in running a social democratic institution. It certainly did that and some of them ran in local elections under the party banner. It also enabled them to form some very useful long term linkages with Muslim democrats, Mindanao being a predominantly Muslim region. These Christian-Muslim associations have continued down the years, run by the same social, Christian and Muslim democrats, and formed an essential part of President Gloria Macapagal-Arroyo's ruling party the Lakas-CMD (Lakas- Christian Muslim Democrats) which merged with and incorporated Arroyo's own party Kampi (Kabilikat ng Malayang Pilipino or Partner of the Free Filipino) in June 2008. The current Philippine government has lost the plot entirely.

Richard Hughes

In Hong Kong on my way to Saigon I ran into a number of journalists who were to remain friends of mine for many years. Foremost among these was the celebrated veteran Australian Richard Hughes. I had an introduction to him from Geoffrey Fairbairn. He warned me not to be fooled by the buffoonery and drinking of this very rotund and much larger than life character who once was described as an amiable blend of Alfred Hitchcock and Robert Morley and who liked to produce a monocle to look down upon those whose opinions he thought suspect. Underneath it all, said Fairbairn, was a very serious man of unusual abilities. John Le Carre reputedly called him a "journalistic Eiffel Tower". Today he is famous for his World War II exploits, his discovery of Burgess and Maclean in Russia, for being cast by his friend Ian Fleming as Dikko Henderson in *You Only Live Twice* and by Le Carre as Old Craw in *The Honorable Schoolboy*, for his entertaining articles, long, long lunches and much more. Every Saturday he hosted and presided over a very generous Chinese lunch at the Cosmo Club to which he invited journalists, diplomats, academics, military officers, actors, businessmen of note and a procession of visiting firemen. He referred to these lunches as meetings of Alcoholics Synonymous. Some of the most famous people turned up including Fleming and Le Carre and actors like Yul Brynner and Sean Connery. Politically, they were an eclectic lot ranging across the ideological spectrum.

Most of the Australian journalists and diplomats working in the region disliked Bob Santamaria, indeed some of them hated him for being a "rightist" who they, wrongly, thought had split their beloved Australian Labor Party in 1954. Dick was different. He had begun his career working for the Victorian railways editing its magazine and leading its debating team. This had bought him into contact with many of the labor figures who were to lead the breakaway DLP after the split including DLP senator Frank McManus against whom he debated. He was always sympathetic to the anti-communist Groupers and, therefore, Santamaria, and eagerly produced his monocle for some of Santamaria's critics. I fondly remember turning up late to one of his lunches at which a number of Santamaria's detractors were present, including a John Pilger-like Viet Cong sympathiser and an Australian WASP establishment diplomat who disliked Santamaria for religious, political, class and, I suspect, racial reasons. As I came though the great wooden doors into the dining room the fifteen or so guests were seated around an inverted U shaped table with Dick at the head of it. He saw me and stood up. He raised a goblet full of red wine about the same colour as his face and said: Gentlemen, let us stand and raise our glasses to the arrival of the emissary from Dr. Santamaria in Melbourne. And they had to follow, however sheepishly. What a man! As we now know, Dick's lunches, like a lot of other things in his life, were generously financed by MI6.

Apart from Hughes, I met up with two other fine journalists on this visit to Hong Kong. One was the novelist and China expert Robert Elegant who was the Hong Kong based correspondent for the *Los Angeles Times* who I had first met in Melbourne. The other was Robert Shaplen. Shaplen wrote for *The New Yorker* and based himself in the Repulse Bay Hotel in Hong Kong where, apart from Saigon, I met him on a number of occasions. These were two of the finest journalists to cover Asia and the Vietnam War. And like Dick Hughes, they understood what the war was all about. Meeting these people had a significant, stimulating influence on me, broadening my horizons. I have said before that the Vietnam War was the greatest experience of my life and this was just a small part of it. I can't describe it exactly, but if I mention some of these people, all of whom appear in my diaries or notes, perhaps you'll get a feel for what I'm saying. Among the Australians I haven't already mentioned in this book were Ian Ward who wrote for the London *Daily Telegraph* and kept a gun under his pillow for protection against angry husbands; Phil Koch, the more experienced brother of the novelist Christopher; Don Hook, a cool ABC hand whose film I carried many times out of Indo-China to Bangkok or Singapore; Hugh Lunn who never understood what was happening; Peter Hastings; and Dennis Warner, a brilliant journalist who too often lowered his colours. And then there were the Americans, Europeans and Asians, some of whom not only influenced the way we looked at things but inspired us to keep thinking grandly, just as Santamaria, Knopfelmacher, Serong, Rodulfo and

Clark had. Here I count in journalists like Henry Camm, Ray Coffey, Keyes Beech, Sol Sanders, Arthur Dommen, George McArthur, Robert Trumbull, Dennis Bloodworth, Ton That Thien, Francisco Sionil Jose, Max Soliven, Kukrit Pramoj and global academics like Robert Scalapino, Patrick Honey and Dennis Duncanson.

Coming into contact with these highly talented, often forceful, hard-headed and extremely knowledgable people in exotic Asian locales was pretty heady stuff for a lad from East Coburg. As I've said it changes you. It's like doing a university degree, in say economics. You will never look at things the same way again, but it is hard to describe exactly how it has changed you. A couple of things I can say, however. One is that through meeting these sorts of people and others as well as my general experiences in Asia I learned how differently different nations and peoples viewed the region geopolitically at that time. Americans looking out at Asia saw primarily China and Japan and thought little of their old colonial possession The Philippines and the rest of Asia. Until the sixties, most of them had never heard of Vietnam or the other countries of Southeast Asia. The Europeans saw primarily their old colonial possessions – the French Indo-China, the British India and Malaya, and the Dutch Indonesia – and they thought little of anything else in the region. Mirror-like, the Asians looked out primarily at their colonial conquerors turning away from or ignoring their Asian neighbours. So The Philippines looked to California and Spain with little interest in the South while the elites who ran the Philippine plutocracy tried to pretend that Taiwan, China and Japan didn't really count. Malaya looked west to Britain and rarely anywhere else. There was very little geo-strategic thinking being done in Southeast Asia, indeed anywhere in the region at that time. This changed with the gradual development in the mid-late sixties of regional co-operation through institutions like ASA, ASEAN, the ADB and ECAFE (Economic Commission for Asia and the Far East) and the intensification of the Vietnam War.

Guns, Money and Women

The other thing I quickly discovered in the mid-sixties was how radically different politics in the Asian countries was to that in Australia. In Australia everything was quiet and orderly and political affairs were conducted strictly in accordance with the requirements of law and order. Politicians, parliamentarians and governments came and went usually without much fuss. The military and police forces operated quietly and were subject to civilian control while gangsters and criminals usually went to jail or lived in fear of doing so. While all the countries of Asia were different in culture and sometimes temperament, I soon found that in nearly all of them political power, from the national to the local levels, rested with those who had the greatest access to guns, money, goons and women. It was these and not votes or popularity that decided who ruled. It took me a while to adjust to this and it partly explained to me why so many Australian political, governmental and military leaders were not comfortable with Asia. I tried to explain this in another way, and rather dramatically, in an unpublished novel I wrote in 1981 centred on the disappearance of Prime Minister Harold Holt in 1967. One of the first things Holt did on becoming prime minister was to try to cut the Menzian eurocentric knot and drag Australia into Asia. To this end he embarked on a tour of Asia. In his very good book *Pacific Destiny, Inside Asia Today* (Crown, New York, 1990), Robert Elegant quoted from my novel saying, "Mount wrote at white heat in a fiercely apocalyptic vein:

> [Intelligence] reports, usually British or American, revealed to Holt an Asian world of convoluted intrigue, of political murders and assassinations, of both endemic and spectacular corruption, of military organisations financed by drug running ... of secret funds laundered through apparently respectable financial institutions ... All of this was played out in a world of spies and counter-spies, agents and double agents, information and disinformation, and cast against a backdrop of poverty social injustices and human degradation ...

... it came as quite a culture shock to this essentially straight and decent man. He now believed that if Australia was to play the role (in Asia) of his vision, it would have to come to terms not only with Asian cultures and patterns of thought, but with the kind of intrigue, corruption, rapaciousness, and lack of institutional restraint most Australians would find disorientating at best and probably distasteful in the extreme.

Given the orderliness of Australian politics, even at its most vicious and divisive times; the timidness of a bureaucracy steeped in legalism and inflexible procedures; the ultra-conservatism and Euro-centricity of the nation's managerial elite; and the country's general insularity and arrogant indifference towards Asia, Holt feared that if ever Australians were to (find) a place in Asia, it would take a long time.

Another thing I should say is that in every country in the midsixties, ultimate national power lay with the military, even in countries like Singapore and Malaysia which had the advantage of Westminster institutions. This is not only because they had the guns, but because the military was the principal and in most countries the only cohesive institution in the country, one in which its members had some trust in each other because they had trained together for years either at home or in places like Sandhurst and West Point.

One more thing, when I first visited Southeast Asia, the most prosperous nation in the region, by far, was The Philippines, thanks to the United States. Indonesia was one of the poorest, thanks partly to the Dutch. Yet even in the sixties I always felt that Indonesia would eventually overtake The Philippines, as in many ways they have, because they just seemed to me to be a more hard-headed and more committed people. I don't know why I thought that way, but I've since learned that I wasn't the only one who did so. Did it have something to do with the fat, indolent, 'tolerant' Spanish friars as against the tough Javanese and Dutch colonialists? Or was it that Indonesia gradually opened up its economy to the world, under the influence of people like Sir John Crawford, while the Filipinos, under the influence of their old phoney Left, took a strong protectionist road in effect throwing out American multinational manufacturing investors like Ford.

8
The 1968 Tet Offensive and its Aftermath

When I arrived from Hong Kong at Saigon's Tan Son Nhat international airport at 9am on Saturday, June 29, 1968, both the tall, dark Clyde Bauer in an olive green safari suit and the short, stocky, sandy-haired Ted Serong in his customary immaculate long-sleeved white shirt, were standing there to welcome me. Ted had his usual bunch of recent newspapers and a satchel of 'select', classified documents for me to read and return. This was my first visit since the January Tet Offensive and the subsequent 'mini-Tet' offensive in May-June, and I expected to see a great deal of destruction all around the place. But nothing seemed to have changed much except for more sand bags and barbed wire barricades along the already choking tree-lined streets full of a nasty blue haze from belching, horn-blaring giant US Army trucks. I commented to this effect to Ted who said he'd give me a briefing on the Offensive and a tour of the city the following afternoon.

They dropped me off at the Continental Palace where I had booked a room. The Dakao apartments were no longer available as the building had been shot-up and extensively damaged during the Offensive. The VC/NVA apparently knew it housed the HQ of the Phoenix program and it was one of the first targets they attacked. They'd swarmed over the bridge and up the lane to in effect assault our bedrooms. Monty Rodulfo, Patrick Pohla, Tommy Wright and others were holed up there for a week or more fighting off the VC/

NVA and with heavy US air support, they eventually prevailed without any casualties. But the building, while still intact, was left like a bomb site. I ascended to my hotel room via an old French hydraulic elevator to find I had appointments to meet, separately, that afternoon Ngo Khac Tinh and Senator Tran Van Lam in their offices. They were both pharmacists but were very different people, despite mixing similar political potions. Lam would become Foreign Minister in 1969 and years later he was to be the head of the South Vietnamese negotiating team at the Paris Peace Talks. Tinh was to become Minister of Information in 1969, then acting Foreign Minister at various times and was Minister of Education when Saigon fell in 1975. Both of them were Pacific Institute members and we would have discussed the war, the region and the Pacific Institute conference then scheduled for Hong Kong in October. When I got back to the hotel I decided to dine on "the Shelf", as the Continental Palace's open-sided sprawling terrace was called by journalists and foreign diplomats, and read the newspapers Ted had given me. I had just started when Kate Webb slid in beside me. She looked into my eyes and said so softly, huskily and innocently, "Hello Frank", and that was that. Once again, we drank, smoked and talked late into the night well past curfew.

The next morning, Tinh picked me up at 8.45 for I had agreed to address a Sunday morning meeting of the Central Committee of the Nhan-Xa Party at the party's national headquarters on Tran Minh Giang Street on the subject of Regional Strategic Issues. Almost all the party's national leaders and key supporters were there including a number of cabinet ministers and generals. Basically, we talked about many of the things I've been raising in this book. They had a good appreciation of the regional strategic issues involved in this war and much better than any American or Australian general I have ever met or read about, perhaps because they had been talking with Serong. At the end of our meeting, Tinh told me the Committee wanted me to visit branches throughout the country and that he was already organising a week- long tour that would begin the following Sunday and take in the Central Highlands, Nha Trang and Cam Ranh Bay on the coast and the 'ancient' capital Hue in the north. This was to be the first of many Nhan-Xa tours I would undertake and which carried me through every province and major city and town in South Vietnam – while giving me a chance to ascertain what was really happening at the grass roots level.

Jack De Silva

Following this meeting I had lunch with the Malaysian charge d'affaires, the irrepressible Jack De Silva, probably at the Cercle Sportif overlooking the busy tennis courts where we often dined together, and Ted Serong then took me on a tour of the Tet Offensive's 'destruction' of Saigon. On TV sets around the world we had seen dramatic pictures of Saigon ablaze and rent asunder by the VC (no mention of the NVA). But amazingly the city was intact. Ted picked me up in a green and white Police Field Force jeep and drove to the US MACV (Military Assistance Command Vietnam) Headquarters at Tan Son Nhat air base. There in a highly classified room he had access to, and with the aid of detailed maps and aerial and other photography, he gave me more than an hour's briefing on the military movements and developments over the months prior to Tet and then during both it and the later 'mini-Tet' offensive. There is no point in going into all of that here as it would take many pages and bore the average reader while the specialist should be able to access it elsewhere. It is well known these days. But something can be said briefly. From observations of VC/NVA military movements and deployments and from excellent intelligence, it was known that North Vietnam's General Vo Nguyen Giap, through a ruthless strategy involving the sacrifice of many thousands of VC guerrillas and NVA soldiers, planned a major offensive attacking urban centres across the country aimed at sparking a General Uprising, the overthrow of the

Saigon regime and an NVA-led communist victory to end the war he was until then losing. The Americans knew it was coming, they knew the cities were being infiltrated, but they did not know exactly when the attacks would begin.

Ted Serong said he had looked forward to the attacks, declaring well beforehand that they would be the best thing that could happen and that they would lead to the destruction of the VC/NVA (subsequent independent sources have long confirmed that Serong said this before the attacks). Ted said that three weeks before Tet, he had advised the US Commander General William Westmoreland, to whom he was still officially attached as chief counter-insurgency advisor, and US General Frederick Weyard, the commander of the Saigon region, to deploy 15 battalions to protect Saigon, which they did. When the attacks failed to come before Tet, the Lunar New Year, almost everyone thought they'd come after it. No one, including the foreign correspondents, thought that Giap and the NVA/VC would violate Tet of all things. Tet was the quintessence of Vietnamese tradition and culture, for which there is no comparison in the West. So revered is Tet that to this day I don't believe the South Vietnamese have ever forgiven the North Vietnamese communists for their outrageous violation of it.

The offensive began in the early hours of January 31, and involved attacks on cities and urban centres throughout the country. Despite the TV images shown around the world giving the impression that the whole of Saigon was subject to fighting and bombardment, if not ablaze, the fighting took place in only sections of the city and even there life went on more or less normally. The city never ceased partying. The people in effect said a pox on both your houses. The same could be said for the rest of the country with the exception of Hue which was occupied by the NVA resulting in the massacre of thousands of the middle class and particularly the educated. The VC was smashed beyond repair and the NVA driven out. They suffered a massive military and political defeat for the masses refused to rise up and those who did came out in support of the Saigon government. The US military estimated that the VC/NVA took over 50,000 dead. Not only did the Western media refuse to accept and report this figure but they misrepresented the Offensive as a stunning VC/NVA military and political victory over the US and South Vietnam from which the latter would never recover. After the war, however, North Vietnamese leaders acknowledged that the 50,000 figure was correct and that it had been a stunning defeat for them. So much so that a shocked Giap organised a second, 'Mini Tet', offensive which he launched a couple of months later by sending tens of thousands of very young NVA soldiers down south and across the borders in surge-like direct attacks on Saigon. These attacks were also repulsed in a number of battles outside the city, although a few NVA units did get into parts of the city, especially in the Chinese Cholon district. In this defence of Saigon, Australian forces performed extremely well in the battles of Coral and Balmoral north of the capital. (See Paul Ham, Chs. 27, 28, 29). If any Western general performed even once like Giap did throughout his career, wilfully and lazily wasting the lives of tens if not hundreds of thousands of his country's young men, they'd have been court marshalled. How much has Giap cost Vietnam today?

After the briefing at MACV headquarters, Serong drove me around the city to inspect the damage. Our first stop was the US Embassy which had been one of the VC's major targets because of its symbolic value. Like millions of people around the world, I had seen TV images of it being attacked along with commentary that the VC had stormed into the embassy fighting the Marines guarding it, thereby humiliating the US military. Well it wasn't true. In the dark, early hours of the morning, when the building was almost empty, a unit of about 20 VC did break though the outer, lightly-guarded wall but that was 30 metres all round from the building itself which was surrounded by another inner highly protective reinforced 'breeze blocks' wall which allowed in light but blocked views of the building. Supporting the VC on the ground between the walls were other VC in buildings across the street with automatic rifles and rockets which cannoned into the 'breeze blocks' wall.

None of VC on the ground were able to breach the inner wall or the embassy itself because of fire from Marines on the roof top. When dawn broke those still alive were killed in face to face combat with paratroopers who had been dropped in, while the VC in the buildings across the road were killed or forced to flee by air strikes. Contrary to sensational Western media reports, no VC ever entered the embassy itself. As we drove by one could see the extensive damage to the various walls, repairs to which were already well underway. We then headed out through hectic traffic to Cholon where two or three high density blocks of Chinese shops and apartments had been destroyed or heavily damaged, mainly during 'Mini Tet'. Some of the streets were still a mess littered with bricks, fire hoses and gutted vehicles of various kinds, but people just seemed to work around it all. Other spots we visited were much the same. All told the damage was much less than I expected to see, which in a bizarre way was somehow disappointing. When I returned to the same Cholon blocks at the end of the next September I was amazed to find that they had been mostly rebuilt. You had to marvel at their resilience, enterprise and optimism. I'm sure that's what carries Saigon and southern Vietnam today.

Before leaving the subject of Tet, there is an incident that seems to have been totally forgotten, erased from the Australian memory. That is the cold-blooded killing by a VC commander of four foreign journalists, three Australians and a Briton, in a Cholon street on May 5 during 'Mini Tet'. The Australians were Michael Birch, 24 years old, who was working for Australian Associated Press (AAP), John Cantwell, 30, a *Time* magazine correspondent and Bruce Pigott, 23, who was a Reuters correspondent. The Brit was Ronald Laramy, 31, who had recently arrived and was another Reuters correspondent. They and a fifth journalist, another Australian, Frank Palmos, 28, a freelancer writing for the *Sydney Morning Herald*, drove into Cholon, against US military advice, in a small open-aired jeep-like French Mini Moke on the morning of May 5. Reportedly, the vehicle carried a large sign above the windscreen saying "Bao Chi" which meant journalists or newsmen. As they drove in, US Huey helicopter gunships were strafing nearby VC/NVA positions. Local Vietnamese fleeing in the opposite direction warned them not to proceed. But they did for some time. They were about to retreat when they turned a corner into narrow Confucius Street and ran straight into a VC/NVA unit. It quickly surrounded them. According to eye witnesses, some of whose accounts in some details were contradictory, the journalists were dragged out of the jeep shouting "Bao Chi, Bao Chi". Palmos says the VC/NVA commander shouted "Bao Chi" and started shooting them with a .45 pistol. Others then joined in with automatic weapons. Palmos claims he survived by playing dead and then suddenly running away into the fleeing crowd amid gunfire when he got his chance.

It is interesting how these Australian journalists and their British mate, brutally executed by Vietnamese communists, have been forgotten while the Balibo Five in East Timor who were travelling with and, at least in one case, supporting the Marxist/communist Fretilin forces and who were killed in uncertain circumstances presumably by Indonesian and pro-democracy East Timorese forces, are lauded in many circles as heroes.

Touring with the Nhan-Xa

On every day of the week leading up to the trip north with the Nhan-Xa Party, I lunched with Monty Rodulfo at a different restaurant each day and dined in the evening with Kate on the Continental's open terrace. Monty's various operations for Ted Serong were such that the two of them took great care not to be seen in public together. Whenever I was in town, and at times in the future I lived for weeks in the Continental Palace, I would act as a go-between, dropping in on Ted at his office on Nhat Linh Street every couple of days. I assumed that when I wasn't there that others, like Clyde Bauer perhaps, performed this role. To enable me to get around town especially after curfew if I needed to, Ted would give me a PFF jeep which I would park behind the Continental. Monty had a very good network of agents in Cholon built around, so I was told, his elegant and beautiful Chinese girlfriend. Prior to the Tet Offensive he was able to warn Serong of strange political and financial transactions going on in Cholon, especially in relation to the price of gold. Like Serong he had an excellent and intuitive intelligence and counter-insurgency mind and had anticipated the attacks on the Dakao apartment block. Over the week he filled me in with what he thought was happening in the places I was about to visit. He was a lot more pessimistic than me.

On Sunday morning I flew out on Air Vietnam for Dalat with Professor Truong Cong Cuu, the party chairman, Ngo Khac Tinh and a couple of rough looking Nhan-Xa bodyguards whom I was assured were needed as VC terrorists and assassins were never far away. I was also well aware of the hazards of flying in the crowded war-driven skies of South Vietnam as I had seen war planes collide in balls of flame over Tan Son Nhat when I was staying in the Dakao apartment and had experienced them fly in, under and around other small aircraft I had been in. So I was glad when we touched down – as always in these circumstances. We were met at the airport 15 miles from Dalat and driven through the beautiful cool hills to the Nhan-Xa provincial headquarters where I addressed party leaders from all over the province. Never did I attempt in any way to tell the South Vietnamese how to run their party or their nation's affairs. That would have been a true disaster. As I explained before, I spoke about how we did things in Australia and how important their struggle against communist totalitarianism was to the future of all of Asia and to their own long term political freedom and economic prosperity. In all of these out of Saigon speeches I had local interpreters and I constantly wondered just what they were telling the people I had said. There again, did it really matter when there were thousands of dialects and many of them couldn't understand each other. It is often forgotten that when Lee Kuan Yew became Prime Minister of Singapore the colonial boy spoke only English and many Singaporeans couldn't understand him. The same was true of Soeharto when he came to power. He spoke Bahasa which was then the language of relatively few Indonesians. But there was always the sense that I might be being seriously misunderstood. And I never doubted that the VC/NVA would be at the meetings wherever I went. I had done enough political organising and infiltration of my own over the years to know that.

At the end of the day the bodyguards drove me to the University of Dalat where they said I would stay overnight. The university was in recess and I was given what I was told was one of the "special" staff bedrooms on account of it having its own bathroom and toilet. I was most appreciative of this gesture until I opened the bathroom/toilet door to be confronted by a cloud of literally thousands of mosquitoes. It was simply unbelievable. I battled my way in with the aid of two swatters made of the day's newspapers and by the time I got to the loo the walls were covered in blood. I got out of there and was tidying the mosquito nets around the bed when there was a demur knock on the door. In came a beautiful, lissome long-haired young girl with a tray of food. Delicious basic Vietnamese fare with a magnificent nuoc mam fish sauce you can't buy anywhere in the world today because the North Vietnamese communists destroyed all the decades-old "capitalist" vats when they overran the South in 1975. After finishing the meal I got into bed, tucked the netting in around me and was dosing off when all hell broke loose. On the concrete roof directly above me a machine gun on a tripod was going off firing somewhere and banging loudly on the roof. The ear-splitting noise was horrendous and bone-jarring. More of Mini-Tet I wondered? I got up, worked my up the stairs to the roof and with my arms open wide in case they didn't understand English, I asked what was happening. One of two young 18-20 year old male students said in quite good English, "We're just practising". In hindsight, I think they might have been assigned there to protect me. After all, only a few months earlier the VC/NVA had attacked Dalat killing hundreds and they were never far away at any time.

The next day I was taken to meet the local Bishop and then on a tour of a number of local hamlets in each of which there was a Nhan-Xa branch. The branch chairman was usually the local tribal elder or chief, most of whom were highly colourful old men. As usual I was asked everywhere to say something and a local interpreter was produced to translate my words into the local dialect. Whether or not they understood anything I said, they all applauded politely. What impressed me was how well Ngo Khac Tinh, who although a Confucian and a cousin of the Catholic President Thieu, got on so easily with the mountain tribal elders whom I imagined to be all animists of one kind or another. Having heard the phrase before, I thought of him as an intellectual politician with a common touch. Having a quick-witted, droll sense of humour he was always laughing or chuckling with most of the people he met. He was truly my best Vietnamese friend and when he later came to Australia he stayed in my house. Truong Cong Cuu was a horse of a different colour – while friendly, he was much more reserved, always in a suit, stern and long-faced.

From mountainous Dalat we flew the following morning down to the spectacular ocean beaches of Nha Trang where Bishop Thuan was in residence and waiting for us. After conferring with the bishop and later the province chief, we spent the next two days meeting Nhan-Xa officials and members including leaders of the ancient local Cham community which involved more talks, lunches and lavish dinners. Centuries ago, this coastal region of Indo-China was the seat of the glorious Kingdom of Champa which in the twelfth century had invaded Cambodia and captured Angkor. So the Cham were a people to be respected. At the end of each day we'd wander down to the wonderful sprawling beach and either walk along the sands or take a swim while loud, wok-wokking US Huey helicopter gunships swept low up the coast. On Thursday we headed down the coast to the US naval base at Cam Ranh Bay where we were given extensive briefings on how the US military there saw the war. They were also interested in our views on local political developments.

On the Friday, we flew into Hue, the old Imperial Capital of the Nguyen Dynasty full of temples and palaces on the wonderful River of Perfumes. What a place except that the centre plantations of the beautiful tree-lined boulevards and streets were covered with thousands of shallow half-peanut-shell graves of those who had been massacred by the VC/NVA during the Tet Offensive. I got out and walked among these graves of people, including women and children, who had given up their lives for the hope of a democratic future. The VC/NVA, like the Khmer Rouge later in Cambodia, sought to eliminate anyone with a French, Western or any other kind of education – that is, the whole middle class. The figure is now put at between three and six thousand people in a population of about 130,000. It seemed you could still smell cordite and rotting flesh in the air of which I was familiar. Our party was in a sombre mood when we arrived at the family home of the parents of Bishop Thuan. Thuan was a nephew of the assassinated President Ngo Dinh Diem. His mother was Diem's sister Elizabeth Ngo Dinh Thi Hiep. This was an aristocratic family of high Catholic mandarinal lineage, Diem's father and Thuan's grandfather having been the Grand Chamberlain for the Emperor Thanh Thai. Later in life Thuan was to become a Cardinal in Rome and a confidant of Pope John Paul II and today, posthumously, he is the subject of a beatification process. When I was introduced to members of his family – his mother and father both dressed in dark traditional long Vietnamese robes – I expressed through an interpreter condolences to them for the recent Tet atrocities. They nodded and then Elizabeth slowly explained that their family history went back at least to the seventeenth century – for some reason she mentioned 1698 – and that many members of the family and its friends had been "martyrs" over the years. She said blood had been shed by the family for centuries. I suddenly realised that what I thought had been 30 years of continuous internecine warfare in Vietnam had in fact been 300 years, at least in this part of the country. I walked out of the house wondering how long will it take for a people and a nation like this to recover. And, secondly, how will democracy come from these people.

The next morning I arose to the rushing sounds of the majestic Perfume River outside my window and the acrid smells of hot nuoc mam sauce on street vendor stoves below. After a pho breakfast and the usual round of meetings with local Nhan-Xa and government officials, including the Province Chief, I was taken to the Hue Cercle Sportif for a Nhan-Xa organised reception for a couple of hundred "notables" as Ngo Khac Tinh called them. I was asked to talk for ten or fifteen minutes this time without an interpreter. I don't think they understood anything I said. But again they clapped, this time with real emotion. Looking around the brick and concrete building, there were bullet holes in the walls everywhere. The next morning I was given a tour of the early nineteenth century walled Citadel, the site of the old Imperial Capital, by a Major Tung of the Vietnamese Black Panther (Hac Bao) Company. He spoke quite good English. Units of the South Vietnamese Army (ARVN) 1st Division, including the Black Panther Company, backed up by a couple of undermanned battalions of US Marines fought 10,000 to 12,000 North Vietnamese and Vietcong in an epic block by block 25 day battle for control of the city and the Citadel. The NVA was slowly driven out of the city and it came down to the Citadel above which the NVA/VC had raised the VC flag at the start of the battle on January 31.

According to Tung, fighting in and around the walls of the Citadel went on for the whole 25 days. Inside the sprawling Citadel sat the headquarters of the ARVN 1st Division, the buildings of various institutions including museums, art schools, the Thai Hoa Palace of the emperors, other monuments and temples of considerable note and the Tay Loc airfield. A calm but clearly excited Tung gave me a detailed description of the battles culminating in his own Black Panthers tearing down the VC flag and replacing it with the yellow and red striped South Vietnamese flag on February 24th. The South Vietnamese had done most of the fighting he said and without much US air or artillery support because of the weather and other local geographic and logistical factors and because they didn't want to destroy the Citadel. Tung proudly explained that the Black Panthers won the Citadel while the ARVN 1st Division and the Marines had defeated more than a whole NVA division who had enjoyed the advantage of surprise. The NVA/VC are thought to have lost over 5000 killed in Hue and another 2-3000 outside of Hue later on. It was a clear, and for Tung a magnificent, Allied victory. But it was one which at the time went almost totally unreported in the Western media because there were no Western reporters of any kind in Hue at the time. The Western press didn't start reporting the battle until late February when it was over!

Even years later, some of them were still misrepresenting things. One example is Gabriel Kolko. He wrote for the *New York Times* and other publications during the war and in 1986 published a much acclaimed book *Vietnam, Anatomy of War 1940-1975* (Allen & Unwin, London, 1986), the cover of which promotes him as "an historian and scholar, and a committed anti-war activist". Among many errors and distortions throughout the book, he says, without citing any evidence, that American forces totally destroyed half of Hue. This is sheer nonsense, to which I can attest having been driven around the city not only in early July 1968 but another two or three times in the following year. The same can be said of the Mekong Delta city of My Tho, which I visited many times in 1968 and 1969. Kolko says, quite wrongly, that the US flattened half of the city (Kolko pp. 308-309).

After we I arrived back in Saigon aboard an Air Vietnam DC4, Truong Cong Cuu dropped me off at the Continental Palace where shortly afterwards I had dinner with Monty Rodulfo in the adjacent La Dolca Vita Italian restaurant. Later that night, I went to work in my extra large room typing away on my little Adler as the window-mounted air conditioner whirred and cluttered away and a large fan clicked above the eight foot square double bed. I admired the French style and from that day on I have always bought a bed of about those proportions. They make life so much easier. At midnight, long after curfew, the phone on the mahogany desk rang. This was surprising for most of the time the blasted things never worked. Maybe someone from Australia, I thought, had somehow got through to me at last. But it was Kate. She said she thought she'd just give me a call and wondered if I'd come over for a drink. As I looked out the window over the square below to the Caravelle Hotel and down To Do Street to the Saigon River, I said slowly that I was working on a long piece and that I'd have a drink with her tomorrow after lunch. We chatted about friendly nothings for a while and when I went back to the typewriter I can remember wondering … Is she in love with me? It distracted me from my thinking for the rest of the night – and after midnight was the time in those days when I did most of my writing, reading and thinking. But what a delicious distraction!

***

The next morning, I had breakfast with Ngo Khac Tinh at the Cercle Hippique followed by an early lunch with a voluble and excitable Italian journalist, Corrado Pizzinelli, who wrote for a major paper in Rome and constantly sought my advice on the course of the war, and then the drink with a jeans-clad Kate early in the afternoon which went on for a little too long. I had been invited to a 5pm cocktail party for the diplomatic community at Tran Van Lam's palatial residence not far from the Cercle Sportif. Ambassadors came and went, while Lam spent a lot of time eagerly introducing me to his daughters. But as beautiful and rich as they undoubtedly were they moved me not at all. Stiff and formal, they lived on a different planet to me. At 7.30 I was due at Ted Serong's house for dinner. When I arrived I was shown by a servant into a large room to meet Ted in his usual, immaculate long-sleeved white shirt, Monty Rodulfo in a dark green shirt and unexpectedly, a surprised Kate whom Ted had invited late that afternoon. We were then joined by two other intriguing people. The first of them to come through the door was Laurie Crozier who had established the failed Ben Cat dairy farm north of Saigon, and was now officially working as an agricultural advisor to the South Vietnamese and Cambodian governments, but unofficially was also an advisor to Ted Serong's unofficial group. Ironically, it was he who was to be a principal behind-the-scenes figure, along with a few others, including Keith Hyland, to secretly negotiate through the North Vietnamese and whoever else in Cambodia and Vientiane, for Kate's release when she was captured by the Viet Cong in Cambodia on April 7, 1971. Crozier told me this in Melbourne in mid-May 1971 when he was angling for an invitation to my wedding a few days later. I don't know the details of the deal, but I suspect it was financial.

As far as I know, Kate and her companions were the only journalists ever released after capture or disappearance during the war. In 1970 alone 24 journalists died or disappeared in Cambodia, not to mention Vietnam and Laos. Hyland himself had been captured by the VC/NVA shortly after the 1968 Tet Offensive and was held for many months before being released, again as a result of negotiations led by Crozier. A highly intelligent and cultured man Laurie was the brother of Brian Crozier an acclaimed journalist who had been an editor of

The Economist in London, a lecturer at Oxford and who had written an excellent 200 page Penguin Special in 1965 titled *South-East Asia in Turmoil* (Penguin, London). Brian had described Southeast Asia as a "political volcano" in which democracy was a far away, if not impossible, dream and especially in Indonesia. Laurie was of similar views.

Following Crozier through Ted's door was the respected South Vietnamese General Pham Van Dong whom I had interviewed on a previous visit after an introduction from Ted. Dong was a member of the Nung ethnic minority which had a reputation of being fierce fighters. He was born in Tay Son west of Hanoi and grew up in Hanoi where for several generations members of his family had been teachers at the Imperial Court. Dong joined the French Army and became the first Vietnamese officer to command French troops. Later he commanded the ARVN 3rd Division, made up entirely of Nungs, was then appointed Deputy Commander of South Vietnam's III Corps and after that Commander of the 7th Infantry Division. In 1964 he was promoted to Major General becoming the Military Governor of Saigon-Gia Dinh District and Commander of the Special Capital Zone. He was known to Serong in all these capacities. I can't remember what position he held at the time of this dinner, but when I lived in Saigon between 1972 and 1975 with my wife Eileen, he'd become Minister of Veteran Affairs in the Thieu cabinet. He was then a number of times a guest at our dinner table. He sported a an extremely long, razor sharpened finger nail on the third finger of his right hand with which, his bodyguards claimed, he could "cut you in half". Dong always respected Serong because he saw Serong as being sympathetic to the cause of the Nung and the Montagnard hill tribes in the highlands of Central South Vietnam, and especially the Rhade in Darlac province where Serong had posted some of his first AATTV officers including Major Barry Petersen in 1963. During the Tet offensive Dong had been unable to get the Saigon

Government to provide protection against the VC/NVA for the small Nung community in Cholon, but Serong had come to the rescue with weapons and ammunition.

For three hours over dinner we wrestled with the war. Ted, as usual, took an arrogant centre stage describing a round table session he had recently attended along with six Vietnam-based US generals and other senior US officers and officials. He said he asked all the generals, pointing to them one after another, what was the grand objective in this war. He said he got six different mumbling answers. He went on to analyse the US military saying that because of the Woodstock-era drug culture that permeated the military like so much else in the US and Europe, the US was incapable of putting one fully effective division in the field anywhere in the world. Despite this, he argued that the way to win the war now, given its escalation from a guerrilla war to a mainforce war, courtesy of both the North Vietnamese and the US, was to defeat and destroy the NVA divisions and the best way to achieve this was to entice them all into South Vietnam, to us, in II Corps and III Corps. There were already 13 seriously weakened NVA divisions in South Vietnam and he wanted the rest of them to come down.

As it turned out this is precisely what happened during the 1972 Offensive. General Dong after a few drinks complained that since the assassination of Ngo Dinh Diem in 1963, a guerrilla war had been allowed to escalate into a global conflict between the USA, USSR and China with Vietnam a pawn between them. Dong also said that from the start the Americans had never learned any lessons from the French whose experiences they completely ignored and he went on to give some telling examples. He also let out a number of criticisms of the Saigon Government whose anti-Montagnard biases and actions he deplored. As we sipped on our black market St. Emilion red, Monty's grey British military moustache chipped in with his analysis of the reaction of the Chinese to the Tet Offensive and its aftermath. He was talking about the Chinese in Cholon where he had excellent sources among both the pro-Taiwanese and pro-communist communities, including some of their respective intelligence operatives. While he was personally pessimistic about the war as a whole, because he never liked or trusted the Americans, he said Chinese communist intelligence sources reported Tet as a massive defeat for their cause and that the NVA/VC could not win the war. At the time there were over 300,000 Chinese soldiers in North Vietnam, releasing the NVA to fight in South Vietnam.

With Kate seated on my right, I didn't have much to say except that with the destruction of the VC infrastructure during the Tet Offensive, it further opened up the possibilities of building grass roots democratic parties and institutions like the Nhan-Xa and other democratic socio-economic organisations like trade unions to ultimately support a liberal democratic government. I spoke briefly about the Philippines and Indonesia and what the Pacific Institute was doing in those places. This was generally well received and a few weeks later I was to repeat it all, but mainly the Vietnam related material, to Sir Robert Thompson, who I was glad to see took it on board in his 1969 book *No Exit From Vietnam* (Chatto & Windus, London, 1969). I came to note that Thompson in his books even wrote up some of Ted Serong's anecdotes as his own. Ted didn't seem to mind this as long as Thompson took on or incorporated his theories and analysis accurately which generally he did. Laurie Crozier, who had extensive Cambodian contacts, didn't have anything to say around the table. But he was seated on my left and said quietly to me that Sihanouk had to go because he was not only impoverishing Cambodia through his own indulgences and neglect, but that he and his wife, Monique, were selling out to the North Vietnamese by allowing them to use Cambodian territory to develop the Ho Chi Minh Trail and ship arms in for the VC via Sihanoukville port. He gave me introductions to a number of Cambodians in Phnom Penh, including the National

Police Chief General Sosthene Fernandez, Prince Sirik Matak and General Lon Nol, all of whom I later met on a number of occasions.

As the various guests were leaving, Ted said Monty would run me back to the Continental Palace – it was already after curfew – in his PFF Jeep. Then he said, "I'll look after Kate". But she said, "No. I'll go with Frank." And so it was. When we got back to hotel she whispered to me in the lift while squeezing my arm, "You're a backroom macro-manipulator, Frank". I shrugged and said "Not really". But in hindsight she was probably right.

The next morning I flew out to Bangkok where I again met John Myint and a true backroom manipulator, and I suspect much more, General Chat Chavangkul, before a week later taking a train through Northern Thailand to Vientiane in Laos; then back to Bangkok for more lunches and a very enjoyable meeting with the beautiful Shan Princess Ying Sita (who was looking for guns for her Shan State Army mates); down to Kuala Lumpur, Singapore, and Indonesia for three weeks (which I described earlier in Chapter 4); then back up to Manila for, among other things, more political formation discussions; then across to Saigon again for more meetings with Ted, who was now living at 176 Pasteur near the Palace, Cuu and Tinh, and of course Kate. Then over to Bangkok for more lunches with Bill Klausner of the Asia Foundation and George Tanham, and down to Singapore for even more lunches with Alex Josey, Dennis Bloodworth and George Thomson and then on to Melbourne just in time for the 1968 Grand Final between Carlton and Essendon. All of this time I was writing every day not only for newspapers around the region from Jakarta to Tokyo and India but my pieces were now being syndicated around the world through the US *National Catholic News Agency* (NCNA) courtesy of the wonderful Father Patrick O'Connor, the NCNA's correspondent in Saigon who wrote extremely well informed forensic 'intelligence' articles on the VC and Vietnam.

9

The 1968 Pacific Institute Conference and on to APEC 1989

In late October Bob Santamaria, Bill Smith SJ and I flew out of Melbourne for the 1968 Annual Pacific Institute Conference in Hong Kong. Bob and I sat next to each other, as we were to do a number of times on long flights over the years, so I got to talk with him about a lot of things mainly relating to Australia, international affairs, theology and economics. He also spoke candidly about his family, his wife, Helen, and other personal matters and since they were off the record, they will forever remain so. This three day 1968 conference from October 26 to 29 was to be the first of three held in successive years in Hong Kong. In 1968 we met at the Jesuit Wah Yan College and in 1969 and 1970 in the Sun Ya Hotel, a moderate Chinese establishment on Nathan Road in Mongkok. These three conferences go together because it was during and between them that we gradually developed what became known as the 1970 Pacific Institute Resolution through which we sought to give effect to our vision of regional cooperation in the form of an Asia Pacific Community or "confederation".

All the conferences through to the last one in 1976 took basically the same shape. Bob would act as chair and deliver an opening address on global and regional strategic developments followed by extensive discussion. Representatives from each country would then report on political, economic, social, security and other developments in their respective countries. Questions and discussions followed each of these. Then we discussed our overall conclusions which led to the 1970 Resolution. It was hoped that whatever conclusions we came to would be acted upon by delegates and that they would strive to have them implemented in their own nations. As far as I was concerned this was the whole idea of the Pacific Institute. I was the Executive Secretary and no notes or minutes were kept of any of the proceedings as I have explained earlier. Quite a number of our people and visitors were members of or close to intelligence organisations and national leaders and we wanted them to speak openly and frankly with no fear that anything said would be repeated outside. No notes of any kind were taken by anyone during the meetings.

By bringing together this particular group of people the Pacific Institute achieved many things in a number of countries related to the building of liberal democratic institutions – quite extraordinary really – but, in my opinion, the most important and influential thing was the 1970 Resolution advocating and articulating broader regional strategic, military, economic and political cooperation. This was moved officially in 1970 by Ngo Khac Tinh, then South Vietnam's Minister of Education, and later Acting Foreign Minister, and seconded by Jusuf Wanandi, then a personal assistant and advisor to Major General Ali Moertopo. Later Wanandi was to become a founding director of Indonesia's Centre for Strategic and International Studies (CSIS) and, in effect, the executive secretary of the Pacific Economic Cooperation Conference (PECC). The Resolution was passed unanimously.

I explained the 1970 Resolution, which was titled The Pacific Community, and the influence it subsequently had on the gradual development of APEC which was launched in 1989, and on other forms of regional cooperation, in a paper I wrote in 1994 called "The Genesis of APEC: An Australian Viewpoint". This was published that year by the U.S. Global Strategy Council in Washington which was run by Ray Cline, a former Deputy Director of the CIA whom I had known since Vietnam and Taiwan days. In this paper I wrote:

> APEC, like ASEAN, is economic in tone but strategic in conception. As with ASEAN, its genesis goes back to the early 1960s. APEC, established in 1989, grew out of the idea of economic, political and eventually military cooperation between Australia, Japan and Indonesia. Its aim was for ASEAN members, cooperating regionally, to hold the balance of power against larger states including Japan, China, India, Russia and the United States.
>
> ASEAN, established in 1967, emerged from the need for the non-communist nations of Southeast Asia to group together for protection against North Vietnam backed by China and Russia, both of whom were seen as expansionary communist states. These Southeast Asian countries believed in the domino theory which they rightly saw to be a political probability theory and not the military inevitability theory caricatured in the West.
>
> The APEC concept was born of much grander and longer-term strategic view than ASEAN's by people who correctly foresaw the general trend of developments in Asia over at least the succeeding thirty years. This concept was gradually developed during a number of annual conferences of an international organisation called the Pacific Institute in the late 1960s and early 1970s.

I wrote that the major objectives of the 1970 Resolution were:

> 1. That ASEAN supported by Australia and Japan should hold the balance of power in the Asia Pacific region and could do so because of the position of its members on the strategic waterways. That is, it could be a sort of cog in the wheel balancing off the major powers within and outside the region, namely Japan, China, India, Russia, and the United States. And it could be said that most of us in the Pacific Institute, and certainly all of the Asians, understood that in the very long run China would be a major problem because until the modern European era it had always been at the centre of the world and most of us on the periphery.

2. That ASEAN should form a Common Market. Some constructive movement in this direction is now obvious with the development in recent years of the ASEAN Free Trade Area (AFTA) among other things.

3. That there be appropriate economic cooperation between ASEAN, Japan, Australia and New Zealand, partly to find ASEAN outside markets and sources of finance and investment in the Pacific and beyond. This has been done in many ways over the years and is now being effected more broadly through APEC and other trade liberalisation mechanisms such as the Cairns Group in the shadow of the General Agreement on Tariffs and Trade (GATT) talks.

4. That there be formal and informal defence 'understandings' between Japan, Australia and Indonesia (leading ASEAN) in the fields of strategic air and naval power, designed primarily to keep open the Sea Lanes of Communication (SLOCs). In effect this would run parallel to the politico-economic cooperation in the Asia Pacific Community.

The Resolution's framework of economic cooperation (most aspects of which have now been superseded) was written by Colin Clark who attended most of the conferences. At the time he was a Research Fellow at Monash University, having been Director of the Institute of Agricultural Economics at Oxford University between 1953 and 1968. The Resolution said that in pursuit of a Common Market, "South East and East Asian countries should agree:

(i) From now onwards not to increase tariffs or impose any new restrictions on the importation of industrial goods or handicrafts produced in other Southeast Asian countries.

(ii) Within a period of two years to replace all existing quota import licensing, exchange control and other restrictions on such trade by an open General Licence to import subject to tariffs at a rate not exceeding 40 percent ad valorem.

(iii) At the end of the initial period of two years and annually thereafter, all tariffs on such trade to be reduced by 10 per cent of their original amount, to disappear completely at the end of ten years."

Clark's great 1970 regional free trade vision was truly the seed and in some respects the blueprint from which APEC and the ASEAN Free Trade Area have grown. He developed it consciously within the context of our grand regional strategic framework. Thereafter, his prescriptions for the developing economies of Asia were taken back to these nations by PI delegates and associates and in many cases acted upon by Western educated economic technocrats. We encouraged him to travel around the region to talk with economists and policy makers about his free trade and trade liberalisation ideas and gave him every support possible. But it is doubtful that even he foresaw how rapidly some of these economies would grow once they got their policies right and eventually opened up to the world.

The principal architects of the Resolution's structure of military cooperation aimed primarily at securing the Sea Lanes of Communication (SLOCs) flowing through the Malacca Strait, the Indonesian waterways and the South China Sea, were Ted Serong, Bob Santamaria and, if I may say so, in a small way, myself. The diplomatic posture came from mainly from the Indonesians and the Australians.

Ali Moertopo's Asia Pacific Triangle

Following the conferences, and especially the 1970 Hong Kong and 1971 Saigon conferences, members took the resolution back to their home countries and endeavoured to have it acted upon. In some countries it was laughed at, but in Indonesia, generals Ali Moertopo and Soedjono Hoemardani, both personal assistants to President Soeharto and his closest advisors, and co-chairmen of the CSIS, immediately took it up. Moertopo for his part launched his concept of an "Asia- Pacific Triangle" linking Indonesia, Australia and Japan.

Explaining it in a 1973 CSIS publication entitled, *Indonesia in Regional and International Co-operation: Principles of Implementation and Construction*, he wrote:

> Basically ASEAN is the first form of co-operation, through which Indonesia will extend its net of co-operation ... In the extension of (this net) Indonesia views the Asia pacific region as an enlargement of Southeast Asia. As it has been described before, and looking at the compositions of the strengths and weaknesses of the five most important countries in the region ... we realize that the present condition makes it possible for Indonesia (and ASEAN), Australia and Japan to create co-operation among them. This concept is called the Asia-Pacific Triangle. This structure of co-operation could be beneficial not only to Indonesia (and ASEAN), but could also serve the interests of Australia and Japan, both now and in the future.
>
> As a previously isolated country and as one seeking new contacts in Asia, Australia needs Indonesia (and ASEAN) through which Australia will make meaningful contacts. On its part, Indonesia (and ASEAN) needs aid from Australia in the form of technology and capital. In order to be connected to Southeast Asia, Japan also feels the need for closer co-operation with Indonesia and ASEAN ...
>
> In general, it can be said that in this connection the geographical position of Indonesia serves as a foundation of this triangular structure. Viewed from ... Japan and Australia, Indonesia serves as the nexus of the Asia-Pacific region, similar to the position Korea possesses in East Asia ...
>
> For Japan this is not impossible ... In such a situation, ASEAN and China will see each other as rivals, each fighting for the acquirement of capital and investment, the import technology from Japan, and also the export of primary goods to Japan. This should explain why ASEAN ought to prepare as soon as possible the infrastructure of this triangle.

From my many conversations with both Ali Moertopo and Soedjono Hoemardani, I know they appreciated not only the grand strategic scope of the Pacific Community endeavour, but the Australian role in its conception.

PECC

Over the succeeding years, the Indonesians and others kept plugging away and eventually in the late 1970s, the Japanese Prime Minister, Masayoshi Ohira, proposed a Pacific Economic Cooperation Council (PECC) and got immediate agreement from Australian Prime Minister Malcolm Fraser, with whom Bob Santamaria had a close working relationship.

PECC held its first conference in Canberra in September 1980 and became a tripartite body of businessmen, academics and government officials aimed at building mutual understandings and therefore cooperation in the region and eventually the sort of Pacific Community envisaged in the Pacific Institute's resolution. There is no doubt that PECC came about largely as a result of the influence in Japan and South Korea of Wanandi, Moertopo and Hoemardani and generally of the eminent Australian economist Sir John Crawford. It ranks as one of Malcolm Fraser's real achievements. Since its creation, PECC has been run efficiently and brilliantly by Wanandi and without him, it would have died long ago. With the assistance over the years of his CSIS colleagues Dr. Hadi Soesastro, Dr. Mari Pangestu (now an economics minister in the Yudhoyono government), Dr. Sujati Djiwandono and Dr. Clara Joewono, he ensured that it later played a valuable role within the APEC framework.

During the late 1970s and 1980s the people associated with PECC and other regional bodies such as the Pacific Basin Economic Council (PBEC) and the Pacific Trade and Development Conference (PAFTAD) – and there was a great deal of overlapping membership – advanced the causes of structural adjustment and trade liberalisation in East and Southeast Asia. Indeed, within their own countries, it can be said that, from the mid-70s onward, they and their Western educated technocratic colleagues gave effect to many of the free trade and domestic prescriptions recommended by Colin Clark, Sir John Crawford, Professor Heinz Arndt, Ross Garnaut and others, gradually opening up their economies to foreign trade, investment, know-how and technology bringing them high rates of growth – and therefore their people greater prosperity and enhanced individual freedoms. This was achieved while protecting national economic interests and fledgling domestic enterprises from foreign exploitation.

The PECC and other regional bodies managed to keep the idea of a Pacific Community going among a gradually widening circle of people in an increasing number of countries – but they were mainly businessmen and academics. Despite its tripartite structure, the PECC was never able to attract government involvement or political interest in its ideas of Pacific cooperation, and without governments and political action there could be no Pacific Community as it was essentially an inter-governmental geopolitical concept. By the mid-1980s, therefore, the PECC had gone about as far as it could go on its own.

In fact, it can be said that the movement towards a Pacific Community gradually lost momentum from the late 1970s onwards and was very much on the back burner by the mid-1980s – notwithstanding the efforts from time to time of governmental leaders, including Indonesia's then Foreign Minister Mochtar Kusumaatmadja, to generate government interest through such things as his proposal for a grouping to be called ASEAN-Pacific Cooperation (APC).

There were many reasons for this loss of interest. To begin with, the Australian Liberal Party and government under Malcolm Fraser was never really committed to the idea, basically because it lacked strategic thinkers and people interested in Asia; Ali Moertopo gradually lost his influence with President Soeharto, as well as his health and died in

1984; some of the ASEAN countries were very nervous about a larger Pacific cooperative grouping for fear that it would be dominated by the developed countries and perhaps threaten ASEAN itself; and a number of the original Australian Pacific Institute thinkers, including Bob Santamaria, simply lost interest after the fall of South Vietnam and the defeat of the Americans.

So by the early 1980s it seemed that the idea of a Pacific Community was a lost cause. However, in 1986 I began travelling again throughout Southeast Asia after a break of four years and discovered that interest in the concept was certainly not dead, especially in Indonesia where it had been kept alive by Wanandi and the CSIS. I reported this not only to our friends all around the region, which included the leadership of most of the countries of ASEAN and North East Asia, but many times over many months to senior politicians, including cabinet ministers, trade union leaders, academics, foreign affairs department officers and high level Intelligence officials in Canberra, Washington, London and Paris. I distributed copies of the Pacific Institute Resolution to all of these people and more. But even before that, I had forwarded a copy with attached notes along the lines I have written in this book to Bob Hawke in mid-1982 who was then the ALP Federal member for the Melbourne electorate of Wills in which I lived. I did this through John Maynes, one of the most respected and powerful trade unionists in the country, who was then President of the Federated Clerks Union (FCU). Maynes, who was also a long serving senior officer of Bob Santamaria's National Civic Council, was an old mate of mine and a regular Friday night drinking companion. He had also visited me and my wife in Saigon and Manila regularly. Maynes told me in mid-1982 that he was in secret discussions with Hawke about bringing the four pro-DLP unions, the FCU, the Shop Distributive and Allied Employees Association (SDA), the Carpenters and the Ironworkers into the ALP in order to counter the Marxist Socialist Left in the state of Victoria and thereby help him become leader the ALP and hopefully prime minister.

In the event, these four unions didn't rejoin the ALP until 1986, well after Hawke became prime minister in March 1983, but these discussions set in train many behind the scenes maneouvres that nevertheless contributed significantly to Hawke's election as ALP leader and prime minister. When Maynes told me he was to have a meeting with Hawke in his Clerks Union office in Queens Street, Melbourne, in mid-1982 to discuss the above matters, I gave him a copy of the Pacific Institute Resolution papers along with an accompanying 'strategy paper' to give to Hawke. He later told me that he had done that. However, I have no idea what happened with these papers and what impact, if any, they had on anyone. Certainly, nothing seemed to happen for many years.

Hawke Launches APEC

Nevertheless, I kept pushing the ideas and concepts wherever I went, especially in Jakarta after I started travelling again in 1986, and then seemingly out of the blue, Hawke launched APEC in Seoul in January 1989. In his 1994 memoirs, Hawke gives his version of how this came about (see *The Hawke Memoirs*, Bob Hawke, William Heinemann Australia, 1994, pp.230-233).

Hawke says that between 1983 and 1989 he was constantly talking about closer relations between Australia and Asia which he labelled "enmeshment with Asia". He said he spoke a lot about the need for greater global free trade and trade liberalisation. He explained that with the guidance of Ross Garnaut and other senior internationalists in his office, he and they continually pursued these objectives.

Hawke said he made his first international move towards these objectives at a conference in Thailand in November 1983 where he spoke about the General Agreement on Tariffs and Trade (GATT) and the needs of food exporters like Australia and Thailand. Following this a number of meetings between countries in the region took place which led to Australia convening the agricultural Cairns Group in 1986 and then APEC in 1989. These developments, he argued, were all parts of the same conceptual policy drive towards enhanced regional co-operation in search of greater free trade which fitted in with his government's broader foreign policy aims.

Further light on Hawke's launching of APEC and whose idea it really was is to be gained from the recent book on his prime ministership written by his wife, the novelist Blanche D'Alpuget (*Hawke The Prime Minister*, Melbourne University Press, 2010). D'Alpuget quotes a number of Hawke's advisors on the subject. The first is Sandy Hollway, Hawke's Principal Private Secretary at the time. He is quoted as saying in effect that the concept of some kind of Asia Pacific community had been discussed in academic circles for about a year.

So the idea didn't come from Hollway, as a number of people have suggested. In fact, Hollway suggests that Hawke had been thinking about it himself for some time as he goes on to say that for many months before the trip to South Korea Hawke had been talking about Australian economic relations with Asia, and had kept repeating the phrase "enmeshment with Asia". Hawke and his advisors knew there was an opportunity for a major speech in Seoul and during one late night discussion between them in Canberra someone, perhaps Hawke, said that the trip could be a good time for Australia to say there should be some kind of community for the Asia Pacific.

As I mentioned earlier, over these years in which Hawke was formulating and shaping his ideas on regional co-operation, I was talking to the Pacific Institute Indonesians in Jakarta, notably Harry Tjan Silalahi and Jusuf Wanandi in the CSIS, while they, in turn, were talking to the Australian Embassy and visiting Australian diplomats, politicians and journalists and others including Japanese and South Koreans. The Australian diplomats in Jakarta, and perhaps elsewhere, were reporting back to Canberra what these Indonesians were saying via secret cables and reports which presumably were read by Hawke. At the same time various academics and journalists associated with

Bob Santamaria and myself were pushing the idea with foreign policy bureaucrats and politicians in Canberra.

Accompanying Prime Minister Hawke on his visit to Seoul in January 1989 were Mike Codd, the Head of the Department of Prime Minister and Cabinet; John Bowan, Hawke's Foreign Affairs Advisor; and Sandy Hollway. D'Alpuget quotes Codd as to the way the four of them worked together on how to raise what Codd called Hawke's "great idea" with South Korean President Roh Tae-woo, so as to encourage a structure of regional economic co-operation that would bring Australia further into the region. D'Alpuget (pp. 193-194) quotes Codd saying that on the night before a scheduled meeting with South Korean President Roh Tae-woo, Hawke gathered his advisors together to discuss the subject with him. Codd said the proposition put, initially to Roh, came from that meeting. He added for the record that often there are prime ministers or leaders who have a great idea but rarely do they call together their senior advisors to discuss how to implement it.

So the idea for the organisation of states they called vaguely "Asia Pacific Economic Co-operation" (APEC) and launched in Seoul came from Hawke himself and not any of his advisors. He is truly the father of APEC, which was later further developed into a heads of state meeting by his successor Prime Minister Paul Keating.

One of the most interesting things Hawke had to say in his *Memoirs*, from the point of view of this book, is that a major guiding influence on him was the liberal, free trade economist Dr. Ross Garnaut who for many years was his Principal Economic Advisor. D'Alpuget goes further and makes it quite clear that it was Garnaut who persuaded Hawke in the early stages of his parliamentary career and prime ministership to take seriously Asia and Australia's need to become more heavily engaged in and with it. Before that, Hawke, according to the D'Alpuget book, had little interest in Asia and the region politically or economically. So we can say that Garnaut was a major influence in getting Hawke to think more about Asia and ultimately what led to APEC.

As a result of his involvement from the late 1970s in trade and other talks with ASEAN countries, and his involvement with PECC, Garnaut had for years been close to and influenced by Jusuf Wanandi and the CSIS generally in Jakarta. So the wheel went round. Consequently, it can fairly be said that Bob Santamaria in promoting his Pacific Community or Asian Pacific Community concept in the early sixties and following it through politically, now stands as one of the great international strategic visionaries in Australian history. It is true that the Japanese advocated a general idea of a Pacific Community in the early sixties, but while later supporting PECC, they did little to materialise it politically.

The Strategic importance of ASEAN

As I wrote in the 1994 U.S. Global Strategy Council paper, despite all of the efforts to disparage it and play it down,

> ASEAN will be pivotal in any pattern of security cooperation because it sits on the strategic waterways where the interests of the major powers impacting on the region converge. As mentioned earlier, those powers include not only Japan, the United States and China, but also Russia which remains a Pacific power with global interests. India promises to emerge as a major economic and military force having finally thrown off the socialist central planning nonsenses of Nehru and his successors. Because ASEAN sits on the strategic waterways, it can be a major instrument helping to balance these powers off against each other – a role which should also help the ASEAN states maintain harmony among themselves – which already has been no small feat in itself.
>
> Over and above all, it can be said that APEC together with parallel defence and security cooperation – that is the Pacific Community as outlined by the Pacific Institute in 1970 – is aimed at creating

a political framework to take in Japan and China so that they are welcomed and accepted as parts of the comity of Pacific nations and thereby prevented from dominating the region either individually or together or, if left alone, from feeling obliged to act as sole balances to each other. In other words, they would be held safe from both the region and each other. The European Community, NATO and a network of transatlantic understandings have, of course, played not dissimilar roles in Europe.

As all of this was discussed, and more than conceptually, at numerous Pacific Institute gatherings, it can be seen that we have come a long way over a long time. And there is still no hurry. As ASEAN keeps telling us, the key to success is to 'hasten slowly' so that concepts can take root, trust and understanding can germinate, and cooperation can blossom bringing peace, freedom and prosperity along with resilient regional and national independence for all.

Today, we are told that the future of regional security and strategic co-operation lies with the "East Asia Summit" which will now include not only China, but India and the US as well. Two points here. The correct title of the East Asia Summit is the ASEAN East Asia Summit, underlining the point I've made above. It grew out of the ASEAN Plus summit meetings. Kevin Rudd, having been strongly rebuffed in Asia over his urgent but vague and ignorant call for new regional co-operation architecture he called Asia Pacific Community in effect replacing APEC and ASEAN, now says the ASEAN East Asia Summit is in effect his Asia Pacific Community idea since it includes the US, China, Russia and India. But all of that has long been on the ASEAN agenda. Indeed, APEC should have included India from the outset, a point long ago recognised by the Pacific Institute when at its 1969 Conference it argued over whether the Pacific Community should be called the Indo-Pacific Community.

Back to the PI Conferences

During the early annual PI Conferences, we decided not only to develop a grand strategic resolution, but to also produce a quality quarterly journal and a monthly newsletter on developments around the region. The first issue of the quarterly called *Pacific Community* appeared in June 1969 and the last of them in Winter (June) 1971 which included an obituary to Monty Rodulfo who had died in Hong Kong in late 1970. It was printed by the Hawthorn Press in Melbourne whose owner, John Gartner, was one of its major financial supporters. It was edited over the years by either Christopher Clark or myself. In its short history it built up an impressive list of contributors which included, apart from members of the Pacific Institute, some of the best international authorities on Southeast Asian affairs, including P.J. Honey, Justus M. van der Kroef, Frank N. Trager, Jeffrey Race, Alex Josey, Ton That Thien, Monty Rodulfo, Frank C. Darling and Rodolfo Severino Jr., a Filipino diplomat who was later to become Secretary General of ASEAN. It folded in 1969 because it was costing too much to produce and distribute and we were not prepared to sacrifice its quality.

The monthly newsletter was called *Pacific News*. Unlike Pacific Community, it was a cheaply produced roneoed and stapled foolscap affair carrying ostensibly "confidential" reports, mainly from PI members, on current strategic and other issues and what was happening in countries around the region. We tried to get members to send in reports every month, but this didn't always work out. In fact, I wrote many copies of it entirely myself. As my travelling grew more extensive and long-lasting in the late sixties, the production and distribution of PN moved over to Fr. Bill Smith at Belloc House where it remained until the PI was wound up in the mid-seventies. PN was an extremely well received bulletin. We distributed it to people all over the world in Asia, the US, Europe and elsewhere, to foreign affairs and defence departments, intelligence organisations, prime ministerial and other cabinet offices, journalists, academics and so on. It was read by presidents, prime ministers, foreign ministers and Intelligence chiefs. Seventy-three issues were produced and we would like to think it had an influence on things, especially in preparing Asia for the sort of cooperation that led to APEC.

It is worth noting here that the 1968 conference decided: "The 'guiding philosophy' of the Pacific Institute is the gradual building of a Pacific Community, a voluntary association of the nations of the Indo-Pacific Region which will extend to each other mutual assistance in the fields of social justice, economic development, political cohesion, democratic institutions and security against internal subversion and external aggression, while respecting each other's national aspirations." (See PI files in the Frank Mount Papers).

The 1969 Conference declared:

> The international policy objective of the PI is the creation – through the political, diplomatic, economic and other actions of government – of a Pacific Community. The Pacific Community is envisaged as an economic, social and ultimately political association of S.E.Asian states, itself associated in different ways with India, Japan, Australia and Latin America. The objective of such a Community shall be not only a growth in the economic wealth of these states, but a greater measure of international justice between them. In the light of this objective, the PI opposes imperialism of every type – communist or capitalist.
>
> The internal policy objective of the PI is the creation of states which, whatever their political form, are pluralist in relation to minority groups – ethnic, political, social, religious and cultural – social democratic in economic policy, whether agricultural or industrial, and therefore anti-communist and anti-totalitarian in political organisation.

The 1971 Conference was held in Saigon in October and what a pleasant time we all had. There is nothing like a war atmosphere to get the adrenalin pumping and we simply loved tree-lined downtown Saigon, the lissome girls in their pastel-coloured Ao Dais, long white gloves and dainty parasols held high above their scooter bikes as they weaved in their dozens through the steamy traffic amidst the smells of diesel, nuoc mam sauce and hot chestnuts.

While the usual delegates turned up, there were of course many more than the usual number of South Vietnamese. They included apart from Tinh, Cuu and Bishop Thuan, local PI associates Senator Tran Van Lam (later Foreign Minister) and Ambassador Tran Kim Phuong, who together were to lead the official South Vietnamese team at the Paris negotiations, Dr. Phan Quang Dan, the Minister of State, General Pham Van Dong, the Minister for Veteran Affairs, Phung Nhat Minh, a senior Foreign Affairs Department officer and Nguyen Ngoc Linh, a dynamic local entrepreneur. Others who came as observers were Malcolm Morris, the Australian Ambassador and Keith Hyland, the tall, Gary Cooper-like swashbuckling duck feather king. Most people in the Australian foreign affairs and Intelligence communities in Asia thought that Keith Hyland was a self-made Asian-based millionaire. But, in fact, as noted earlier, he was the wealthy scion of the family that produced frozen foods in Melbourne and had a feather processing factory in Sydney. Hyland, who was a friend of Cawthorn's, was happy to quietly support the Pacific Institute in whatever way he could. He and I often got together for a meal (see Frank Mount Diaries).

While the conference didn't make any changes to the 1970 Resolution, it added some policy recommendations regarding the global and regional strategic situations at the time. However, in the long run these became outdated.

More importantly, we decided to set up a Vietnam Chapter of the Institute under Ted Serong and to appoint him Director of Studies of the whole Institute. The next time I came back to Saigon I found a bronze plaque on the high white brick fence beside his fortified gates saying "Pacific Institute".

10
Living in Saigon

In early 1972, the Pacific Institute's backers, at my initiative, agreed that I should move my base to Saigon. Until then, I had worked out of Melbourne on extended overseas tours. However, in May 1971 I had married Eileen Gleeson, a Melbourne history teacher introduced to me by John Myint in the lounge of the Windsor Hotel in Melbourne. I was sure that being based in Southeast Asia, in fact in Saigon because that was where the action was and where so much was to be decided, was the thing to do. So on April 23, 1972, we arrived in Saigon and set about finding a house to live in.

We had arrived at the height of the NVA 1972 Easter Offensive when all US ground combat troops had been withdrawn and the South Vietnamese Army (ARVN) was left to fight the NVA with only US air and some naval support. One of the first things that struck me at this time in Saigon and when travelling around nearby provinces were the 100 metre long queues of young South Vietnamese lining up at recruitment centres to join the ARVN and defend their nation. These were the South Vietnamese who according the Western press wouldn't fight. Needless to say these queues were never reported in the mainstream Western media even though some international press agency reporters had to walk past them to get to work.

While Eileen and I looked for a house or an apartment, we lived very graciously in the Continental Palace. On some evenings, we'd dine in the rooftop restaurant of the Caravelle Hotel across the square where we'd watch allied aircraft dropping flares to protect the city from VC/NVA rocket attack and listen to the crump, crump of artillery on the horizon which would go on every night as we went to bed. As the days went by, we sat in amazement as the ship carrying our crate of possessions was commandeered by the South Vietnamese government and diverted to Danang in support of the war effort. Would we ever see our stuff again? Luckily, three weeks later the slow old rusty trader sailed up the Saigon River and after paying the usual outrageous bribes the crate was delivered to us.

In the meantime, we had been lucky enough to rent a three story apartment at 9A Phung Khac Khoan which was at the top of the street behind the US and French embassies and just down the street from the Australian Consulate Annexe. At the bottom of this beautiful high tree-lined quiet and narrow street was the residence of the US Ambassador. But more importantly, it was just a few blocks around the corner from Ted Serong's residence and now the Vietnam Pacific Institute office at 134 Phan Dinh Phung. So for the next two-and-a-half years Ted and I were in easy walking distance of each other and we got together often – on average two or three times a week. As he had said earlier, "I'll look after war, Frank, and you look after the politics, Southeast Asia and regional cooperation." And so we did. We had Thieu's liberal democratic Dan Chu Party now to support and develop throughout South Vietnam, along with the democratic trade union movement led by Tran Quoc Buu. Regionally, we supported liberal and social democratic parties and organisations of various kinds in many countries from Taiwan down to Indonesia over the years and with enormous success. Much of the kudos for this rests with Americans like the CIA's Ray Cline and his mates who played significant roles in transforming Taiwan and South Korea from martial law to the rule of law bringing them economic growth and political liberalisation and thereby inspiring much of Southeast Asia, including Indonesia.

As the South Vietnamese Army smashed the NVA, driving it back over the borders, and people throughout the country rallied to the Saigon government, we settled into Saigon. There was a confident air about the place. In between typing articles for the increasing number of newspapers, magazines and various outlets I was writing for around the world, one of my early jobs was to organise the first official conference or meeting of the Saigon Chapter of the Pacific Institute. This meeting eventually took place on July 14 in Ted Serong's residence. About 25 prominent Vietnamese politicians, academics, and businessmen attended and we elected Ngo Quoc 'Mike' Phong President, Professor Nguyen Van Chau, First Vice President, and Vu Quy Ky General Secretary. Had South Vietnam survived, these people would have had brilliant futures, especially the American-educated Phong who had prime ministerial material written all over him. The same could be said about others at the meeting including Nguyen Ngoc Linh and the cultured French-educated intellectual politician Ha Nhu Chi who had spent years in jail following the overthrow of Diem and who had written for *Pacific Community* in 1969 ("The Situation in Vietnam", *Pacific Community*, Number 3, Summer 1969). What I'd give to have another lunch with those two remarkable people. My notes show that Ted Serong nominated Clyde Bauer as an invitee to the first meeting of the Chapter, but that this was rejected, probably not to overload the meeting with foreigners.

It also seems from the notes I have from the early meetings that our intention was to have not only a PI Chapter in Saigon led by Serong, but to establish PI chapters in cities throughout the country, with the help of Tran Quoc Buu's trade union network which was being funded generously by US sources, and to build a parallel national liberal democratic youth movement to support the Dan Chu and any other liberal or social democratic parties with the aim of creating a civilian-led liberal democratic nation after the war.

Just when all of this seemed possible and promising, the Paris Peace negotiations, which had begun under President Johnson back in May 1968 following the Tet Offensive, began to weigh on the nation. However, before going into that, my diaries show that shortly after the July 14 PI meeting, I was off to Singapore where I met with S.R Nathan, the head of Singapore Foreign Intelligence (SID) in his office in the military barracks on Sherwood Road where we discussed not only Vietnam, but East Timor, regional co-operation and our planned PI annual conference in Singapore the following December which could not be held without the approval of Singapore security (a subject I also discussed with Tay Seow Huah, then the Director of Special Branch known as the Internal Security Department, ISD).

A couple of days later, I was with Indonesia's Lim Bian Kie (Jusuf Wanandi) and General Ali Moetopo for similar discussions in Jakarta and the next day with General Soedjono Hoemardani on the cushions of his black and purple lounge for more philosophical-theological meanderings. Another couple of days later I met with Harry Tjan and dined with P.K. Ojong, the editor of Indonesia's largest selling newspaper the Catholic *Harian Kompas* which continued to translate and publish my articles. The following day I was back in Singapore, this time lunching with S.R. Nathan at the Cockpit Hotel where I was staying, his assistant having met me at the airport (which he was to do often in the future). We ranged at length, and on conditions of strict confidentiality and secrecy, over developments in Vietnam, Indonesia and East Timor and on our long-term thoughts about ASEAN which centred on Indonesia, and the future rise of China.

Back in Saigon we continued supporting the Dan Chu Party and developing the local PI network. However, as mentioned earlier, our efforts were distracted by the pressures surrounding the Paris peace negotiations which had intensified as President Richard Nixon and Henry Kissinger ramped up the pressure on Thieu to sign an agreement he, quite understandably, didn't like. Heavily involved in the negotiations were two of our most prominent associates, Tran Van Lam, the Minister of Foreign Affairs, and the Vice Minister of Foreign Affairs, career diplomat Tran Kim Phuong, who was to become the Ambassador to the United States on July 21, 1972. Both

Lam and Phuong had served as ambassadors to Australia and had been very well known to us for years. Lam became Foreign Minister when Prime Minister General Tran Thien Khiem, an active Nhan-Xa Party member, formed his cabinet in September 1969. A 1973 declassified US State Department Briefing document I downloaded in November 2009 from Google, said, "Lam's performance as Foreign Minister was good. He is regarded personally as an intelligent, polite and cultured gentleman."

Henry Kissinger apparently had a different opinion. The release of more secret Richard Nixon tapes in mid-2009 reveals that at the height of Nixon's efforts to force Thieu to agree to the Paris deal, Kissinger indicated it would be easy to strong-arm Lam into signing the document. Kissinger told Nixon, "the foreign minister is an ass and he won't be able to do anything." While Lam, very reluctantly, did eventually sign the agreement on behalf of the South Vietnamese government in January 1973, he was a couple of months later in Washington with President Thieu where, along with Ambassador Phuong, he helped the visiting Thieu persuade Nixon to promise in writing that the US would come to the defence of South Vietnam and Saigon if it was ever seriously threatened in the future. What Kissinger didn't appreciate was that while Lam wasn't any sort of intellectual, and didn't respond much in conversation, he was nevertheless a quiet, serious Tammany-type political thinker who came to conclusions slowly, sometimes days later, and, surprisingly, usually to the right conclusions, and then saw it through – which explains his amazingly successful career. Nor did Kissinger understand the quiet, darkly handsome Phuong, a cultured intellectual diplomat and a totally different person to Lam. Having been born in Hanoi in 1926, Phuong joined the South Vietnamese foreign service when it was formed in 1954. The above mentioned US State Department Briefing document accurately described him as an "extremely gracious", "rising star" close to President Thieu who "promotes the Vietnamese position with vigor and can be quite aggressive."

So when Nixon said the US wouldn't let South Vietnam down in the future, Thieu, Lam and Phuong together in effect slammed Nixon's fist on the hook by getting him to put it in writing. Unfortunately for them, South Vietnam and the region generally, when the crunch came in early 1975 after years of Watergate, it was not Nixon, a man accustomed to taking very unpopular decisions, who was president to deliver on his promise but Gerald Ford. There was no way that the weak Ford was ever going to defy media and popular opinion and send US air support, let alone ground troops, back into South Vietnam to honour Nixon's solemn promises. Thieu, of course, believed that he and his nation had been profoundly betrayed.

For Eileen and myself, much of the second half of 1972 was taken up with preparing for the PI Annual Conference in Singapore and prior to that a visit to Saigon by Bob Santamaria and a party including his wife, Helen, daughter Anne, and Fr. W.G. Smith SJ. We had tried to get some of the local Saigon PI Chapter leaders, notably Mike Phong and Ha Nhu Chi, to the Singapore conference, but time and the exit visa requirements of an impossibly authoritarian and corrupt bureaucratic state defeated us. However, when Bob and his party arrived on Monday, December 4, we were ready with a well prepared and very interesting schedule which Ted Serong, Clyde Bauer and I had put together over the previous months (see PI Files, Frank Mount Papers). Unfortunately, Bob arrived thoroughly depressed as the Australian federal election on December 2 had just elected the ALP's Gough Whitlam as prime minister. Even though we still had five DLP senators in the parliament, giving us significant leverage over government policy, Bob was to remain subdued for most of the rest of his tour. However, news that I had succeeded in arranging a meeting for him with President Thieu on the following Saturday cheered him up a bit.

In the meantime, there were various lunches and dinners, including a dinner hosted by Keith Hyland (reading my diary I am surprised at how many meals and meetings I had with Keith in the last few months of 1972). Bob was also to visit Tran Van Lam in the Foreign Ministry, Prime Minister Tran Thien Khiem and various parliamentarians and journalists while the whole party including Serong, Eileen, Helen, Anne, Fr. Smith and myself went on an up-country tour to Qui Nhon and Hue aboard a South Vietnamese C130 military aircraft. The highlight of this tour was Hue where we stayed overnight in the Presidential guesthouse following a lavish 12 course Vietnamese banquet which concluded with a magnificent Lotus Duck as we gazed across the moonlit gun metal waters of the River of Perfumes.

Among the hosts around a great oval table were the Local Province Chief, the Mayor of Hue, the magnificent General Ngo Quang Truong who was the Vietnamese Commander of Military Region One, or "Eye Corps" (I Corps) as it was known, and one of his country's greatest soldiers (see Google), and not least of all the US Military Commander of I Corps whose name escapes me at the moment. However, I can see him very clearly for the next morning in a highly fortified bunker complex at US Headquarters across the river he and his staff gave Ted, Bob, Fr. Smith and me an extensive secret briefing on the military situation in the country. We walked out of that two hour briefing confident about the military future of South Vietnam. They confirmed that the NVA had been pulverised by a very impressive South Vietnamese Army performance during the Easter Offensive earlier in the year. The overall military picture was consistent with that given in the excellent paper that had been prepared for the Singapore Conference.

Following a buffet brunch for a selected list of guests at my house in Saigon on the Saturday morning, Bob Santamaria and I went off to the Presidential Palace for the meeting with Thieu. I sat in and simply listened while Bob and Thieu quietly conversed in French (see photo). My French was pretty rusty and from where I sat I could pick up very little. My notes on this are spare. But Patrick Morgan discovered in researching his books on Santamaria that Bob had subsequently written to Thieu, Lam and myself about "The Plan" he had discussed with Thieu. At the time Morgan was writing his book, I could not remember what it was, but now after researching this book I have a much better idea. Simply put, Bob was saying to Thieu that there needed to be a lavishly funded international campaign to win public support for democratic South Vietnam against totalitarian North Vietnam and that the major political target in this effort had to be the US Congress in the same way Taiwan had so successfully targeted the same institution. But these ideas had been put to Thieu over many years by his political and diplomatic advisors and it seems he simply didn't understand the need for this sort of political action, nor perhaps even its nature.

The 1972 Singapore PI Conference

Until now, I've always thought of this conference, held at the Singapura Forum Hotel on Orchard Road, as more or less a non-event. But I was wrong. Reading today through my notes and the papers presented to the conference there are some items that could be of continuous interest to serious historians. One is the paper presented on Vietnam and another is the report from Indonesia presented by Jusuf Wanandi.

While the Vietnam paper was titled "Evaluation of the Political Situation in Viet-Nam (1972)" it in fact covered both the military and political situations (see copy in Frank Mount Papers). This paper was put together by myself combining back-to-back two papers – one a short analysis written by Ted Serong and the other a much more extensive and brilliant report written by Vu Quy Ky, who apart from being the secretary of the Vietnam PI Branch, was a paid part-time assistant of mine with access to a brief of top secret documents provided to him, and me, by the ever helpful and cheery General Dang Van Quang, the Head of South Vietnam Military Intelligence, who had been another supporter, if not member, of the Nhan-Xa

Party. The major conclusions of Ky's paper, which contained no input or editing from me, were:

> 1. The Pacification and Vietnamisation programs were "going in the right direction" despite weakness (all analysed in some depth).
>
> 2. The South Vietnamese Army (ARVN) had achieved victory in 1972 in "adverse conditions".
>
> 3. "In 1972, the ARVN proved that with air and naval support it could successfully repel massive enemy forces armed with modern and heavy weapons. This is another way of saying that the ARVN now is able to take the greater share of the war.
>
> "In the months to come, it will have to prove that it could take the whole burden of the war on its own, provided it is as well equipped as the communists other conditions remaining equal. This is the crucial meaning of Vietnamization."

It is clear from this paper that Ky understood the Vietnamisation and Pacification programs very well. It is also clear from this paper and the Hue briefing mentioned above, that it was very reasonable to conclude at the end of 1972 that the war was won, despite the very unsatisfactory Paris peace negotiations and the continuing anti-war movement in the US and the West. Both Ted and I certainly felt that way. Who could have predicted Watergate and its consequences?

In the Indonesian report to the conference Jusuf Wanandi made some very interesting comments. Firstly, he revealed that the Soeharto government, acting on Moertopo's advice, planned to reduce the size of the Indonesian army from 500,000 to 250,000 over the next five years and to phase out the army's political role (that is, the dwi-fungsi or dual role) over the next ten to twenty years. This did not really surprise me as I had always seen Moertopo not so much as a soldier but a politician in uniform.

Wanandi also made it very clear that despite Konfrontasi in the past, Indonesia's official diplomatic posture of non-alignment and its continuing anti-colonial rhetoric, it privately strongly supported the

Five Power Defence Arrangements (FPDA) which had replaced the Anglo-Malaysian Defence Agreement (AMDA) of 1963. The FPDA had come into force in April 1971 after three years of talks beginning in Kuala Lumpur in June 1968 between Australia, New Zealand, Singapore, Malaysia and the United Kingdom. It was not a formal alliance, but provided for immediate consultations in the event of the threat of an attack on Malaysia or Singapore. It also provided for an Integrated Air Defence System (IADS) covering Singapore and Malaysia and an intelligence sharing arrangement. Members and associates of the Pacific Institute played not insignificant backroom roles in Australia and Southeast Asia during and between the talks from 1968 to 1971 as we and the rest of Southeast were concerned by the British Labour Government's decision in January 1968 to withdraw its military forces from "East of Suez" by 1971. In 1968, there were over 3000 Australian, 2500 British and 1000 New Zealand forces based in Malaysia and Singapore.

In late October 1969, Bob Santamaria and I visited Bangkok, Kuala Lumpur and Singapore on our way home from the PI Conference in Hong Kong and held many discussions with highly placed political, civilian and military security figures on how we would deal with the British withdrawal and update AMDA. Back in Australia, Santamaria pursued the matter with senior Liberal party politicians including the then Foreign Minister and later Prime Minister, William McMahon, with whom he had a working relationship, as well as senior figures in the foreign policy and intelligence establishments, some of whom, like Bob, had holiday houses on the Mornington Peninsula.

There were times when I carried messages and material between Bob and McMahon and some of the others. There was one extraordinary interaction in March 1972 – I cannot recall the exact date, although I've always thought it was a on a weekend. Bob and I were standing and chatting on the front verandah of his home on Burke Road in Kew when a black car pulled up at the gate. Prime

Minister McMahon got out of the driver's seat in a dark suit and a thick black satchel in his hand. He walked up the drive and handed it to Bob saying something close to "When you've read it, Bob, get Frank to return it to me". He turned and hurried off. Bob then shocked me by saying, "He is the greatest prime minister we've ever had". Like so many others, I thought he was one of the worst we'd ever had. Bob was never a good judge of people. I left shortly after.

A few days later in his office, Bob gave me the satchel, suggested I read its contents and return it to McMahon which I did, under instructions, through Sir Wilfred Kent-Hughes. Inside the satchel was a large Commonwealth Government brown envelope and inside of that forty to fifty classified Intelligence documents, some of them stamped Top Secret, covering the Vietnam War and developments in Southeast Asia generally. Some of them were quite familiar.

Nearly forty years later, the FPDA has now evolved into something much greater that the original consultative forum and IADS. One academic described it in 2005 as "Southeast Asia's unknown regional security organisation" while another, Carlyle Thayer, called it "The Quiet Achiever" in contributing to regional security and "an important component among the plethora of regional multilateral security organisations". Thayer wrote: "The FPDA has gradually expanded its focus from the conventional defence of peninsula Malaysia and Singapore air space, through an annual series of Air Defence Exercises (ADEXs), to large-scale combined and joint military exercises designed to meet emerging conventional and non-conventional security threats extending into the South China Sea."

Thayer described many of these joint exercises saying of the augural Ex Bersama Padu in September 2006: "This was undoubtedly the largest and most complex FPDA exercise to date. Twenty-one ships, eighty-five aircraft, one submarine and 3500 personnel including ground support elements, took part ... The aim of the exercise was to meet various threats to maritime security and to enhance coordination in the defence of the sea lines of communication." That is, the SLOCs running through the Malacca Strait, the Indonesian waterways and the South China Sea.

Thayer added: "Australian defence officials argue that the FPDA has become the oldest and 'only multilateral arrangement in the region with an operational dimension in Southeast Asia'," with the possibility of adding "counter-terrorism and peacekeeping components" to its exercise structure. (See Carlyle A. Thayer, "The Five Power Defence Arrangements: The Quiet Achiever", *Security Challenges*, Volume 3, Number 1, February 2007).

A Kissinger Parade and a Dialogue of the Deaf

Well before Bob Santamaria and his party arrived in early December 1972, Henry Kissinger and Alexander Haig had been through Saigon in October to twist President Thieu's arm to sign a Paris agreement that had been conjured up behind his back by Kissinger and North Vietnam's Le Duc Tho. Kissinger arrived on October 19th and left on the 23rd. He stayed in the residence of the US Ambassador, Ellsworth Bunker, which was at the end of my tree-lined narrow street, Phung Khac Khoan. When Kissinger and his entourage travelled between the ambassador's residence and Thieu in the Palace, they passed so close to my front gate that I could have almost touched them. Thieu had them going back and forth like the Boston shuttle as he kept rejecting the terms of the agreement and demanding many changes.

Despite the seriousness of the issues, it was a bit of fun, even if at times it was difficult to get out of my house. On one occasion, Thieu kept Kissinger and Bunker waiting for six hours before telling them he couldn't see them that day and that they should come back the next. Naturally Kissinger got angry. Thieu's major objection was that the agreement allowed North Vietnamese troops to remain in South Vietnam. His major advisor in this was Ambassador Phuong who had flown back from Washington for these meetings. Foreign

Minister Tran Van Lam was also, of course, involved, so we were well informed of what was going on. We also had information from the American side. The Australian Embassy was useless. When Thieu objected to the continued presence of NVA troops, Kissinger argued that he had in effect agreed to this when agreeing to a "ceasefire in place" in May 1971! It got very nasty. The day after Kissinger left, Thieu told the nation he would never accept the agreement and called for direct negotiations between Saigon and Hanoi. But, of course, in the end he had to accept because he could not afford to totally cut off the Americans. So on January 27, 1973, the unsatisfactory, flawed agreement was signed in Paris by Tran Van Lam and Le Duc Tho.

I should say here that before the meeting between Thieu and Bob and myself on December 9, I briefed Bob in detail about Kissinger's visit and the continued US pressure on Thieu to sign the agreement. The pressure Thieu was under may well have explained his lack of response to Bob's suggestions concerning a 'The Plan' to raise US and international awareness of South Vietnam's position. Whatever, the US pressures continued right to the signing of the agreement in late January 1973 and those applying it in Saigon, Paris and Washington included not only Nixon, Kissinger and Haig but also William H. Sullivan, U. Alexis Johnson and Marshall Green.

The pressure was not only continuous, but in many respects disgraceful. For example, even before Kissinger arrived in Saigon in October, Nixon had sent a letter to Thieu reminding him of what had happened to Ngo Dinh Diem in 1963. (See N.T. Hung and Jerrold L. Schecter, *The Palace File*, Harper and Row, New York, 1986, p. 376). In his book, Bui Diem, a former South Vietnamese Ambassador to the US, the publisher-editor of the *Saigon Post* and at the time an emissary from Thieu, says that following a friendly luncheon session in Washington on January 6, 1973, Alexis Johnson had turned the screws on him. Diem and Johnson had been close friends and professional diplomatic collaborators for a decade going back to 1964-65 when Johnson had been the US Deputy Ambassador in Saigon under Maxwell Taylor. Diem said Johnson had been one of the few people to oppose the escalated American military intervention in March 1965 with thousands of US combat troops. Diem saw him as a man of principle, perception and understanding for whom he had a great affection. Yet here he was applying intense pressure on Diem to persuade Thieu to accept Nixon's agreement with a veiled threat that failure to do so could end their friendship. But Diem knew there was no way Thieu in principle could concede anything. It was hard and sad and they just kept talking past each other (see Bui Diem with David Chanoff, *The Jaws of History*, Houghton Mifflin Company, Boston, 1987).

11
Eight Scenarios

The 1973 PI Conference

Apart from Watergate, the rest of 1973 saw no outstanding or significant events as far as Eileen and I were concerned including the December PI Annual Conference in Hong Kong. It can be said that this conference, like those that followed in Singapore, December 1974, Hong Kong, December 1975 and again Hong Kong in December, 1976, produced some extremely interesting papers, but nothing of any great historical interest. However, they were still very useful in bringing our friends and associates together once a year and therefore improving regional co-operation. Eileen and I enjoyed living in Saigon, with its French Indo-Chinese culture and restaurants, and travelling regularly around the region through a variety of Asian cultures as I reported and commented on political and other developments for an increasing number of publications. This continued into 1974. As I talked with many people in high and low places, from presidents to jungle guerrilla leaders, as well as countless diplomats, intelligence officers and well-connected journalists, I came to see that the Soviet Union was cultivating good relations with anti- and non-communist governments across the region, including even South Vietnam, because, it seemed, they never thought the US would let South Vietnam fail.

However, as Watergate revelations, one after another, kept dominating the headlines, radio and TV, we slowly became aware in the later months of 1973 and early 1974, that what was now at stake was not the long term political future and liberal democratic shape of South Vietnam to which I was emotionally and intellectually attached, but its ultimate survival as an independent state. The NVA had been smashed in 1972, but now Watergate, Nixon, Kissinger, the Washington establishment and the Western media generally were giving it back to Hanoi by undermining the South. By March 1974 some parties in Canberra, Melbourne, London and Washington were becoming very concerned. In mid-April, I was asked by Bob Santamaria, Ted Serong and Sir Robert Thompson to write an urgent paper on what I thought the next twelve months held for South Vietnam. I hurriedly put together *Vietnam Prognosis, April 1974 to mid 1975: Eight Scenarios*, dated April 23, 1974 (see Frank Mount Papers). This document was subsequently distributed on a secret/highly confidential basis to senior members of the Pacific Institute as well as the most senior political, military and Intelligence figures in the Western alliance.

Re-reading the document today, it stands up rather well. After an introduction and the laying down of some general assumptions and definitions, including an esoteric but nevertheless valid distinction between a major and a general NVA offensive, I go into some detail through eight possible scenarios. These ranged from "NVA General Offensive in 1974 – South Quickly Defeated" through "NVA Major Offensive in 1974 – Eventual Defeat of the South" and "NVA General or Major offensive 1975 – Quick or eventual defeat of South Vietnam" to "NVA Offensives But GVN (Government of South Vietnam) Will Hold With a Gradual Hanoi Fade-out" and "No NVA Offensive in Next 2-3 Years – South Strengthens" and finally to Scenario VIII, "The Analyst's Scenario". In this scenario I wrote the following:

> My own estimation is that we are likely to see a major or a general NVA offensive in 1974 or 1975 and that the ultimate outcome of that offensive will result in either the fading-out of the North and the consolidation of the South (as described in Scenario V) or

the decline and eventual defeat and dissolution of the South (as described in Scenario II).

The decisive factors as to which way it will go, are likely to be the following:

(a) The extent to which the Russians have supplied the North since the 1972 Invasion.

(b) The degree to which Hanoi believes the Russians will be prepared to supply them after the offensive – this effecting, perhaps, how much Hanoi will throw into the offensive.

(c) The state of NVA morale and the level of its combat skill.

(d) The levels of US economic and military aid up to, during and after the offensive.

Unless Russian military aid to Hanoi since the 1972 Offensive has run at levels much higher than prior to it, the most important of the above factors is probably the last, (d). But point (c) – the general 'shape' of NVA forces on the borders should not be underestimated.

In other words, my estimation has not, basically, altered since March 1973 – with the possible exception that the NVA offensive may come somewhat earlier than anticipated at that time, that is, in 1974 rather than 1975-77.

I think the balance of evidence clearly points to an offensive. The Paris Agreement never meant an end to Hanoi's war effort. It was always clear that having not been able to obtain during the negotiations a settlement of the central issue of the war – namely, who controlled Saigon – in its favour, Hanoi simply used the Agreement to obtain a unilateral US withdrawal from Vietnam. Most captured documents in the South (e.g., those on and related to Resolution 12) make it clear that while political and economic strategems will be used within Vietnam and internationally, victory can only be achieved through war: "The revolution in the South can only be won by means of armed violence in close co-ordination with the political violence of the masses" (Document based on Resolution 12, dated February 5, 1974, and captured in Binh Thuan province late in February or early March, 1974). The current NVA work and build-up on and within the borders of South Vietnam, as well as Hanoi's need to clearly demonstrate to its sceptical military commanders and increasingly war-weary, partly demoralised soldiers, that the Paris Agreement was in fact "a turning point" and "a great victory", are among the reasons an offensive is likely. Fifteen months after the signing of the ceasefire agreement, it must be clear to Hanoi that the GVN (Government of South Vietnam) although facing serious economic problems and perhaps declining US economic aid, is not going to collapse or crumble through its own weaknesses. Its rapid or gradual collapse will not come about without the application of external force. The VC/NLF cannot do the job. As is admitted in internal Communist Party documents, the VC/NLF structure in the South is weak. It alone cannot threaten, or be used as an effective weapon to bring down the GVN.

The only way the GVN and RVN (Republic of Vietnam) can now be defeated – at least within a reasonable time frame (and given the internal problems within the NVA on the borders, time has probably become a factor for Hanoi) – is through a major or general offensive which hopefully will crack ARVN and destroy the GVN or at least take so much territory from the GVN that morale in the South irretrievably collapses. If such an offensive is not undertaken, the old men in the Hanoi Politburo must accept the very real probability that their "revolution" has failed – and that, as I have argued elsewhere – is something they will never accept. Therefore, as long as the present Politburo remains in power, there will in all likelihood be another major or general offensive within the next twelve months. This will be so irrespective of the quantities of Russian supplies Hanoi has been receiving since the 1972 Invasion. The timing and strategy of the offensive are more difficult subjects for analysis. But they are subjects of critical importance as this could be Hanoi's last chance.

The prime objectives or major targets of the offensive are likely to be South Vietnamese cities, towns and urban centres, except in the Highlands where the objective will be to grab real estate.

Earlier this year when a very strongly held general and professional opinion argued that there would definitely be no NVA offensive in 1974 this analyst said an offensive was a 'possibility' ... 'at least until the end of March'. That rough date was based on weather factors. Around the end of March, the author changed his mind believing that the weather might no longer hold the importance it once did in Hanoi's military calculations. If that is so, then a general or major offensive is a possibility anytime in 1974 or 1975. However, if it is not so, and the old weather factors still hold good, then I would suggest that a major offensive is a possibility in 1974 up to approximately early September and that the most likely period for the launching of a general offensive is January-early April 1975.

Hanoi launched a general offensive, involving a full scale invasion of South Vietnam in late January 1975 with Saigon falling on April 25 after the US cut off all aid.

Historians might find it of interest that Scenario VI of the Prognosis, entitled "No NVA Offensive in Next 2-3 Years – South Strengthens" was the scenario espoused "with great confidence" by US diplomat William H. Sullivan (see Reuters dispatch, 28/3/74) when he was Ambassador to the Philippines. The impossibly good looking, Tyrone Power-like and disarming Sullivan, a protégé of Averell Harriman, had been one of the architects of the Paris Agreement and one of those who had outrageously heavied Thieu and his associates into signing it. He, and some others, simply misread the situation completely, arguing that the North was now too weak to fight a war, that the Russians and Chinese had backed off – and that Hanoi had shifted from a "war policy" to an economic reconstruction policy (see *Vietnam Prognosis*). This never really surprised me. I had first met Sullivan in Laos when he was Ambassador there for five years in the late sixties. The then Australian Ambassador, John Ryan, who was in effect a subscriber to *News Weekly*, introduced me to him over lunch and we had many repeats. I was never impressed. The man was too full of himself with, seemingly, little understanding of geo-political realities and little rapport with or understanding of the local Laotians. (He was later to say arrogantly "We ran Laos" when obviously no one had ever really 'run' Laos and its tribes). After the Vietnam War, when Eileen and I moved to Manila in 1975 where Sullivan had been Ambassador since 1973, I met him again a number of times. All I can say is that his understanding of Philippine politics was even less impressive than his understanding of Vietnam and Indo-China.

It should be noted in respect of what is said above in "The Analyst's Scenario" that some of the captured NVA documents referred to were obtained by trained sources of mine who had infiltrated COSVN through a series of cut-outs. After I wrote *The Prognosis* I thought about it for a couple of months and then became so convinced that it was on the ball that I decided to move Eileen and my house out of Saigon back to Melbourne at the end of the year and then set up in Manila, and to combine the move out of Saigon with Santamaria's visit to the country prior to the December PI Conference in Hong Kong.

It was not long after I wrote this paper that Ted Serong returned in June 1974 from his visit to Washington where he met the leaders of the CIA, the Pentagon and numerous Congressmen and presented his thoroughly pessimistic and dramatic 'you will not be sitting here' reports on the Washington paralysis to Bishop Thuan and President Thieu and his generals as I described earlier in Chapter 3.

12
The Fall of Saigon

Bob Santamaria flew into Saigon on November 28, 1974, and had meetings and dinners with the Foreign Minister of the time, Vuong Van Bac, Keith Hyland one of our most generous, faithful and unquestioning business supporters, Bishop Thuan, and a number of other cabinet ministers. But the scheduled meeting with President Thieu, which I had arranged through his assistant Hoang Duc Nha failed to eventuate. Bob wasn't in the brightest of moods because the previous May, the DLP had lost all of its Senate seats in a double dissolution election and hence he had lost his leverage in Australian politics. From that moment he was never the same man again. Always a pessimist, he became increasingly pessimistic with the world at large. What depressed him most, it seemed, about the election was that, against his judgement, the DLP leadership had supported the double dissolution of both houses of the parliament without securing certain conditions from the opposition Liberal Party – or so he claimed (see his letter to me, April 10, 1974, Frank Mount Papers).

In his post-election analysis to his NCC colleagues he said Australia faced "complete economic collapse" (NCC Paper, "Federal Election: Preliminary Analysis and Middle-Term Significance", Late May, 1974). It coincided with what was to my knowledge his first outburst of anti-Americanism when he said on television in late May, "For more than a decade, the Left was held. It broke through politically in Australia only when – and because – the Americans permitted themselves to be defeated in Vietnam" (see TV Script *Point of View*, May 26, 1974). This he said a month after receiving a copy of my *Prognosis* and a year before Saigon actually fell. He was to become increasingly anti-American as the years went by.

We flew out on December 2, 1974, for the PI Conference in Singapore. As I mentioned earlier, this conference didn't produce anything in itself except a couple of interesting papers, but it kept us together and enabled the establishment of some very useful contacts relating, among other things, to saving some of our friends in South Vietnam which all of us knew by then was going down the drain due to Watergate.

Back in Australia Eileen and I prepared to move house to Manila, but as the situation in South Vietnam worsened I was pressured to go back for a number of reasons. One of them was that hundreds of Australian-based Vietnamese were clamouring on Bob Santamaria's door for someone to help their seemingly doomed families in South Vietnam. Many were in tears. When I boarded the plane at Melbourne airport I was carrying countless letters, parcels and tens of thousands of US dollars for Vietnamese families. I had cleared this with Australian authorities, but I still had to pass through two international airports to deliver this illegal cargo to its various recipients in Saigon. I was met at Tan Son Nhat airport by Ted Serong and on the drive into the Continental Palace where I was staying, he gave me the usual run down on the military situation after which I gave him a cheque from Bob Santamaria for ten thousand US dollars which is about two hundred thousand dollars in today's money. This was to help him and some of his friends and associates escape the country. We already knew that he had flown to Hong Kong to charter an aircraft to get people out and this was to further help his cause (for more on this see Anne Blair's books). When he saw the cheque he gave me one of his best smiles of all time. He was an incredibly tough, courageous, resourceful and intelligent Alan Ladd-like soldier who could be very charming when required. But he could also be incredibly arrogant, rude and dismissive towards even his best friends and often publicly. He and I had a gritty love-hate relationship over ten years right to the end of the war while seeing each other almost every other day I lived in Saigon.

In an unpublished espionage novel written in 1981, I wrote a chapter on the Fall of Saigon. This fictionalised account was based very closely on my actual experience. There is nothing in it that didn't actually happen to me – only dates, times and names have been changed. Hardly anything else needs to be said. The following is an edited version of the original text:

> Sad, resigned and resentful but still elegant and stubbornly arrogant was Saigon in the dying days of the Republic. Nearing the culmination of a massive invasion of South Vietnam, sixteen North Vietnamese divisions had moved within striking distance of the city. The South Vietnamese Army had disintegrated; Thieu was on the verge of abdicating and fleeing the country; 'Big' Minh promised peace through a coalition with a non-existent Viet Cong; and the American Congress had finally terminated all economic and military aid to an 'ugly, undemocratic and corrupt regime'.
>
> He stood on the balcony of his tenth floor room in the Astor Hotel on Tu Do Street. It was six-thirty in the morning and he wore only his pyjama shorts. It was hot and humid. The normally air conditioned room was like a sauna, the electricity having been cut off, as it was every evening at nine for twelve hours. For more than a week he had found sleep elusive. Not so much because of the heat or the incessant thump crump of artillery and fighter-bomber strikes that wafted across the skies from Xuan Loc twenty miles away where the South Vietnamese were fighting a hopeless, last ditch battle, but because he has been consumed by an eerie, surrealistic sensation unlike anything he had ever experienced. Saigon, the charmed, bedraggled city he loved was there – he could see it, feel it and smell it – but it was 'falling' and he felt a part of himself was falling with it, slowly, but inexorably into a vast, open translucent and mindless void. Next week, or the week after, or the one following that, South Vietnam, a once prosperous nation with all the potential of another South Korea, and the free-wheeling, carefree society of Saigon with its rich, ambivalent Sino-French-Vietnamese cultures, its intelligent, artful humour and erudite urbane

sophistication would begin to disappear under the boots of a cabal of dour, doctrinaire and unimaginative communist totalitarians. Here today, gone tomorrow. Not the city physically, of course, but its life, its civility, its many independent newspapers and journals, its soul. 'It can't happen here,' he kept telling himself. 'Societies just don't disappear before your eyes.' But it was happening. He struggled to imagine how his Vietnamese friends must feel as they and their families awaited the inevitable and terrifying nightmare that lay ahead. That nightmare, its panic and hysteria would not come for Haig in the same way it would for the Saigonese. He was free to leave the country at any time; they were entrapped. They knew what had already happened in Da Nang and other places to the north. There an awesome line of tanks had rumbled down streets as frenzied mobs had rioted and torn savagely at each other in a grotesque scramble to flee the faceless totalitarian monster they had long feared and fought viciously for a quarter of a century. They knew that when the tumult subsided the nightmare would not pass quickly; that it would go on into a dark, hopeless future, illogically changing forms but relentlessly demanding more and more until it took everything – their possessions, minds, their individuality and their souls, leaving them exhausted with nothing. They knew that families would suicide, that countless thousands would be taken prisoners and more thousands would scurry like rats into the seas and the jungle.

But for now, Saigon was outwardly calm, silently fearful and desperately introspective. He looked down on Tu Do, along its treetops and over the cathedral. The Vietnamese were an early rising people and even at that time of day the traffic of small cars, cyclos, motorcycles and trucks was usually quite heavy. But it was now thinner and less frenetic than usual as if it, too, was waiting and thinking. There were few pedestrians and not a soldier to be seen anywhere.

He had another luncheon appointment that day and he did not look forward to it. Every second day for more than a month, or so it seemed, he had lunched with old and dear Vietnamese friends who had paid for marvellous meals in expensive restaurants or provided cheap fare in modest little houses with one thought in mind: to ask or beg for assistance. They wanted him either to help them leave the country or adopt their children and take them to Australia. Always polite and beautifully dressed, they were quietly plaintive and despondent, but rarely tearful, distraught or insistent. They too, sat in a daze, benumbed by the circumstances in which they found themselves, incredulous that this could be reality. In English or French, his sombre reply to the pleading, empty black eyes that again and again stared at him from shattered minds was the same: "I am sorry, madame."; "I do not have influence with the Australian government, monsieur"; "There's nothing I can do, madame."; "Perhaps the embassy…". He had told the truth, there was nothing he could do, as much as he would have liked to have been able to tuck them all under his arm and carry them off to their imagined paradises across the seas. The embassy he realised was powerless to help these people, and probably would do little for any Vietnamese even though four Royal Australian Air Force Hercules aircraft sat idle at Tan Son Nhat airport. The Australian Labor government clearly wanted no truck with what it considered to be right-wing South Vietnamese refugee 'Balts'. When Saigon fell, most of the Hercules flew out empty, deserting even many of the locals who for years had served faithfully on the embassy staff. Some of those so callously abandoned were later to be imprisoned and persecuted. Others became 'boat people', either making it safely to freedom or drowning at sea. Far more compassionate were Ben Strong and the irrepressible Henry Draw. Haig knew that Draw had sailed his ferro-cement yacht from Hong Kong and, at that moment, was plying the high seas on a dangerous voyage to Singapore with a boatload of his Vietnamese friends. Unfortunately for Haig, he had been more than fully subscribed. Ben Strong had been to Manila in an effort to charter an aircraft to fly out his friends. It had been a brave and admirable endeavour, but because of the chaos of the times and the unreliability of the available private aviation operators, he had so far failed. Yet he was still there, in Saigon, plugging away.

Haig had not, however, been rendered entirely useless. A few weeks earlier he had flown to Australia to collect from hundreds of Vietnamese students letters and money for their stranded families in Saigon and its surrounds. Accompanied by his old friend Tran Ngoc Phung, who was now the Minister for Trade, he had spent a day and more personally delivering the letters and money to their designated recipients, consoling them and assuring them that their boys and girls were in good hands in Australia.

Having done whatever he could to help his friends, he had decided it was time to leave. He could see no point in waiting around for the 'last day', which he was sure was not far away. There were thousands of foreign correspondents in Saigon of all nationalities lounging around the bars, restaurants, massage parlours and brothels waiting for the day many of them had longed for – when they could finally dance on the grave of South Vietnam and tell the world what it felt like. When the end came, Haig knew there would be an ugly, horrendous fight to get out of the place as the American evacuation was put into effect. He had seen what had happened in Da Nang and had been in Phnom Penh shortly before it had fallen a few weeks earlier.

As he leant against the hotel balcony rail, his mind turned to Phung. The previous morning he had dropped by Phung's house to tell him that he was leaving the country the next day. That evening they had dined together for the last time in Guillame Tell, a small French restaurant by the Saigon River. The café's only patrons that night, they had chatted nostalgically across a small, red-clothed, candlelit table about mutual friends and what might have been with South Vietnam, with the Nhan-Xa, and with Kissinger and the Americans, for Phung had been one of Thieu's advisors during the Paris peace talks. The future was never mentioned. At the end of the evening, Phung had insisted that he would accompany Haig to the airport and told him to come by the trade ministry two hours before the departure of his aircraft. Being a cabinet minister, Phung himself could freely leave the country and Haig had implored him to do so. But he was determined to stay until the very end – whatever Thieu did. In any event, he had said softly, the

American embassy had promised they would provide him and his family with safe passage out of the country.

Tired and disconsolate, Haig turned from the balcony, packed his suitcase, picked up his portable typewriter and checked out of the hotel. He paid the bill with a fistful of piastres. The cashier was clearly unimpressed and seemed surprised that he had bothered to pay at all. A bevy of bar girls sat listlessly around the lobby, business obviously being slack, and he wondered what was in store for them. He doubted that they would find the North Vietnamese Army and the Russians quite as generous as the Americans and the foreign press corps. He walked up Tu Do to the ministry on Le Thanh Ton Street, through the doors and up a flight of stairs to the ministerial office as he had done many times. There he was confronted by a scene he was never to forget. Phung, his secretary and two Assistant Ministers, all in dark suits, were frantically pulling files out of a dozen open cabinets and tearing their contents to pieces with razor blades. The ragged mess on the carpeted floor was being stuffed into extra large brown paper bags, presumably for burning, by pretty girls in pastel blue ao dais. The same thing was happening in government offices throughout the city.

Few words were spoken as they slowly drove to the airport past the Goethe Institute where baroque ensembles and choral groups had regularly performed, the Francais Institute which taught French, drama and fine arts, a number of independent TV stations and numerous hospitals, orphanages and schools run by dedicated Christian nuns. "What would happen to them all now?", Haig wondered despondently.

The chubby little Boeing 737 rocketed out of Saigon with a rate of ascent more appropriate to a moon launching. There was an eerie silence in the cabin as the aircraft rushed towards Singapore. The passengers, most of them businessmen, diplomats, foreign government officials and journalists, sat like stunned mullets staring about the aircraft. Haig leaned back against the headrest. Throbbing through the numbness of his mind were the words of an old friend, spoken to him only a few weeks earlier as they had sipped cold champagne from ancient silver chalices on the Palace patio overlooking the Tonle Sap in Phnom Penh: 'My only mistake, Jeffrey, was to trust the Americans.' A few days later, his friend, a highly sophisticated and cultured Khmer patriot, declined a lift to safety on an American helicopter out of Phnom Penh. He elected to remain with his people as the murderous Khmer Rouge stormed into the city. Within hours he was summarily executed by Pol Pot's Marxist 'liberators'. His name was Prince Sirik Matak.

In the novel, the character of Ben Strong is based on Ted Serong while Tran Ngoc Phung is a thinly disguised Ngo Khac Tinh. After the Fall of Saigon on April 30, Tinh was to spend the next thirteen years in gaol, nine of them in solitary confinement, sometimes with his leg chained to a wall. Bishop Thuan, who was made Archbishop of Saigon as the city fell, had an almost identical period in gaol and in solitary confinement and wrote a moving and uplifting book about it called *The Way of Hope*. Ted Serong was evacuated out to a US ship in the South China Sea and moved to Perth, Western Australia, while I was living in Manila by the end of May.

We had two more Pacific Institute Annual Conferences, in December 1975 and December 1976, both in Hong Kong, but they were minor affairs. It is fair to say that after the fall of Saigon, Bob Santamaria lost interest in Southeast Asia and turned away from the great free trade and strategic visions of the Pacific Institute. He became increasingly anti-American, isolationist, protectionist and disconsolate to the point where he eventually said there was no hope for the world or the Catholic Church or anything else and, as far as I could see, he more or less gradually opted out of anything of any substantial political or religious significance. In 1978, he started a fight within his own organisation, the National Civic Council (NCC), which eventually led to a disastrous split from which it never recovered politically (see Part Two, Chapter 13). Bob continued on writing and lecturing until his death in February 1998.

13
Life in Manila

After the fall of Saigon, Eileen and I moved to Manila where we based ourselves for six years while continuing to cover the region.

Manila is an ugly city but the people are a delight. It's a hopelessly disorganised society, but one with the atmosphere of a fiesta and many laughs a day. At least that's how we found it, despite all the political and domestic violence and various guerrilla wars going on across the country. It had its demands and difficulties of course, but they were far outweighed by the pluses. From Manila, we continued to travel throughout Southeast and East Asia reporting for an ever growing number of publications and agencies around the world. Everywhere we went, I endeavoured to quietly and diplomatically advance the Pacific Institute's policies and ideas and to support liberal social democratic forces wherever possible. Eileen travelled with me on most of these trips.

However, it can be said that between 1975 and 1981 when we left Manila, the region generally sat stunned and more or less paralysed following the American debacle in Vietnam. Nothing much happened. The exceptions to this were the continued low key gradual movements for greater 'openness' and democracy in Indonesia, Taiwan and South Korea, the developing anti-Marcos movements in the Philippines led by Jesuits and the Light-a-Fire Movement (see Thompson Mark R., *The Anti-Marcos Struggle*, New Day Publishing, Manila, 1996) and the Indonesian invasion of East Timor which I discuss in Part Two. As with today, there was a general perception that American power, influence and even interest in the region was in decline. Then it was said that Japan could take over. Within a decade, by 1987, this was regarded by many sober commentators and highly paid experts as "inevitable" with some of them predicting that Japan would become the greatest economy and super power in the world surpassing the United States.

On another subject, it was in 1977 that I got my first inkling of the nature of radical Islamist totalitarian thought and action. These insights arose from discussions with two Filipino Muslim academics I got to know, the moderate Dr. Michael Mastura and the less moderate Dr. Alunan Glang. They were concerned at the prospect of anti-Marcos radical Islamic terrorist attacks in Manila against the Catholic Church and other targets. It was a real threat because of what was happening in Mindanao and other parts of the Southern Philippines. They described in detail the totalitarian nature and the capabilities of these terrorist groups and their links to Saudi Arabia and the Yemen. It is interesting that out of these groups grew the Manila-based terrorists, including Khalid Shaikh Mohammad, who planned the attack on the US World Trade Center in 1993, planned to hijack 12 US airliners over the Pacific and crash them into US west coast cities and who helped mastermind 9/11. At the same time as these Muslim Filipinos were talking to me, I knew that Ali Moertopo was attacking Islamist terrorists in Indonesia where he arrested and gaoled Abu Bakar Bashir in 1978 (see Part II). From Manila, I sent confidential reports on these subjects to Bob Santamaria, who forwarded them on to his political and Canberra connections and thanks to Ted Serong, Ray Cline and others from Vietnam days to some senior people in Washington and London. The response from everywhere was "no interest". A senior Canberra diplomat told me that nothing that happened in The Philippines was of any interest to Canberra or anywhere else in the world. Radical Islam, he said, was "not important".

16. With Fr. Joseph Beek and some of his students at a Jakarta training house, April 1977.

17. With Australian economist Ross Garnaut and Jusuf Wanandi, co-founder and member of the Board of Trustees of the Indonesian Centre for Strategic and International Studies (CSIS), Jakarta, 2004. Wanandi was a member of the Pacific Institute in the sixties and seventies.

18. With Harry Tjan Silalahi, co-founder, former director and member of the Board of Trustees of the CSIS Jakarta, 2004. Tjan was a Pacific Institute member in the sixties and seventies.

19. General Benny Moerdani, Indonesian Armed Forces Commander, 1983-1988, Minister of Defence and Security, 1988-1993. Earlier, Indonesia Army Intelligence Chief. Photo circa 1980.

20. Eileen about to board a South Vietnamese helicopter in the Mekong Delta, 1974, smiles at me, the photographer.

21. With future Indonesian president, General (Ret.) Susilo Bambang Yudhoyono, Jakarta, 2004

22. The green and white Police Field Force jeep loaned to me by Ted Serong in 1967-1968.

23. With former Indonesian President and long time friend, Muslim cleric, scholar and leader, Abdurrahman Wahid, Jakarta, 2004.

24. With National President of the Nhan-Xa Party, Dr. Truong Cong Cuu, and members of the Chau Doc Province Central Committee deep in the Mekong Delta on the Cambodia border, 1969.

25. With a painting of Gen. Soedjono Hoemardani in the CSIS building, 2000. Soedjono was a special advisor to President Soeharto on financial matters and Javanese mystic beliefs, and with Moertopo, a co-founding Honorary Chairman of the CSIS.

26. Ngo Khac Tinh, the Nhan-Xa Party National Secretary and later Minister of Education and Acting Foreign Minister photographed by me while on an inspection tour of Nhan-Xa branches, South Vietnam, in 1968. Tinh spent 12 years in solitary confinement after the war.

27. In CSIS office, Jakarta, 2002

14
From Manila to Melbourne

In September 1978, Eileen and I adopted a son, Patrick, in Manila and the next year a daughter, Lucy. With nothing much from a journalistic point of view happening in the region, except the gradual solidification of ASEAN thanks mainly to our Indonesians colleagues, Eileen and I began thinking about returning to Australia to allow our children to grow up with their new relatives. At the same time, Bob Santamaria and some of my business backers were thinking along similar lines. We could have stayed in Asia with a lifestyle and atmosphere we loved, for I still had plenty of outlets and supporters, but in the end we opted to return to Australia.

Back in Melbourne in April 1981, I had no intention of taking up a position with Santamaria's NCC which was then engaged in a nasty internal fight involving friends on both sides over issues I didn't fully understand (see Part II). I also disagreed with their increasingly protectionist, anti-American and anti-Asian positions and their promoting of people like the intolerant John Pasquarelli. My plan was to find a job in the corporate world which was then replete with positions suitable for me and which went under such headings as International Relations Officer and Public Affairs Officer. I was told in the late seventies by a number of senior Melbourne businessmen that I'd have no difficulty finding a slot. However, no sooner had I settled back in Melbourne than the economy went into recession and these sorts of positions were the first to go. However, I kept hunting and in early 1982 sought a position with Control Risks, the international private security advisory company. This was headed in Melbourne by the patrician Alfred Brookes, who had been the founding Director

General of the Australian Secret Intelligence Organisation (ASIS). Brookes invited me to his office where we had a long and seemingly fruitful conversation. Towards the end he asked if he could invite me and Bob Santamaria, whom he had never met, to lunch if I could get Bob to agree. A couple of weeks later on March 10, he hosted the two of us in the decorative upstairs Mural Room of the elegant Florentino restaurant on Bourke Street.

The conversation ranged across a number of international issues, chats about mutual friends and what might be done in the Asian region and the world. Brookes had obviously kept himself well informed on issues, especially Indonesia and fellow local Yarraside political people. Towards the end, he said to Bob, while wagging a finger and a gin and tonic swizzle stick in my direction, "I'm sure Frank will do what you want him to do". Bob replied, "Frank's his own man. No one can tell him what to do. He's afraid of no one." At the time, I thought this was a compliment. After three more lunches with Brookes over the next twelve days, all of them at the Melbourne Club, with more wagging fingers and swizzle sticks, nothing happened. The job prospect evaporated like a poorly concocted zabaglione. Eventually, I began to think that Bob's comment hadn't helped. However, at one of these lunches, and at my prompting, Brookes did make an interesting comment. He said that he had been sacked as Director General of ASIS on the instructions of Allen Dulles the then Director of the CIA on the grounds that he was interfering in Indonesian politics and CIA operations in that country.

An Encounter with ONA

I kept chasing jobs and in July 1982 applied for an advertised position as an Intelligence Analyst with the Office of National Assessments (ONA) in the Prime Minister's Department. Surprisingly, I was granted an interview in late August and they flew me to Canberra. The interviewers were two senior public servants and former academics I held in high regard. Questions ranged over the Southeast Asian region. One of the many questions I was asked was who would be the next ABRI (Armed Forces of Indonesia) commander when the current man, General Mohammad Jusuf, retired in early 1983. I said Benny Moerdani (because Harry Tjan, Jusuf Wanandi and Father Beek had told me so, although I did not tell them that). They said "impossible" – even a man who was concurrently the Head of Indonesian Military Intelligence (AsintelHANKAM), the Head of Kopkamtib (the Operational Command for the Restoration of Security and Order) and the Deputy Head of BAKIN (National Intelligence Coordinating Board), as Moerdani was, could not jump ranks to become ABRI commander, they said. I said I understood that personality, force of personal authority and connections counted for more (because Harry Tjan had told me so.) They shrugged their shoulders and wished me good luck.

Three weeks later, while I was living in Ocean Grove with my toes in the water and my young children running across the sand, I received a call from one of the ONA interviewers to inform me that I had failed in my application. He said that it was clear that I didn't understand Indonesia and other parts of Asia and reminded me of my "silly remarks" about Moerdani. In March 1983, Moerdani became ABRI Commander replacing Jusuf. A couple of years later I was to run into this same esteemed academic bureaucrat who in a plummy Yarraside voice apologised for "our mistake", but did not give me any satisfactory explanation, leaving me to wonder whether my Santamarian background had been a factor. Looking back, it was the best thing that could have happened to me. As with the many the corporate jobs I applied for, I probably avoided a fate worse than death – and worse still, I would have had to move the family to that bureaucratic fantasyland Canberra. While all this was going on I was writing the unpublished novel I mentioned earlier. I had two children to educate and, if nothing else happened, perhaps a novel might help.

As it happened, a sympathetic old diplomat whom I had come to know well in Southeast Asia and who was a regular reader of *News Weekly*, and who had read many of my articles, offered to help me out. He found me an "at least temporary" job doing highly classified research and analysis for the Foreign Affairs and Defence departments in Victoria Barracks in Melbourne. So I had joined a bureaucracy! However, it was an extremely interesting three year period and I learned a great deal I could never have found elsewhere, and that is a vast understatement. I could write a book about it.

Despite enjoying my secret time at the barracks, I was not born to be a desk bound bureaucrat and wanted to get out again into the field in Southeast Asia. To this end, I left the barracks job and set up Austasia Consultants which I advertised as being an organisation of "trade and research consultants to the Asia Pacific region". Having signed up a few corporate, academic think tank, trade union and governmental clients in Australia and Southeast Asia, I eventually flew out of Melbourne for Manila on June 26, 1985. Standing in the rear galley of the Qantas aircraft with the smokers, including myself fully puffing on my curved Petersen pipe, I thought to myself "I'm back". For the next ten years I travelled on and off around the region reporting to my many customers, including some of my old newspaper clients, in Australia and around the world on what was happening in the region economically, commercially, politically, militarily and socially. It went well. In this ten years, only two major public political events occurred: the overthrow of Marcos in 1986, as a result mainly of the activities of my social democratic and Jesuit friends, about which I wrote earlier, and Prime Minister Hawke's launching of APEC in 1989, which I have also already covered in this book.

Between 1994 and 1995 I lost a couple of my major clients for reasons best known to themselves and I decided that I'd had enough. I was travelling away from home a lot and my kids had just about finished their schooling. So Austasia Consultants faded and I decided to set up something else, the Asia Pacific Strategy Council and its email newsletter *Asia Pacific Report* (APR). Before talking about that I should say that about this time I had lunch in Melbourne with two highly placed Australian Foreign affairs and Intelligence officers. Journalists are always running into Intelligence people for, in many ways, they are looking for the same thing. These chaps said to me that the trouble with my articles was that I was still too concerned with Islamic radicalism and one of them said: "Islamic radicalism is not important in Southeast Asia and is totally irrelevant to the future of Australia". What could one say to such supposedly secretly well informed people? A few years later in 2001, a well connected senior Australian international journalist whom I highly respect, repeated this view a couple of months before 9/11, when he told me in the Florentino Cellar Bar in Melbourne that his high level Foreign Affairs and Intelligence contacts in Canberra regarded my writings in APR as "obsessed" with the "non-existent issue" of radical Islam. Well the bomb went off and they like me even less today.

The Asia Pacific Strategy Council was a loose grouping of associates in Australia and Asia and the original idea was to lock into Ray Cline's Washington organisation the United States Global Strategy Council as he had been a Deputy Director of the CIA and a friend since Vietnam days. However, no sooner had we decided to do this than the Global Strategy Council collapsed for whatever reasons. Nevertheless, we continued to use the Asia Pacific Strategy Council moniker to put out *Asia Pacific Report*. This proved a huge success, effectively exploiting the internet technology of the time. The days of the printing press for this sort of thing were now past. At one point we were sending out APR to about a thousand people on our address book and they were sending it on to thousands of others. In 2000, we received an email from a girl in the Australian Department of Defence saying she "loved" *Asia Pacific Report* and that she networked it to "every member" of the Defence Department.

Then there were the academic networks. We got emails from all over the world from academics, journalists and others, most of whom we had never heard of, asking for more information about some of the things we had covered. As I travelled less in Southeast Asia, and my inside knowledge of what was going on there declined, so did the frequency of issues of APR. The last one, Number 72, went out in October 2007. However, we continued to email to our readers carefully selected newspaper and magazine articles of interest which we thought conveyed information or analysis they might not otherwise have seen. Many articles published overseas and in Asia are not seen in Australia and vice versa. Over the years we sent out, under the rubric of "With the Compliments of Frank Mount & the Asia Pacific Strategy Council" about a thousand such emails, most of which were well received by our readers – or at least they said so in many cases.

PART TWO

Addenda, Vignettes and Anecdotes

1
The Burchett Case, Saigon and the CIA

On January 26, 1973, Bob Santamaria sent letters to Ted Serong and me in Saigon where I was then living saying that journalist Wilfred Burchett had taken out a "libel action" against the New South Wales DLP Senator Jack Kane. Kane, who was the Federal Secretary of the DLP, had published an article in the DLP magazine *Focus*, which he edited, written by Peter Samuel which quoted DLP Senator Vince Gair saying in the parliament that Burchett was "a communist KGB agent" and much more. Burchett claimed this was defamatory. Santamaria asked us if there was any chance of persuading a "celebrated VC defector", Bui Cong Tuong, about whom Serong had written to Santamaria "a long time ago" to come to Australia to testify against Burchett on the grounds of his collaborations with the VC. Tuong had defected to the South from the VC in September 1970 when he was member of the Ben Tre Province Party Committee, having been for several years the Chief of Propaganda, Training, Culture and Education for the VC in Ben Tre. Serong passed his copy of the letter to me for "action" saying something like "you know more about VC defectors than me", which was true, for among other things, I had interviewed a number of them in the past. A few weeks later Bob informed us that Burchett was suing Kane for one million Australian dollars. If he won, he would establish a precedent enabling him to sue many others who had similarly described him. He could retire with endless bottles of Scotch. If he lost, he would be totally finished.

We heard nothing much more about the case for over a year. On April 17, 1974, Bob wrote me another letter saying that Kane's lawyer, John Traill of the Sydney firm of solicitors Murphy and Moloney, had left Australia for Washington, London, Paris and Saigon to collect evidence and would be in Saigon sometime in mid-May. Traill duly arrived on May 14. Because of the short notice I had of his arrival and the general uncertainties of his travel schedule, I was not able to make many appointments for him. I met him at the airport and on the way into town the very big, balding, jovial and bespectacled lawyer gave me a long briefing on the case both in the car and later in my office. As my records show, I rang President Thieu's assistant Hoang Duc Nha, who was now the First Deputy Prime Minister and concurrently Minister for Information and Open Arms. He politely put me through to his Deputy Director of Overseas Information who turned out to be Nguyen Ngoc Bich whom I knew very well. He was the brother of businessman Nguyen Ngoc Linh and journalist Nguyen Ngoc Phac (who today lives in Australia). Within a day a heavily sweating but happy Traill and I had conducted, through an exasperated interpreter, a two hour plus interview with a difficult Bui Cong Tuong. Between Bob's letter to me of April 17 and Traill's arrival, I had interviewed a number of other defectors including To Ming Trung on April 30, 1974. Trung had defected to the South Vietnamese government in November 1973 and he claimed to have known Burchett. I sent the transcript of this interview to Bob and gave Traill a copy on his arrival in Saigon. I was never impressed with any of these defectors on the Burchett issue and leave it to others who were there to judge their value in the court case.

As I explained in a letter to Bob of June 3, 1974 (see Santamaria-Mount correspondence, Frank Mount Papers), Bich was chasing up photographs of Burchett taken in Tay Ninh province and anything else in South Vietnamese Intelligence and Military Security files. I also had my own man, the will-of-the-wisp Ky on the job. In the event, we never found any photos, but we discovered records of the existence of films of Burchett with the VC in Cambodia and perhaps South Vietnam and set about locating them. On July 13, Eileen and I flew out to Singapore, Jakarta, Kuala Lumpur, and Bangkok on one of my irregular regular trips. On this tour I met up with George Thomson and S.R. Nathan in Singapore; in Jakarta with Ali Moertopo, Harry Tjan, Jusuf Wanandi, Fr. Beek and the Malaysian Ambassador, the erudite and clear-headed Zainal Sulong whom I had known for many years; and others in Kuala Lumpur and Bangkok. All of them were concerned about Vietnam and secondarily about East Timor because of the civil conflict there and the fact that it was a Portuguese colony ruled, now, by a pro-Soviet soft socialist government in Lisbon.

When we got back to Saigon in late July, Bich and Ky had found the films in South Vietnamese Military Intelligence files, as they put it. We now had to work out how to get permission to take them out of the country and, secondly, a way of getting them out of the country. The key to the first was moon-faced General Dang Van Quang, Thieu's Security Advisor and in effect the Head of South Vietnamese Military Intelligence. I suggested to Ky that he work on Quang, for whom he was doing some research, while I worked on Tran Van Lam and Ngo Khac Tinh. Within a couple of weeks Quang, whom I had met a few times, and General Cao Van Vien, the Chief of Staff of the South Vietnamese Army, reluctantly agreed and soon we had two canisters of film in our possession. To get them out of the country we would clearly need American assistance. I had smuggled many things in and out of a number of countries, but privately hand-carrying two large 12 inch diameter canisters with South Vietnamese military markings through Tan Son Nhat airport past immigration, police and customs officers whose allegiances one could never trust, was just not on. It was also unnecessary. Eileen and I were both accredited journalists with the South Vietnamese government and with the Americans who gave all accredited journalists the honorary rank of major. We were entitled to fly on any US military aircraft at any time anywhere around the world if a seat was available. So, theoretically, we could have flown on a US Hercules to Sydney or Melbourne with the films, but no planes were going there at that time.

There were suggestions that they could put on a special, but visa, immigration and time factors ruled that out. So the CIA, through people like Douglas Pike, Don Rochlen, Clyde Bauer, Ted Serong, Ray Cline and their associates, decided to fly the films out to Bangkok on an Air America Volpar aircraft. Eileen and I could have gone on it too, but that raised complicated visa problems with South Vietnamese and Thai immigration. So while the films went on Air America, Eileen and I flew out to Bangkok on Thai International on August 26, 1974, and booked into the Erawan Hotel not far from the US embassy. At 9am on Wednesday, August 29, I was in the office of the rosy-cheeked, bespectacled and soft-hearted US Ambassador to Thailand, William Kintner, accompanied by a wild friend of his and mine the Errol Flynn-like US Major Larry Tifverman, who was always hidden behind yellow sunglasses, to explain the situation to him. An academic and professor of political science, the timid Kintner wanted to know what was happening on his patch and whether we knew what we were doing. What we were doing in this case was really not very much, but he obviously had no idea of some of the much larger things that were happening on 'his patch'. Anyway, he was very diplomatic and supportive and took us to lunch.

On August 30, I rang Vu Quy Ky and General Quang from CIA headquarters in Bangkok to tell them that the films had arrived safely. This I did through, I think, a satellite phone, supposedly the first of its kind ever. I also directly dialled my parents in Melbourne as if I was in Melbourne. Unheard of! Had I invested in that technology then, Warren Buffet would be working for me today. The next day, Eileen flew out of Bangkok for Sydney with the films tucked under her arms where she said she had no trouble with customs and had a wonderful time with the Traills in Sydney and later her own family in Melbourne. All this time I was still interviewing political, military and other people and writing articles for my stable of newspapers and magazines around the world. After Eileen left, I locked myself in my room overlooking the hotel pool and a bevy of bikini-clad Scandinavian Airlines hostesses and did nothing else but write. I returned to Saigon on September 2 and after meetings with Bishop Thuan, Tran Van Lam and Ted Serong, I found myself on September 7 in General Quang's office on the Saigon River. He asked gruffly, "When do I get my films back?" I said whenever the case was over but that no dates had been set down for it although it was scheduled to be heard in the New South Wales Supreme Court. In the event, I don't think he ever got them back. History simply engulfed us all.

After the films arrived in Australia we got messages from Traill and Santamaria that they wanted the defectors To Minh Trung and Bui Cong Tuong in Australia for the case as well. This was not a surprise for they had always been talking about this and the defectors had always said they were happy to testify. But getting them out of the country was yet another matter. Fortunately, we had been working on it for a long time. It was never easy for any South Vietnamese to get a passport and an exit visa, for that was what was required. After getting a passport, which usually took months, you had to get clearances from about eight taxation departments before you approached immigration and stood in line for 2-3 days in stifling heat (as I did myself a number of times) for a hard to get expensive exit visa. And these people were VC defectors! So how could we to do it? Fortunately, we had started early in the process, although that didn't seem to be helping us much. On October 18 I bought, out of my own pocket, two open return economy class tickets for the two defectors on a UTA flight via Noumea to Sydney through Patrick Harper Smith, an Englishman I knew, who was head of the newly established American Express Travel Agency in Saigon. (The details can be found on an attachment to a letter I wrote to Traill on November 19, 1974, outlining my expenses claims, a copy of which exists in my Burchett Court Case file, Frank Mount Papers). So here we had an unusual Vietnamese war combination: a British national representing an American travel agency putting Vietcong defectors on a French airline paid for by an Australian. It worked beautifully. By going through American Express, which was my choice because I knew them to be a thoroughly professional company, and using one of their credit cards, I put their monthly accounts in Saigon in the black for the first time ever.

Being in Saigon, I had no idea what was happening in Sydney with the case. In fact, it had begun in the Supreme Court of NSW on October 21. Despite constant proddings on my part the Vietnamese authorities had still failed to produce the travel documents for the defectors. According to my diary, that evening I received a telephone call from Bob Santamaria asking what was happening and saying that Denis Warner had been trying to contact his friend Dr. Phan Quang Dan, the Second Deputy Prime Minister, about the matter. I told Bob that Dan was my next door neighbour on Phung Khac Khoan street and that I'd go in and see him. Until this time, I had no idea he had anything to do with Burchett. Dan wasn't home, so I rang Traill in Sydney for an update on the case (Saigon telephones, thanks to the Americans, now worked a lot better than five, or two years earlier). He said they still wanted the defectors. I went back in to Dan's villa and sat in his lounge until he came home. That was 1.30 am the next morning, hours after the curfew and he looked a bit dishevelled. We were both tired, but we discussed the case at length, about which he knew nothing. He said he had not spoken to Warner for over a year. At nine that morning Dan and I met Prime Minister Tran Thien Khiem in his office on Thong Nhat and within thirty minutes passports and exit visas were provided for the two defectors and their interpreter/security guard. I rang Traill to let him know that they would be on the

UTA flight the next morning, which actually had been chosen by the CIA because of its Pacific routing. The CIA was afraid that if they travelled through Asia the KGB might try to kidnap or assassinate them. After they took off, Prime Minister Khiem, Ngo Khac Tinh, who was then Education Minister, and myself met President Thieu at the Palace to brief Thieu on the Burchett case. At that time Thieu and South Vietnam were under tremendous military pressure because of Watergate and all I wanted to do was hand Thieu a Brief on the case which I had thrown together. However, he, Khiem and Tinh sat there talking in Vietnamese for over an hour – I hoped about the war and not Burchett. A week later, on October 31, I was back in Khiem's office explaining to him the outcome of the court case. In a complicated decision, Kane had won. The jury decided that Burchett had been defamed, but that Kane and Samuel has simply reproduced what Gair had said in the Senate under parliamentary privilege so it was nothing more than honest reportage. The judge ordered Burchett to pay Kane's costs. As he couldn't and wouldn't he was exiled from Australia. Since then much more has been written about Burchett, exposing him clearly as a communist, a Soviet and Chinese operative and a treacherous Australian (see, for example, Tibor Meray, *On Burchett*, Callistemon Publications, Melbourne, 2008).

2

The Beek Organisation in Indonesia

When I first met Father Beek in Manila at the Pacific Institute conference in 1967, he was already fifty years of age. A charming and often jovial, balding, thick set man who spoke a halting, lilting English as well as Dutch and Bahasa, he was seen as a man of the people with a powerful intellect and a remarkable organisational ability. He was also all his life a teacher and disciplinarian and highly regarded as such by his students, trained cadres and associates. A very impressive, commanding, larger than life figure, he stood proudly erect and would kick his head back when making a point or cracking a joke and laughing as he often did. While he always appeared confident, he was also a humble ascetic who lived frugally – except for the bottles of Bols Genever and Corona cigars I and others often brought him from overseas. I was in thrall from the first moment I met him climbing out of a putrid green outdoor swimming pool in the grounds of the Ateneo de Manila University.

He was now a famous figure and renowned for his abilities as a trainer and mentor of young Catholic Action socio-political activists. But when he first arrived in Indonesia in 1936 he was just a 19 year old Jesuit novice, although obviously a very mature one. I don't know why he was sent, or requested to be sent to Indonesia at such a young age. In 1942 he was interned by the Japanese during World War II, an experience that would influence his training methods later on. After the war, he returned to Holland, where he studied theology and other subjects and was ordained in December 1948. After he returned to Indonesia in 1952, he began setting up, in cooperation with other Jesuits, groups of Catholics to promote the anti-communist social justice ideas of the social encyclicals *Rerum Novarum* and *Quadragesimo Anno*. The principal organised enemies of such ideas were The Indonesian Communist Party (PKI), the Marxists of the PSI (Indonesian Socialist Party) and the radical Islamists in Muslim organisations like Muhammadiyah and Darul Islam, the latter having fought a rebellion in the 1950s against the predominantly Javanese secular government in Jakarta. Similarly inspired social justice organisations were being set up by Jesuits at much the same time in many countries around the world including Australia, the Philippines, Taiwan, Thailand, South Vietnam, South Korea, Japan and Taiwan. Often they were found under the titles Institute of Social Order (ISO) and Asian Bureau. They in turn supported activist lay organisations like the NCC in Australia, the Catholic Party (Partai Katolik) in Indonesia, and the FFF and FFW in the Philippines.

By 1967 Beek had gone well beyond the usual ISO seminar and weekend courses for students, intellectuals, academics, bureaucrats and others who might be interested. He had established an incredibly impressive cadre network throughout Java, Sumatra and the islands of Nusa Tenggarra. Over time, he explained it all to me and I was on a number of occasions to spend 3-4 days at a time staying with him and his students during their courses held at a Catholic convent in Klender, a suburb on the then sparsely populated outskirts of eastern Jakarta. For some reason he and I had hit it off immediately in Manila, becoming instant friends despite our age difference. Over the years we never lost our mutual rapport and spark, respecting each other's confidences amid endless laughs at the follies of others and the enjoyment of cut and thrust philosophical, theological and political discussions. I would invite him for a meal at my hotel and he loved swimming in the pool. I remember talking with him for hours at Klender and around the pool at the Intercontinental Hotel about all sorts of subjects including one of his favourites, the comparative values of different ontologies of 'being' once he discovered I'd read a bit of philosophy and theology. It was great stuff. As far as I was concerned he walked on water and when it came to what was happening in Indonesia, he was the master and I was the pupil.

Over the years, a few of the Jesuits who had begun the socio-political courses and action with him in the early fifties broke with him claiming he had become "too politically involved", especially with some elements of the military, and that they had differing ideas on what Catholic Action involved. Some of them also said that they disagreed with some of his training methods. Similar divisions occurred in other countries. For Beek, in the early sixties the major, immediate threat to the nation and the Christian communities was the PKI and in early 1965 he predicted to Bob Santamaria that it would launch a coup attempt (see Patrick Morgan, *B.A. Santamaria, Your Most Obedient Servant, Selected Letters: 1938-1996*, p.545). This meant he had to co-operate with the anti-communist military leaders most of whom he despised and very few, if any, of whom he had met. He had, for example, never met Ali Moertopo whom he dealt with through his proteges and associates such as Harry Tjan in the Catholic Party and student leaders like Lim Bian Kie (Jusuf Wanandi).

The Courses

What sort of courses did Beek run and what were his methods? The training courses attracted young Catholic men from all over the country. They came by boat, bus, pony cart, foot and train, some travelling for days to learn from the great man. Apart from religion and spiritual and personal formation he taught them leadership skills, public speaking, organisational and propaganda techniques, history, and what we in Australia once called 'civics', which embraced politics, national constitutions, parliamentary structures, the role of the military, religious organisations, trade unions and other bodies in society. I gave a number of talks, through interpreters, on Australian politics and society and sometimes on what happened in other Southeast Asian countries. The aim of the courses was to develop a disciplined, well educated corp of young men who would build trust and respect among themselves as Indonesians citizens and help in the development of the nation economically, socially and politically. Beek ran half a dozen initial or basic courses a year for 30-40 students at a time and followed those with regular up-dating courses for each initial class honing and occasionally culling his cadres as the years went by. Having started out in the early to mid-1950s he had a formidable regularly up-dated organisation across the country by the end of the decade, each of his cadres reporting to him, at least monthly, on what was happening politically and militarily in their regions. Every six months, they had to come to visit him in Jakarta or he visited them in the field. Most of those who survived his initial course, which was tough and demanding, intellectually and physically, came to have a fierce personal loyalty to him. It has been said by some critics of these courses, including some Jesuits, both privately and in some unpublished papers, that they were, to quote an unpublished one, "conducted with a large measure of brutality". It was said that his students were involved in beating each other, "long daily sessions of mutual criticism" and being woken in the middle of the night. It was true that Beek employed a few techniques that I thought were bit strange and probably unnecessary. But "brutality" is too strong a term. He was certainly a tough disciplinarian and perhaps unwisely so at times. But he had been through the experience of Japanese internment during the war and here he was preparing young Christian men to withstand the sort of brutalities and torture he had suffered, in the event of a communist or radical Muslim takeover.

In September 1970, Lim Bian Kie described Beek's long term strategy as follows: "What we and Beek's Bureau are working for is that in ten to fifteen years we, the civilians, through the Functional Groups, will be able to take over from the Army. In the meantime, we have to support the Army and work for change and restrain the present political parties" (see my report to Santamaria of a conversation with Lim on September 21, 1970, in the Beek File, Frank Mount Papers). The Functional Groups later became the Golkar Party, the successful building of which would never have occurred without the dynamic Lim and Ali Moertopo and their mutual co-operation with Beek's Bureau. Beek described Moertopo's OPSUS as "numerically very small. It depends on our Bureau for information and ideas. The Bureau is better for information than what the government has got because military officers don't tell Jakarta the truth." (See my report to Santamaria of a conversation with J. Beek, September 19, 1970, Beek File, Frank Mount Papers). In the same conversation, I report Beek as saying "the major threat to the country now comes from Muslim extremists who want to set up an Islamic State."

An Original Thinker

In my travels around Indonesia I got many assessments of the effectiveness of Beek and his organisation. Most of them were positive. In Jogjakarta in 1970, Fr. Geldorp SJ, the Editor of the Jesuit journal *Basis*, said Beek "is an original thinker in the political field and an excellent organiser. His boys are very good. Without Beek, Lim Bian Kie, Harry Tjan and others would survive and continue to do good work, but they would lose much of their guidance. Beek is the key man. He has saved this country on more than one occasion" (Report to Santamaria, September 24, 1970, Beek File, Frank Mount Papers). Another Jesuit in Jogjakarta, Fr. Huber SJ, was equally enthusiastic. He said: "Beek's boys are very good. Quite effective. But the boys he has here who were born in Jogja are no good. The best ones come from Flores and Sumatra. They are the key boys here. They did an excellent job in West Irian. Here they are extremely well informed and well trained. Of course, they are not known publicly. It is quite secret. They are saving the situation" (Letter to Santamaria, September 21, 1970, Beek File, Frank Mount Papers).

Huber's reference to West Irian (or Irian Jaya and now Papua) is to the 1969 Act of Free Choice. A hundred of so of Beek's specially trained people were sent into Irian Jaya to encourage the locals to vote in favour of integration with Indonesia. They also reported back to Beek and therefore Ali Moertopo on what the military was doing as Moertopo never trusted what he was told by military officers on the ground far from Jakarta. This project was considered a resounding success in every respect. Beek's protégés were later to play a similar role in East Timor where they eventually formed the backbone of a very successful bureaucracy. They were the reason why schools, bus and other services functioned well. In the eighties there was a bus service every half an hour between Dili and Bacau. Unfortunately, when East Timor voted for immediate independence in 1999, this entire 5000-strong, well, and largely Jesuit-educated bureaucracy, including both Indonesians and native Timorese, fled the country for Indonesia. Another Beek protégé to exert an influence in East Timor was Father Marcus Wanandi SJ, Jusuf Wanandi's youngest brother who moved to Dili in the late eighties and became an advisor to Bishop Carlos Belo. Belo was an outspoken critic of Indonesian rule, but he always opposed immediate independence in favour of a gradual ten year or longer transition, which would avoided the disasters of 1999.

Another measure of Beek's effectiveness came in 1974 following the anti-Soeharto riots in central Jakarta that accompanied the January 15 Malari Affair. In a letter to Bob Santamaria dated July 21, 1974, I wrote the following (edited) based on what I was told by Beek and others: "Joe Beek has been under considerable pressure over the last 3 months, although it now seems to have passed. This pressure came from PSI (Indonesian Socialist Party) and extreme Muslim elements who tried to connect his organisation with the inciting of riots in the January 15 affair. He was investigated by local police authorities with one or two very senior anti-generals (i.e., anti-Beek and anti-Moertopo) pushing it along ... Apparently, he was saved by Ali Moertopo, the deputy Head of BAKIN (the National Intelligence Co-ordinating Board) who bluffed and blustered his way through the National Security Council where Joe's organisation came under considerable discussion. A number of generals, including Amir Machmud, the Minister for Home Affairs and before that the Military Commander of the Jakarta District, were shocked to hear Moertopo say that Joe 'had the most extensive and competent network of cadres in the country', that he and not the dispersed generals really ran the country, that he was 'so powerful that if they moved against him, he could organise a takeover' and so on. However, the crisis has now subsided and Joe says things are okay as far as the generals themselves are concerned ... But given the continuing radical Muslim and PSI pressure, some of them will be looking for anything to tie Joe to foreign or 'dangerous' political forces ... " (see Santamaria-Mount Correspondence, Frank Mount Papers).

In 1983, I wrote a file note on Beek. The following are edited extracts:

> I first met Beek in 1967 when Indonesia was struggling to find an identity amidst the effects of Sukarnoist eglomania, PKI Marxism, Islamic extremism, ethnic diversity, grinding poverty and political anarchy ... When Soeharto's assistants, and especially Ali Moertopo and those around him like Jusuf Wanandi, were restructuring the country politically in the early seventies so as to reduce the influence of religious, ethnic, radical Islamic, extreme ideological and other destabilising influences – sometimes a bit too crudely – Beek proved himself to be the best informed man in the country. I was there for much of that, sometimes travelling with Moertopo ... When Golkar was being developed as the major political weapon in support of Pancasila, social and religious tolerance and ultimately, one hoped, liberal democracy, Beek's

network was able to tell Moertopo which generals, governors, mayors and other people were helping and which were hindering the process. Naturally, I threw in a few ideas of my own along the way. Beek was able to translate this sort of capability into significant indirect influence with the predominantly abangan secular military leadership. When Islamist extremist elements pushed their cause for an Islamic State through parliamentary bills and other more forceful means, Beek's counsel to the generals, relayed indirectly and for years anonymously, often proved decisive … Over the years, the more capable and energetic members of Beek's network gradually moved into political, commercial, academic and government posts and many of them have now risen into positions of great national and international importance and influence. To say more would be to embarrass them … I first participated in Beek's courses in 1968 … He invited me to Klender to stay a week and deliver a few lectures on Australia, the Vietnam War and Philippine politics. From that time I began making some lasting Indonesian friends. Every day we'd rise at 5am and join Beek for Mass where he would give his students a short homily on some virtue related to his larger aims such as honesty, loyalty, discipline, sacrifice, tolerance and respect for others. These themes ran again and again through everything he had to say. And as far as he could, and with a disarming smile, he demanded his cadres practise them. So he insisted they be always on time, personally and with their reports, even if they had to walk 500 kilometres" (see Beek File, Frank Mount Papers).

Before leaving the subject of the Beek/Moertopo influence in the world I should quote from a report of mine to Santamaria on September 25, 1970: "Lim Bian Kie said to me, in a car on the way to a secret political meeting: 'We have considerable influence in Malaysia in the fields of foreign policy and domestic policy. We are not worried about the rise of Ghazali's boys because we can control them. The second man in the Indonesian Embassy in Malaysia is our, OPSUS man. He has great influence. Ghazali (Shafie) is very close to the military. If there was any coup in Malaysia, he would become prime minister. Whether he can ever become PM democratically is open to doubt because he is very unpopular with the Malays because of his arrogance and with the Chinese because of his policies'" (see Report to Santamaria, Beek File, Frank Mount Papers). Through such means the Indonesians around Moertopo and Moerdani exerted great guiding influence throughout Southeast Asia.

The first Western journalist ever to write publicly about Beek was the Australian Brian May who spent four years in Indonesia as the Agence France-Presse (AFP) correspondent. In his 1978 book, *The Indonesian Tragedy* (Routledge and Kegan Paul, London, 1978), which I criticised at the time for its ultra-pessimistic view of Indonesia's future, May described how he saw Beek's relations with the generals. He thought the President's advisors had turned to Catholic Action for fear of the Muslims and had found themselves involved with a Dutch Jesuit who soon started influencing their political ideas. He rightly saw Beek exerting his influence through Chinese Catholics but saw no evidence that he advised them or Golkar on specific policies or strategies. He said Beek warned the Muslims were plotting for an Islamic State and had raised the issue of the prospects for democracy and economic development in countries like Indonesia (in respect of which May argued the prospects were zero). He said the activities of Beek and his associates gave Catholics a much greater influence than their paltry two million numbers indicated. May's tone suggested he was pessimistic about that too.

Two years later another Australian journalist, Hamish McDonald, wrote about Beek in his book *Suharto's Indonesia* (Fontana Books, Melbourne, 1980, pp. 101-102). Very much like May, McDonald got the players right but also like May he failed to fully appreciate the nature and weight of the relationships between them. Moreover, he made a number of glaring factual errors. For example, he wrote that Beek was of Dutch-Indonesian descent which is to completely misunderstand the man and his position. He also consistently spelt the name of Lim Bian Kie, later Jusuf Wanandi, incorrectly in both incarnations. Unfortunately, these sorts of factual errors ran throughout the book. And, strangely, no reference to Brian May and his work is to be found anywhere.

Without an understanding of the influence and the nature of the political activities of Moertopo, Moerdani, Beek and the Beek organisation and its protégés including the Wanandis, Harry Tjan and the CSIS and their associates among moderate Muslims, like Subchan, Johnny Naro and Abdurrahman Wahid and the interactions among them all, it is impossible to understand the last half century of politics in Indonesia, the rise and overthrow of Soeharto and the emergence of a democracy. Yet I have met many senior Australian, Western and Asian diplomats and intelligence officers, academics and journalists who have little or no understanding of any of this. It is like somebody claiming to be an expert on Australian post war politics who has never heard of the 1954-55 ALP split and the influence of Bob Santamaria. Consequently senior Australian and American diplomats and intelligence officers, and therefore their respective governments, completely misunderstood the changing dynamics of Indonesia in the decade before and at the time of Soeharto's overthrow. Former Australian Foreign Minister, Alexander Downer, complained about this after his retirement, seeing it as a major Australian intelligence failure (see the article by John Lyons, *The Australian*, September 9, 2008). Some senior Australian diplomats and intelligence officers thought the future lay with Habibie and the most fundamentalist Muslims, which was never going to be the case. Believe it or not, others even thought that the senile Soeharto was still in control, that his resignation was a feint, that Habibie was his temporary puppet and that he would come back to power in a few months time!

Father Beek died a desperately reluctant death in Jakarta on September 17, 1983, in my opinion as a long term consequence of the underwater swim he took in a stagnant green pool in 1967 at Ateneo de Manila University. The mercurial Ali Moertopo died of a heart attack on May 15, 1984, on a couch in his office at the CSIS. He was at the time living in an apartment on the top floor of the CSIS building on Jalan Tanah Abang in which I was later to stay on numerous occasions myself.

3

Ali Moertopo and Abu Bakar Bashir, 1978

Ali Moertopo spent much of his time throughout the seventies fighting radical Islamists striving to establish an Islamic State in Indonesia through a variety of loose organisations and often through violent means. He said a number of times to me, "If we allow these people to go free, they will be a threat to us all, for they seek to violently overthrow the existing society." At other times he was even blunter saying, "If we don't act, they will destroy us all." Abu Bakar Bashir is the spiritual god father of the al Qa'ida connected Jemaah Islamiyah (JI) which has been responsible for many terrorist acts including the 2002 Bali Bombings which killed 202 people and the 2003 bombing of the Marriott Hotel in Jakarta. In the late seventies Moertopo had arrested numerous Islamist extremists and terrorists including Abu Bakar Bashir in November 1978. While Bashir was charged with promoting a radical Islamic state and organising an Islamist militia, others from a number of radical groupings were charged with bombing Christian churches, Hindu temples, movie theatres and nightclubs. Moertopo had a very clear appreciation of what these people represented. He understood their violent Islamist temper, their political objectives, strategies and tactics, their Wahhabist totalitarian origins and that their local inspiration went back to the Darul Islam movement in the 1950s. He saw them as a serious threat as they had friends and secret members in high places in the military and politics and he said that if they ever got a sniff of power (as they were to do in the nineties), chameleons in the general Muslim community, including military officers and politicians, would swing to them.

There is no doubt that had Moertopo had his way, he would have closed down Bashir's Pondok Ngruki and other radical Islamist boarding schools (pesantren) preventing them from brainwashing a generation. Had he been allowed to arrest all the radicals in the late seventies and early eighties, they could not have gone to Afghanistan and elsewhere to be trained by al Qa'ida. Indeed, he might well have effected this throughout Southeast Asia as he had the informal contacts and influence to do those sorts of things in those days. But as Moertopo realised, not even that would have been enough because, ultimately, theocratic radical Islamism has to be defeated, not legally, but politically and religiously within Islam.

Abu Bakar Bashir was eventually tried and sentenced in 1982, but having spent already four years in gaol, he was released shortly afterwards. In 1985 he was convicted again, this time for involvement in the bombing of temples and churches, but somehow fled to Malaysia where he was based until 1999, visiting among other countries, Australia. In the late eighties, I asked a senior Australian diplomat familiar with these matters why Canberra allowed Bashir to visit Australia under a number of aliases and presumably on suspect documents. He rebuked me saying, "He is a respected Muslim cleric who is being persecuted by Soeharto, Moerdani and people like you and we wish to protect him."

The terrorist and political activities of these radical Islamist groups in Asia and the arrests of many of their leaders in the seventies were extensively written about at the time. Australia, however, showed little interest and consequently slept for 25 years. As I mentioned in Part I (Chapter 12) a very senior Australian Foreign Affairs officer told me in Melbourne in the late nineties that radical Islam was "not important" in Southeast Asia and "totally irrelevant" to the future of

Australia. Indonesia slept in much the same way after Moertopo died in 1984. So much so that when I met Dr. Hadi Soesastro, the brilliant Indonesian economist, canny political observer and then Executive Director of the CSIS in Jakarta on November 12, 2001, and said to him that Indonesia had a serious Muslim terrorist problem, he replied, "No, no, the only terrorists in Indonesia are in the military." I got similar responses everywhere else except from Abdurrahman Wahid whom I suspect had always agreed with Moertopo. I'd love to have been a fly on the wall whenever they met.

In view of the above, briefly described, history of Abu Bakar Bashir and Islamist terrorism in Indonesia I was astonished to read in mid-2003 that the then Director General of the Australian Security Intelligence Organisation (ASIO), Denis Richardson, had said that his organisation did not know until December 2001 that Bashir's JI had "transformed itself" into a terrorist organisation, the tone being that until that time there had never been any Islamic terrorist groups in Indonesia (see transcript of *The World Today*, ABC Radio, 30 June, 2003). What conclusions are we supposed to draw from that other than that Australian Intelligence organisations employ the wrong sort of people? If you want military intelligence, employ military people, if you want economic intelligence, employ economists, if you want business intelligence employ business people, if you want scientific intelligence employ scientists, if you want political intelligence get political animals – and then after that, other objective political animals to process it.

One other thing I did in this regard was to organise and finance, through a number of visionary Melbourne businessmen, a seminar in Jakarta in July 2002 to promote Christian-Islamic understanding in view of the Islamist threat to us all. Working through my Indonesian associates at the CSIS in Jakarta, I was able to bring together a group of young male and female Muslim and Christian Indonesian political activists along with some older Indonesians and a couple of Filipino associates of mine, one of them a prominent trade union leader, Tony Asper of the FFW, and the other representing my old mate Norberto Gonzales who was shortly to become Head of Philippine Intelligence (NICA) and later Secretary of Defence under President Gloria Macapagal-Arroyo. The idea was to build an ASEAN-wide network. I also invited two senior Australian political figures, but in the end they failed to turn up. One of them later rose to be an unreliable, delusional and erratic prime minister (which actually as a result of this experience with him I predicted). I also invited Father Frank Brennan SJ because of my Jesuit associations and because I knew he had a keen interest in Indonesian affairs. He came and that was good. This was all before the first Bali bombings on October 12, 2002. None of the Indonesians took the Islamist terrorist threat seriously. They also all rejected the terms "Islamic fundamentalism" and "Islamic extremism" and so on. Privately, the non-Muslims said there were no Islamic terrorists in Indonesia and again that the only terrorists were in the army. So the conference was a fizzer. As later correspondence showed, most of the Indonesians, especially the Muslims, saw it just as an opportunity to ask me for money to advance their pet projects. Then Bali exploded and they all changed their minds. But it was too late. As Harry Tjan had said, "Frank, you'll be infiltrated and it will ruin your retirement."

4
The 1975 Invasion and 1999 Liberation of East Timor: Some Points

The Invasion

When Indonesian forces invaded East Timor in the early hours of December 7, 1975, General Benny Moerdani, a behind-the-scenes unofficial controller of it all, was back in Jakarta providing security for the visit of President Gerald Ford and Secretary of State, Henry Kissinger. A few hours before the invasion, on the evening of December 6, Moerdani's life-long friend and civilian colleague Harry Tjan, the CSIS Director who, among many other things was Soeharto's major advisor on Portuguese Timor and responsible for all diplomatic and political relations with Australia by-passing the Foreign Affairs Department, was having dinner with Bob Santamaria and myself in a hotel restaurant in Hong Kong – following our annual PI Conference. Many aspects of Tjan's role in all things related to Australia, Indonesia and East Timor can be found in the 900 pages of classified and other documents unwisely released by the Howard government called *Documents on Australian Foreign Policy, Australia and the Indonesian Incorporation of Portuguese Timor, 1974-1976*, (Department of Foreign Affairs and Trade and Melbourne University Press, 2000). But in reality many other 'unofficial' things happened, of which the Australian Ambassador at the time, Richard Woolcott, had absolutely no knowledge. Judging from the *Documents on Australian Foreign Policy* it appears that over many months before the invasion, Tjan played the hapless Woolcott like a trout.

My relations with Tjan on Portuguese Timor went back a long way and I had known him since 1967. For example, in a letter to Bob Santamaria on July 21, 1974, immediately following a visit to Jakarta, I wrote:

> Harry has been asked by Suharto to advise him on what Indonesia's position should be on East Timor; what action, if any, should be taken; and how it should be taken. It is clear, however, that Indonesia's position is already decided – Portuguese Timor should be integrated into Indonesia. This is also the official, private position of the Australian government of which they have informed Jakarta. The question is how to bring this about with the minimum of fuss from the international left and left liberals. Indonesia is planning on a political operation in Timor to develop further indigenous claims for integration into Indonesia. The problem is how to approach and handle the international aspects of this and any controversy that might be whipped up by the left and left-liberals. Harry and I discussed this at some length. However, the only points of relevance for you in this letter are the following:
>
>> a) *News Weekly* and the NCC should as far as possible stay out of any discussion or controversy – simply reporting on any controversy should it occur without entering the argument itself.
>>
>> b) Harry said Whitlam should be asked to encourage one or two prominent pro-Labor academics or journalists to be prepared to enter the debate if the left starts a campaign. Their line of argument would not be to support integration outright, but simply to argue that it is, in a difficult situation, as acceptable as the alternatives – independence or a continuation of a colonial arrangement under the Portuguese. That is, if a campaign is whipped up, these pro-Labor academics should argue that those opposed to Indonesia's integration of Timor

are motivated not by their concern for the welfare of the Timorese, but their opposition to the Indonesian government, that they are not being objective, etc. The Indonesians, that is Harry, will put this proposition to Whitlam's advisors. However, before that position is reached, Harry wants to satisfy himself as to the morality of an Indonesian political operation in East Timor. He asked my opinion on this, but in fact it is your opinion he wants. He no doubt feels – and quite rightly – that your moral authority far exceeds mine which is perfectly non-existent. He therefore would like your advice on this matter and all other aspects of the Timor question. (See Santamaria-Mount Correspondence, Frank Mount Papers).

It can be seen from this that the Indonesians were uneasy about the whole East Timor problem. They didn't want to invade the place; they would have been perfectly happy for the Portuguese to stay there for another 450 years. East Timor was never a part of the Dutch East Indies and this was an important factor in Indonesian thinking at the time, which was something I could never fully grasp despite Benny Moerdani explaining it to me (in his strange logic, Vietnam was entitled to rule Laos and Cambodia because they had been a part of French Indo-China). While they didn't want Portuguese East Timor, political and strategic factors at the time, largely associated with the left wing-Marxist military coup in Portugal and the deteriorating situation in South Vietnam (and they had all read my April 1974 Prognosis), and international pressures forced their hand in 1974. Ali Moertopo, Benny Moerdani and Harry Tjan planned a political operation – as mentioned in my letter to Santamaria above. They believed a military invasion would be a disaster because they all realised that the Indonesian Armed Forces (ABRI) weren't up to that sort of project and long term operation and that there were no prospects of any thorough-going civilian follow up (see APR47). They also understood how ABRI would behave in East Timor given its behaviour throughout the rest of Indonesia, especially after nightfall. I don't want to go into detail here about the invasion and its truly horrendous, disgraceful aftermath in which ABRI behaved appallingly and stupidly among other things imitating disastrous US misnamed 'counter-insurgency' techniques in Vietnam including those involving the use of AV10 Broncos, napalm and other inappropriate weapons including probably agent orange. It is simply mind-boggling resulting in extensive and pointless, indeed counter-productive, loss of life, hunger and long term damage to Timorese society. (For more detailed comment of mine on the invasion of East Timor see APR issues 11, 12, 13, 17, 29, 44, 47, etc). Nor do I want to go into the many Fretilin atrocities which are the reason the East Timorese do not want a detailed examination of the past. But some points should be made here.

First, as I travelled around Asia in mid-1975 I was constantly asked in the strictest confidence by government ministers and senior military and intelligence officers as to when my "Indonesian friends" were going to take action in East Timor against the threat of a pro-communist, pro-Soviet Fretilin takeover. They would quite anxiously and bluntly ask, "Why doesn't Indonesia invade East Timor?" They would explain the cause of their anxiety: South Vietnam, Laos and Cambodia, three dominoes, had just fallen to the communists and the Soviet Union was moving to establish a major naval base at Cam Ranh Bay on the South China Sea. If Fretilin took over East Timor they feared its leaders would invite the Soviets to establish another naval base there. This would have given the Soviets bases on each side of the strategic Sea Lanes of Communication (SLOCS) running through the Indonesian waterways between the Indian and Pacific Oceans, the importance of which I have discussed earlier in this book. The thought of the Soviet Union gaining strategic ascendency over these SLOCS greatly concerned them, as it did many other countries including the US, Australia and a number in Europe. Many of them genuinely feared a Cuba in Southeast Asia. One eminent figure in a nearby Asian nation went so far as to say rashly but unforgettably, "If Indonesia won't invade, someone else will".

My diary shows that between July and December 1975 I visited from my new home in Manila nearly every non-communist country in Southeast Asia as well as Japan, South Korea and Taiwan. Among the people I interviewed during this period were the Philippine Secretary for Foreign Affairs, Minister Carlos P. Romulo, President Marcos' Executive Secretary Alejandro Melchor, a raft of senior advisors in the Japanese, Taiwanese and Malaysian foreign ministries, Tun Mustapha, the Chief Minister of Sabah, and in Singapore, Foreign Minister Sinathamby Rajaratnam, George Thomson, Tay Seow Huah, the Head of Special Branch (ISD) and S.R. Nathan, then Head of Singapore's foreign intelligence service, SID. The point of all this is that if most of these people were telling me that the Indonesians should act urgently in East Timor, how much pressure were they applying to the Indonesian directly? My Indonesian friends say it was very considerable. It should also be said that every country with an interest in the matter, including Portugal, believed that East Timor should be incorporated into Indonesia – that there was simply no other workable alternative because an independent East Timor was, at that time, seen to be an economically unviable proposition. In the end a very reluctant Soeharto gave the invasion the green light.

Secondly, the political operation that Harry Tjan mentioned in July 1974 as "being planned" was, in fact, underway shortly afterwards. Moertopo and Moerdani secretly sent political operators into East Timor to politically and electorally support pro-integrationist forces, protected where necessary by armed guerrillas. This was Operation Komodo which was not officially 'formed' until 1975. As the civil war in East Timor intensified and the Portuguese in effect just sailed out, while falsely discussing a number of possible alternative scenarios, the senior Indonesian military decided in August 1975 to push Komodo aside and prepare for a massive joint military operation or invasion involving all the three services called Operation Seroja. Although Moerdani opposed this strongly, wanting to continue a political operation, he was only the Head of Military Intelligence. However, he set out to control it as far as he could and to a very considerable extent he succeeded. This bore out one of the things Harry Tjan had taught me a decade earlier (as I've mentioned before) that in Indonesia, rank or position wasn't the most important thing. Force of personality or charisma and 'an aura of command' based on ability were much more important. Both Ali and Moerdani had it all in spades. One other thing of interest: when the invasion came, two of the senior generals who had forced it on Ali and Moerdani were overseas. General Soerono, the Deputy ABRI Commander, was on a Hajj prilgrimage to Mecca in Saudi Arabia while Major General Leo Lopulissa, the Kostrad Commander, whose troops comprised a core element of the invasion, was off shopping in Paris.

The 1999 Liberation of East Timor

On a visit to Jakarta in July-August 1997, my best and most reliable contact then over a number of years in the Indonesian military, a retired senior officer still working in a very high position in HANKAM (Department of Defence and Security), told me in strict confidence that General Wiranto, the recently appointed Armed Forces (TNI, formerly ABRI) Commander, and the young generals coming to power including Agum Gumelar and Susilo Bambang Yudhoyono were restless about East Timor and might take action to get out. Back in Australia, I wrote a confidential paper in September 1997 on possible options and sent it to them and others. We later published a version of it in APR6, dated July 19, 1998 (see Frank Mount Papers). On May 14, 1998, I flew into Jakarta from Sydney when Jakarta was aflame a couple of days before Soeharto's removal (more about that in the next chapter). During the riots and mayhem, my HANKAM man found his way into to my hotel to tell me, among many other things that the new, coming TNI leaders mentioned above had bitten the bullet and decided that the TNI had to get out of East Timor. They couldn't see why the TNI should keep taking casualties when the Cold War strategic importance of holding the place had long passed – a point we had made strongly to them in 1997. They could always retake the place if necessary. In order to get the TNI out of East Timor – which they all believed to be an irrelevant Catholic backwater – these secular nationalist military officers would offer the East Timorese a referendum on independence, most of them expecting or hoping that the East Timorese would vote for a long period of autonomy as favoured by Bishop Belo, or even peaceful integration with Indonesia. These generals knew that extricating the TNI from East Timor would be a delicate operation because Indonesian military officers posted there over the years had developed many business and other interests in both East and West Timor. Some of these officers now occupied senior military and political positions in Jakarta and they would fight viciously any withdrawal. Further complicating the picture were the thousands of East Timorese members of the Indonesian army who depended for their livelihoods on the TNI. (It is not often recognised that many of the instances of TNI abuse and atrocity in East Timor involved East Timorese killing and abusing other East Timorese as they had done for hundreds of years under the Portuguese). Then there were the tens of thousands of East Timorese who depended indirectly on the TNI and the local Indonesian bureaucracy for their livelihoods. Tens of thousands of these East Timorese would want to retreat with the TNI (as indeed eventually they did, fleeing into West Timor where thousands of them still languish in camps).

So the new TNI leadership wanted time, years of it in fact, before any vote on independence, so they could explain the new policy to the TNI and the Indonesian-dependent East Timorese and generally prepare for the move. But following Soeharto's removal, B.J. Habibie, the Vice President had become President and he had little knowledge of or interest in East Timor. He was happy to go along with the military withdrawal idea as proposed by the new TNI leadership, including Commander Wiranto, but he publicly announced that while he would consider "special status" for East Timor, it would remain "an integral part of Indonesia" and that there would be "no referendum on independence". That was until the smug Australian Prime Minister John Howard, who many Indonesians viewed as "a little Englishman from a remote English village", as Jusuf Wanandi once described him, very unwisely sent him what he saw as a lecturing letter suggesting possible autonomy and an independence vote in ten years. This was one of the greatest blunders in Australian diplomatic history. Habibie was an exuberant, mercurial, unpredictable 'crazy' aerospace engineer and a political 'idiot-savant', as some of his many critics – and friends – called him. He understood little about politics and international affairs and was never going to survive as president, despite the Australian Department of Foreign Affairs thinking otherwise. In a fit of anger and pique at being lectured to by an Australian 'village' Englishman he saw as interfering in Indonesian affairs, he irrationally declared: we'll give them a vote on independence immediately. The thoroughly predictable disaster accompanied and followed the vote held on August 30, 1999.

When the Australian-led INTERFET (International Force East Timor) operation began on September 20, the Australians were met and welcomed by the TNI, first at Dili airport and later at the dock to where some of the airlifted Australian soldiers were transported in Indonesian Army trucks. As INTERFET proceeded, there were two and later three US naval vessels sitting offshore to protect it and ensure that the Indonesians withdrew as they said they would following a vote for independence if it occurred (which most of the TNI didn't expect). These vessels included the USS *Belleau Wood*, an amphibious assault ship which carried four CH-53E Super Stallion heavy lift (16 tons) helicopters, nineteen smaller helicopters and 1800 marines from the Okinawa-based 31st Marine Expeditionary Unit (MEU) with more firepower, medical, hospital, hotel, catering, laundry and other facilities than the entire Australian military effort. None of the 1800 US marines went ashore, but their presence was made known to the Indonesians and the Australians. The *Belleau Wood* processed about 100 pounds of INTERFET laundry a day while providing daily ice runs, hot meals and showers to a constant stream of visitors from onshore where there had been considerable, and predicted, damage to East Timor's infrastructure facilities. I mention the above because there is a growing myth in some Australian circles that the Australians, through John Howard, initiated the liberation process and that the Australian military did it all on their own without any significant help from anybody else and notably the US. The truth is that even in a relatively minor operation like INTERFET, the Australian military was dependent on the support of the US. That would also be true for any Australian military operation conducted anywhere in the Asia Pacific region. (For detailed analysis and comment on East Timor and INTERFET see the book by Don Greenlees and Robert Garran, *Deliverance: The Inside Story of East Timor's Fight for Freedom*, Allen & Unwin, Sydney, Australia, 2002, and various issues of *Asia Pacific Report* (APR), especially APR No. 18, October 20, 1999).

5
The Overthrow of Suharto, May 21, 1998

In the early afternoon of Thursday, May 14, 1998, which was to become known as 'Black Thursday", I flew into Jakarta on an Ansett flight from Sydney. As the aircraft descended into Soekarno-Hatta International Airport, the city looked like the bombing of Dresden as thousands of office buildings, shopping complexes, cars, trucks and piles of tyres were burning sending dozens of cigar like columns of thick black smoke billowing above the city. I had been reading for days about conflicts across the city between demonstrating anti-Soeharto students and the military and in fact had been in touch from Melbourne for many days with some of the student leaders on their mobile satellite phones. On Tuesday, May 12, 'Black Tuesday', the student protests broke out of the campuses on to the streets and up to six students were shot dead at Trisakti University. I then decided to book a flight to Jakarta as I knew this would be the end of Soeharto and much else. By mid-afternoon the next day, Jakarta had descended into anarchy as the student protests gave way to anti-student, anti-Chinese and anti-Christian violence and destructive rioting across the city, including the killing and raping of women and children. It was obvious that these riots were encouraged and supported, if not organised, by various rogue military elements and their cronies with their own agendas opposed not only to Soeharto, but also to the TNI Commander General Wiranto and other secular nationalist (merah putih) TNI forces. It was strangely both complex and simple.

As I walked through the terminal towards immigration most of the disembarking travellers decided to get back on the plane and go on to Singapore. A few of us however continued on.

I had booked accommodation at the downtown three star Hotel Indonesia. Once through customs, I headed to the Hotel Indonesia airport desk where I was told the roads to the hotel were under attack. This did not surprise me as Trisakti and the Catholic Atma Jaya universities which had been under attack for over week were on the main route into town. Everyone seemed to be on the phone monitoring the situation while passengers stood around dazed. There were no taxis about. Eventually, I asked the head man behind the Hotel Indonesia desk whether he was going home that night. He said yes and said he lived on the other side of the city with which I was very familiar. In fact, I knew Jakarta better than I knew parts of Melbourne. I asked if I could come with him and he nodded his head. Over an hour or so, as he spoke to people on his phone, we sat at a table and plotted a wide course around the city which would enable us to approach the hotel from the other side of the city. Then, accompanied by a colleague of his, we headed off in his modest 'unmarked' medium sized car, leaving behind the hotel marked or advertising Mercedes. I sat alone in the back. We drove out of the airport and on to the major road into the city which we had to travel on before turning off on to our circuitous route. Across this major, multi-laned highway roamed dozens of murderous bare-armed thugs, their faces masked by scarves of various colours. They were brandishing machetes, Indonesian swords and krises, water pipes and other weapons. They were hailing down and smashing into any vehicles that looked like they belonged to the rich, especially Chinese and Western rich or were marked "Hilton" or "Sheraton". As soon as I saw them I crouched on the floor as best I could while our driver made our way through. I could hear him talking to the thugs.

Over two hours later, we pulled up at the entrance of the Hotel

Indonesia on Jalan Thamrin, where I had stayed many times going back to the mid-sixties. As I got out of the car the driver pulled my luggage out of the boot. A group of Europeans were standing by the door. One of them said in a sort of startled voice, "You haven't just come from the airport have you?" I said "Yes, I have". He let out an expletive and said, "We've been trying to get out to that F... place for three days". I shrugged, gave the driver a more than generous bundle of US dollars and wandered off. Not that it was necessarily a bad place to be stuck in. The value of the Indonesian currency, the Rupiah, had temporarily collapsed because of the riots and that night an old friend and I enjoyed a wonderful Teppanaki dinner in the hotel's Japanese restaurant for about ten Australian dollars for what would normally have cost us about $150. This hotel was made famous in the Mel Gibson movie *The Year of Living Dangerously* based on the 1978 novel by Christopher Koch. I was a regular in its then wonderfully exotic, darkened downstairs Ramayana Bar in the mid-late sixties where young Soekarno look-a-likes in black Peci caps behind a sunken bar served iced Bintang and gin tonics. It was a haven for foreign correspondents and both local and foreign intelligence officers and the movie captured its ambience very well. I was sure I saw myself in it sitting at the bar near Gibson and Noel Ferrier who seemed to be doing a Richard Hughes impersonation.

The next morning I rang the CSIS to be told by Harry Tjan's secretary Mrs Menik, one of my favourite people and a Muslim who had made many appointments for me over many years, that Harry, the Wanandis and other Chinese had left the county, a few of them for Boston where some of their children had been or were being educated. I asked if she could make a few appointments for me with a number of CSIS officers including Dr. Joseph Kristiadi, a CSIS director and one of Fr. Beek's protégés and Dr. A.M.W. Pranarka, a very smart and extremely well-informed political analyst, and that I'd be over there later in the morning, the CSIS Building being only a few minutes drive away in Tanah Abang. I then rang a few of my other contacts around town including my ever reliable "retired senior officer still working in a very high position in HANKAM (Department of Defence and Security)" as I put it in the previous chapter. He said he'd come to my hotel over breakfast the next morning and that he had a lot to report, secretly of course. We had been in touch by international telephone before my arrival.

Another person I rang was Firduas Wadjdi, an old solid Muslim friend whom I had first met in Saigon in 1973. In his youth Firdaus, a big man in all ways, had been national president of the major Muslim university student organisation HMI (Himpunan Mahasiswa Islam). When I met him in Saigon he was an Ali Moertopo man working in BAKIN. As Indonesia had no diplomatic relations with South Vietnam, Ali had opened a 'Trade' office in Saigon. This was staffed by Firdaus, who was a civilian, and a BAKIN military man, Colonel Pringowirono. Ali told me that I could keep him and Soeharto informed of developments in Vietnam and elsewhere through this office, which I did – gratis of course. The payoff was that they would help me with Indonesia and sometimes with other places and people. It's a wonderful game if you know how to play it. And it's often a long, slow game of patience, as all good games are. Firdaus asked me what I was doing for the rest of the day in Jakarta. I said I was heading for the CSIS building. He said he'd pick me up there at the front door at midday. I said OK immediately, for in this game, as all good journalists in the field know, you never postpone something you've got for something you might have however attractive. When Firdaus came by in his luxurious Mercedes, a car I couldn't possibly afford in Australia, with the city still burning and riots breaking out across the town, he laughed and said, apropos of Jusuf Wanandi, his brother the top Chinese tycoon Sofyan Wanandi, Harry Tjan, Hadi Soesastro and others: "The Chinese conglomerates fly out and Frank Mount flies in." We laughed and sneaked off to lunch.

My HANKAM man had a lot to say the next morning. As I mentioned in the previous chapter it was he who confirmed to me what he had suggested to me in August 1997 and afterwards, that the coming-to-power young secular nationalist (Merah Putih or Red and White) generals, who knew Soeharto was on the way out, wanted to withdraw the TNI from East Timor because of the constant useless casualties the TNI was taking, and eventually give the East Timorese a referendum on their future. But he had some more immediate things to tell me about what was happening in Jakarta. Briefly, to cut a complex situation short, he made a number of points:

1: Soeharto had returned from a visit to Cairo the previous day, that is, Friday 15th.

2: Wiranto immediately briefed him on the riots and other developments. He explained that General Prabowo Subianto, Soeharto's son-in-law and Commander of Kostrad (Army Strategic Reserve) was the principal force behind many of the riots. Having earlier, in Cairo, threatened to have Wiranto sacked on his return because of the riots, he accepted Wiranto's explanation, realising it was really coming from Moerdani, which included a long background on Prabowo going back to his activities in East Timor at the time of the Santa Cruz massacre. Wiranto also warned about the Muslim threat through Vice President Habibie and Wiranto's predecessor as TNI (Armed Forces) Commander, General Feisal Tanjung, a radical Islamist, who was now Coordinating Minister for Politics and Security (POLKAM) and who during a riot earlier in the year had openly encouraged people to attack the Chinese and destroy their buildings. Soeharto kept nodding through all of this. Wiranto went on to explain softly to Soeharto that should he decide to resign and retire at any time, the TNI could and would promise to protect him and his family's security, although not their economic assets.

3: Soeharto is senile and doesn't fully understand what is happening around him.

4: If Soeharto doesn't resign by Monday or Tuesday enormous 'merah putih' pressures will be brought against him in the streets, in the parliament and in his cabinet where there will be resignations. One way or another, he won't last another week.

Over the weekend of the May 16-17 and the following Monday, the anti-Soeharto protests gradually escalated as thousands of students, social democratic labor activists, NGO organisers, religious leaders and others descended on Jakarta and Parliament House. They were supported, fed and transported by mainly 'merah putih' people both military and civilian. It was an impressive display of what could be delivered when necessary. And they kept me informed, by mobile phone, of everything that was happening and, of course we exchanged tactical ideas. At the same time, House Speaker Harmoko, along with the leaders of four parliamentary factions, joined the bandwagon demanding that Soeharto step down. Soeharto got the message and on Tuesday morning announced a "reform package" involving, among other things, a cabinet reshuffle that removed his daughter Siti Hadiyanti 'Tutut' Rukmana, Bob Hasan, General Raden Hartono and other cronies, and new elections in which he said he would not stand for president. But as the elections were not to be held for eighteen months, it meant he would stay in office at least for that period. This was totally unacceptable to the 'merah putih' people. Things could not be allowed to drag on just to suit the Soeharto family. So even bigger demonstrations were threatened, twelve cabinet ministers immediately resigned, and almost the entire parliament and Golkar executive suddenly deserted the man to whom they all owed their positions and fortunes and before whom, until this moment, they had previously grovelled.

On Thursday 21st, Wiranto and his 'merah putih' associates and aides went to Soeharto and politely told him again that the game was up. Soeharto must surely have known that he had lost control of everything and perhaps, as suggested earlier, could no longer grasp what was happening around him. In any event, he agreed. Wiranto offered him the same 'safe passage' compromise deal to protect the family's security but not their vast economic assets. There'd be no prosecutions – that was the deal. Ultimately, but reluctantly for many good reasons, Soeharto said he would hand over to Habibie. Soeharto further agreed that before handing over to Habibie he would demand that Habibie be obliged to confirm Wiranto as ABRI Commander and Minister of Defence, remove Prabowo from the Kostrad command, re-post him to a non-command position and announce a new cabinet excluding 'Tutut' and her cronies. When my HANKAM man told me sometime very late that afternoon that Soeharto had agreed to all of this, I headed for the airport and took an overnight and almost empty flight out to Sydney.

Why was Soeharto overthrown? What led to it? Some commentators have said he was a victim of the 1997 Asian Financial Crash, but that wasn't so, or at least it wasn't that simple. He was always going to be overthrown, and the financial crash just helped facilitate things. In truth, he was overthrown as a result of a ten year campaign to remove him by much the same 'merah putih' forces that put him into power in the late sixties. In the mid-late sixties these forces were led by ABRI generals Ali Moertopo, Sarwo Edhie, Kemal Idris, Achmad Yani, Soedjono Hoemardani and their civilian supporters and associates like student activists Jusuf and Sofyan Wanandi, Firdaus Wadjdi, Des Alwi, Harry Tjan, Cosmas Batubara, Zulharmans, Soe Hok Djie and many others (I apologise here for leaving out the names of many I should be able to remember). In the eighties and nineties they were led by Ali's protégé General Benny Moerdani, who was ABRI Commander until March 1988 and then Minister of Defence and Security, and his protégés, generals Try Sutrisno, Wiranto, Gumelar, Yudhoyono and their civilian associates including Abdurrahman Wahid, Harry Tjan others associated with the CSIS.

For the sake of brief analysis, we can take the ten year political-electoral project to remove Soeharto from power back to the 1987 elections. I was there for those elections and it was a remarkable experience. For many months beforehand there had been a period of political 'openness' after decades of stricter authoritarianism. This period saw the growth of Abdurrahman Wahid's Forum Demokrasi, the establishment of the liberal magazine *Tempo* and the invigoration of a number of NGOs and political organisations including the opposition Indonesian Democratic Party (PDI). As a part of the strengthening of the PDI, Moerdani, then Armed Forces Commander and Abdurrahman Wahid, the leader of 60 million Indonesian Muslims in Nadlathul Ulama, had persuaded Megawati Soekarnoputri, one of Soekarno's daughters, to take over the leadership of the party. But at the same time, Soeharto's family had grown around him and, with his blessing, they had begun taking more and more of what they could, initially commercially which from the start upset Moerdani. As they became increasingly avaricious, crushing any opposition, the public began to react and started rallying to the PDI cause. During the 'open' 1987 election each party was allowed to hold a large campaign rally in Jakarta and to march through the city in support of the party and its candidates. Soeharto's ruling Golkar party held its rally and some days later was followed by the major opposition Muslim parties led by the PPP (United Development Party). The last rally was that of the PDI. Adopting the colour red, Megawati and other PDI leaders encouraged the people to come out into the street wearing something red and to march through the streets in protest against the excesses of Soeharto and his voraciously greedy family. What happened was something to behold and it shook Soeharto to his bootstraps. Well over a million people surged on to the streets having dipped their T-shirts, scarves, bandanas, flags and banners into buckets of red dye. They peacefully marched for hours through the streets on foot and on the back of trucks and lorries demanding the ouster of the Soeharto family in a tremendous barrage of noise, belting drums and colour. Eventually they were addressed by Megawati and other party leaders at a rowdy pulsating gathering.

These demonstrations signalled the beginning of the end of the Soeharto era, and I said so at the time. Moerdani, Harry Tjan, Wahid and company knew it would take another ten years, that is, two elections, to remove him peacefully and usher in an acceptable transition and they planned accordingly. Soeharto had lost his political legitimacy and his authority with the people and the dominant 'merah putih' faction of the military. While Golkar easily won the 1987 election and Soeharto the subsequent Presidential election, he immediately set about superficial things like changing political campaign rules so as to ban marches and the use of trucks. He then led his family into taking over more of the nation. At first they took over companies, then industries, then whole sectors of the economy, public and private, financing it through foreign borrowing and state concessions. Then they moved to take control, both directly and indirectly through crony patronage, of Golkar, the parliament, the bureaucracy and the nation's military and other institutions. In short, they set out to hijack the nation. Family members and their cronies were given positions in the parliament and the cabinet at the expense of moderate pro-Wahid Muslims, Christians, pro 'merah putih' members and other independently-minded people.

The major public family figure in this was Soeharto's eldest daughter Siti Hardiyanti Rukmana or 'Tutut' whom he eventually started grooming as his successor as part of the establishment of a Soeharto dynasty. He directed it throughout. At the same time, Habibie, his 'adopted son', began cultivating his radical Islamist friends through the establishment of ICMI (Indonesian Association of Muslim Scholars) which he chaired, placing them in positions of influence in and around the government, while a naïve 'Tutut' found new friends among the Islamist or 'green' generals whom she got her father to promote through the military, so that eventually, the radical Muslim General Feisal Tanjung became Armed Forces Commander while many 'chameleon' generals, like Raden Hartono, the Army Chief of Staff and a 'special friend' of 'Tutut', swung his way.

At this stage, the radical Muslims, including Abu Bakar Bashir, although a small minority in Indonesia, were not very far away from seizing power if a few things could break their way. If they and their Saudi Arabian and other Middle Eastern backers had come to power, it would have fundamentally changed the whole strategic situation in Asia. But standing in their way were the 'merah putih' generals and their allies, including the CSIS, Megawati and the PDI, who knew that the general public was aghast at the sight of the Soeharto family brazenly hi-jacking the nation and threatening to bring to power the radical Muslims. By the mid-nineties, the public, including students and intellectuals and the mainstream military were becoming extremely restless and demonstrations against the regime began breaking out in many places while radical Islamist forces were bombing and terrorising Christian churches, Chinese shops and businesses and so-called 'Western' institutions like bars and nightclubs as if illicit sex had been invented by the West.

In June 1996, a rattled Soeharto regime attacked the PDI headquarters which resulted in the deaths and arrests of many student activists and the forcible removal of Megawati as the PDI chairperson. This led to a collapse of the PDI which left the Muslim PPP as the only effective centre of electoral opposition to the government and Soeharto. Muslim PDI members joined the PPP en masse. Emboldened by this, Muslim PPP activists ran wild taunting the PDI, torching Christian and Chinese buildings and attacking the Soeharto family for corruption and nepotism. This polarisation between 'political' Islam on the one hand and a secular, Pantjasilist government and family on the other in a volatile atmosphere, alarmed moderate Muslims, the Chinese, Christian communities, abangans generally and the 'merah putih' secular nationalist generals in particular.

With PPP-inspired riots breaking out in many parts of the country, this intensified and came to a head in May 1997 in the lead up to the May 29 House of Representatives (DPR) elections. Abdurrahman

Wahid, the moderate, liberal, social democratic Muslim leader of Nahdlatul Ulama (NU), who had been a friend and an operational partner of mine since the mid-seventies (see Footnote or Comment below), explained it to me in strict confidence in July 1997. Sitting back in a low arm chair in his NU office, with his blind eyes closed, he said Benny Moerdani, Harry Tjan and he went together to see Soeharto in early May to tell him that "if he didn't act and do certain things the nation would burn." Wahid said that Soeharto reacted "positively". The most immediate thing that had to be done was to spike the PPP's electoral guns. Two things were agreed in this regard. One, an open alliance would be announced between 'Tutut' and Wahid in which Wahid would encourage Muslims to vote for 'Tutut's party Golkar arguing that the PPP combined with ICMI constituted a major threat to the nation. Secondly, Soeharto agreed to take simultaneous action against ICMI in a number of ways. Both of these things happened. But of even greater long term importance, said Wahid, was that Soeharto agreed that after the elections, which Golkar won overwhelmingly, he would replace Feisal Tanjung as Armed Forces Commander with Moerdani's man General Wiranto who then held the post of Kostrad Commander.

So it was that in June 1997 Wiranto first of all replaced General Raden Hartono as Army Commander in front of the Kopassus Commander Prabowo among a raft of military promotions favouring the 'merah putih' faction. Then in February 1998 Wiranto replaced Feisal Tanjung as Armed Forces Commander completing this part of the May 1997 deal. Rising through the ranks with Wiranto were generals Yudhoyono, Gumelar, Hendropriyono and others – the men who had already decided to withdraw the military from East Timor. There was, according to Wahid, a fourth part of the May deal – that in early 1998 Soeharto would choose someone acceptable to the 'merah putih' forces as his vice-presidential partner in the early March presidential/ vice-presidential elections and therefore the likely successor to himself.

This meant, specifically, someone other than Habibie or Feisal, either of whom could undo everything. As we know, he appointed Habibie either in a calculated act of betrayal or more likely as a result of advancing senility, for he was obviously unhappy two months later to have Habibie succeed him. Whatever, it angered the 'merah putih' boys which made it easier for Wiranto to negotiate Soeharto's resignation when he returned from his ill-judged trip to Cairo.

The rest is history, as they say. Readers of *Asia Pacific Report* at the time will know that we said that Habibie could not possibly last as president because of his personality and association with radical Islamists and that he should be replaced by a current or former military man, perhaps either Wiranto, Gumelar or Yudyohono who was then the Armed Forces Chief for Social and Political Affairs (SOSPOL). We didn't rate Megawati's prospects highly at the time of Soeharto's overthrow because she didn't seem presidential enough and had been little more than a Moerdani puppet. We changed our minds in 1999 as her new party the PDI-P (Indonesian Democratic Party- Struggle) grew in strength. Nor did we think Wahid could be president because of his eyesight. We thought he could be a good and very useful vice-president in the fight against radical Islam. It is hard to run for president, let alone be one if you can't read or write! Yet it happened – both Megawati and Wahid were elected president. But Wahid couldn't last and he didn't. He did some very good things and some silly things and in the process was treated abominably by some people who should have known better. By any measure he was truly a great Indonesian and one of the more remarkable people I have met. For sound political reasons we never thought Prabowo, at least not then, or Amien Rais who was finished, were presidential possibles. (For more detailed comment on this period in Indonesian history see various issues of *Asia Pacific Report,* especially APR 5, June 19, 1998, titled, "Special Report: Indonesia After Soeharto", but also APR 2, March 3, 1998; APR 3, April 6, 1998; APR 8, October 31, 1998; APR

9, December 1, 1998, titled, "Guns, Blood and Tears on the Road to Democracy"; APR 14, May 27, 1999; APR 15, June 30, 1999; APR 16, August 7, 1999; and APR 19, November 28, 1999).

In regard to the "Footnote or Comment below" (mentioned two pages ago), this is it: I first encountered Abdurrahman Wahid in 1973 or 1974 shortly after he returned to Indonesia following years of leisurely study abroad. A Filipino social democratic associate of mine based in Bangkok was running an anti-Soviet operation within a left wing, Marxist Christian NGO in Bangkok called ACFOD (Asian Conference for Development) which he had actually set up and which was being generously funded by the United Nations Food and Agricultural Organisation (FAO) and heavily influenced by the Soviets. ACFOD's major area of activity and influence was Muslim Southern Thailand and Malaysia where the Soviet had succeeded in penetrating the Malay elite, especially around the Malaysian Prime Minister and Foreign Minister. My Filipino friend said he needed an Indonesian Muslim who could pretend to be a Marxist to help him with his Bangkok operations. I suggested he contact our CSIS friends in Jakarta who sent him the relatively young anti-communist Wahid to play the role – to very good effect. So good in fact, that years later I read somewhere that the CIA regarded Wahid as a dangerous, committed communist, never to be trusted.

Kate Webb

While in Jakarta for the fall of Soeharto, the wonderful and indomitable Kate Webb reappeared in my life. I hadn't seen her for more than twenty-five years and I had had little to do with her for nearly twenty-five years. Since I last saw her briefly in Manila in 1975 where she covered the IMF Conference, she had worked in a number of places including Hong Kong, Jakarta, Baghdad, New Delhi, Pyongyang and Kabul where she experienced a couple of reputedly hair-raising, life-threatening adventures involving Afghan warlords and assassins, about which she refused to speak, at least to me. One of the more intriguing of these stories had her kidnapped by an Afghan warlord and taken to a hotel where she was "brutally beaten and dragged up a flight of stairs by her hair", according to *The Los Angeles Times*, May 15, 2007. She then finally escaped with the help of two fellow journalists and hid out on a window ledge in the freezing Afghan winter, while the warlord and his men searched the building for her, according to another newspaper (*The Independent*, May 15, 2007).

She was now back in Jakarta working for Agence France-Presse (AFP) and I ran into her at a press conference. Thereafter, we got together for drinks and a meal whenever I was in Jakarta, usually at the Zigolini restaurant bar in the Mandarin Hotel and often accompanied by another Jakarta-based Australian journalist, the bubbly, energetic Maggie Ford. The years had not treated Kate well. She was a chain smoker and a heavy beer drinker and she told me that while she felt well she wasn't really – without saying what the problem was and I sort of dismissed it. She hadn't lost that air of vulnerability and there was still some sort of mutually attractive rapport or spark between us, but that's all it was and we enjoyed that. There was plenty of laughter and wit and I particularly liked the cut and thrust of our beery conversations which were usually about anything except Asian politics and often about literature and other journalists and people. Despite our many long conversations in Jakarta over two to three years we never swapped adventure stories about ourselves, despite there being plenty to talk about. In 2001 Kate retired and eventually settled near Newcastle in New South Wales. We kept in touch and she was a regular reader of *Asia Pacific Report*. She died in May 2007 of bowel cancer aged 64. Whether this had anything to do with the health problems she mentioned in 1998, I have no idea.

6
With Ali Moertopo in Bandung

In early May 1969, I was invited to join Ali Moertopo, then Deputy Head of BAKIN, but in fact its boss, and the head of the army's Special Operations unit (OPSUS) on a two day journey to Bandung in the cool hills south of Jakarta. The Bandung Institute of Technology (BIT) was then a hotbed of student discontent with many students claiming to be Marxists, Maoists and Che Guevaraists of varying hues and they universally hated Soeharto. Every now and then this broke out into violence on and off the campus. Bravely, Ali had decided to go out and talk with them which was something Soeharto could never possibly do because among other things, he lacked the language skills, the intellectual capability and the ability to communicate with university students of any kind. This turned out to be one of the more fascinating political weekends of my life. We travelled by train and with Moertopo there was an entourage of military officers of various rank. I wasn't there to talk with or interview Moertopo, especially in front of others, but to observe and this is what I did.

The next day Moertopo delivered a speech to two-three thousand students and political activists from many miles around in a very large theatre in Bandung. I sat up the back. He spoke for three hours without a note and you could hear a pin drop except when he broke out of Bahasa into English to say something like "And I told Kissinger this and that, and he had to agree with me!" when the whole place broke into laughter and cheering. That night, Moertopo sat for hours in the hotel foyer fielding questions from the leaders of the student radicals. It was here that I first realised that he was not so much a military man as a very intelligent politician with a common touch who happened to be in uniform. I have wondered ever since how different Indonesian history might have been had Moertopo, the politician, become president in 1965-67 rather than the man he and his colleagues put into power, Soeharto the businessman and autocrat. We flew back to Jakarta on an Indonesian military Hercules. Moertopo and I sat together during the rollicking flight discussing regional co-operation and I think we made some very useful points together especially concerning the newly established ASEAN and the emerging China.

The Nature of the Military

One of the things Moertopo and his associates taught me early on in the sixties was the nature of the Indonesian military. They started out by saying that the Indonesian military is decentralised and fragmented. This they said was a consequence of the military being forced to finance itself because the central government in Jakarta could not afford to do so because it could not raise the taxes required because of an institutional inability to collect them (a common problem throughout Southeast Asia). Hence divisional commanders and their equivalents were forced to go into business to finance their forces. This also happened in other parts of Asia. But what seems to have distinguished Indonesia is that the commanding general was not only responsible for financing his troops but also their families and maybe their extended families. He had to provide for their employment and cover the costs of their educational, health and other requirements. In other words, thousands of families depended on the divisional commander for their livelihoods.

Most divisional commanders sought out smart well connected local Chinese entrepreneurs to assist them and they set up businesses together (these Chinese partners were called Cukongs). To help them, these generals then charged their colonels and other lower officers with doing the same thing to help lighten the burden. In this way large and small empires were built, depending on the relative abilities and connections of the generals and officers, way beyond the control or influence of Jakarta especially in the days when communication with Jakarta was poor or non-existent. Army generals usually went into local agricultural, mining, timber and other businesses. Their Naval and Air Force equivalents went into what they were best at, namely smuggling, both inter-island and internationally, sometimes on a surprising scale with their military associates in neighbouring Asian countries and states. Some of this still continues today.

In this situation, when General Soeharto rose though the ranks to become the Commander of the Diponegoro Division he was already an accomplished businessman with an impressive network run in conjunction with his Chinese partners Lim Sioe Liong and others who later were to help him build his Presidential empire. Assisting Soeharto from his Diponegoro days, and perhaps before, was another very smart businessman general, Soedjono Hoemardani, who was also his Javanese mystical and spiritual advisor, but a very different man. And Soeharto's major operational and political advisor in the Diponegoro was, of course, another very different man, Moertopo.

So the Indonesian military is a disparate and fragmented organisation. It is nothing like how it has been presented in some Australian and other academic studies where one finds, among other things, neat linear diagrams showing chains of command which have little to do with reality. This fragmentation, where the Indonesian military in effect has been made up of a number of loosely connected armies within which officers often did not know what their own soldiers were doing, has aided, to an extent more so than in other developing countries, the phenomenon of what has been called "rogue military elements". Some of these "rogue elements" have been led by generals, including some based in Jakarta. Benny Moerdani used to say that even when he was Armed Forces Commander there were military operations going on in various parts of the country of which he knew little or nothing. He strongly suspected President Soeharto of running some of these operations, for good or ill, using rogue officers especially in the Jakarta area. General Wiranto ran into the same problem in both East Timor and Jakarta. He knew who was running the militias in East Timor and that the Jakarta-based radical Islamist general, Feisal Tanjung, was responsible for the planning and implementation of the scorched earth military retreat from East Timor. But he was powerless to stop any of it – as would have been any other Armed Forces commander. Fortunately, with the growth of liberal democracy and reforms within the military, things have improved in recent years with increasing institutional accountability.

7
On the Cushions with Soedjono Hoemardani

Major General Soedjono Hoemardani, having been born in Jolo, central Java, in 1919, rose through the ranks of the Diponegoro Division and later Kostrad with Soeharto who was also born in the same region of Central Java in 1921. Soedjono became the division's finance and business officer which led him into doing a US Army Advanced Finance Course at Fort Benjamin Harrison in Indiana in 1963. But he was much more than that being a lifelong animist and Javanese mystic which saw him adopt a prominent role in the Elders of the Universe Parapsychology Foundation. Soeharto was a fellow mystic and animist and Soedjono became his personal spiritual consultant or 'guru' – although I have been told quite strongly by his friends that 'guru' is not the right word. Both Soedjono and Soeharto officially listed their religions as Islam, but that was mainly because of ID card requirements and political expediency.

When I first met Soedjono through an appointment arranged by Harry Tjan, he was a Personal Assistant to the President for the Economy and Trade and also Inspector General for Development Projects. Being Inspector General as Indonesia very slowly opened up to the world following the fall of Soekarno and its aftermath, he was, among other things, in charge of granting franchises and licences to local Indonesians to operate branches of incoming foreign companies in the automobile, petroleum distribution, pharmaceutical and other fields. This put him in a powerful position to help his friends and supporters of the regime. So it was Toyota for you, Mitsubishi for me, Shell petrol stations for someone else and so on. In 1971 he was to become one of the founding Co-Chairmen of the CSIS along with Moertopo who was still Personal Assistant to the President for Political Affairs, Deputy Head of BAKIN and Head of OPSUS. If Ali was a politician in uniform, Soedjono was a businessman financier, if not always in uniform, at least in disguise.

Appropriately enough Soedjono lived on Jalan Diponegoro in central Jakarta. In the late sixties, I'd arrive at his residence in a stifling hot un-airconditioned taxi as they all were in those days and have it wait for me outside his gate. Inside I would be greeted by his receptionist and assistant, Lim Bian Koen (Sofyan Wanandi), who sat at a small desk in a carport outside the side door of the residence with his trusty little scooter bike parked behind him. He'd show me into a lounge and close the door behind me. The lounge, which I visited often, was a dark, scented room strewn with black and purple cushions over purple carpet and dark armchairs and long ceiling to floor curtains to match. It would take a while for my eyes to adjust. As they did Soedjono would appear in a long flowing black gown and gesture for me to sit either in an armchair or on the purple cushions on the floor. A thin, elegant man of easy charm with black curly locks (see photo), he would immediately produce packets of gold-tipped Russian Black Imperial Eagle Sobranie cigarettes. At that time I was a constant Petersen pipe smoker, addicted to Irish tobacco, and I knew he smoked a pipe as well. But I never saw him with one in these meetings. It was Black Sobranie chain smoking all the way. Some of our meetings, often lying on the cushions, would last for three or four hours. His English, spoken in a quiet voice, was quite good and over the years we covered a lot of subjects. I knew he had Soeharto's ear and I played it on that basis. He also had excellent contacts in Japan whose investment capital Indonesia badly needed. He was Indonesia's Mr. Japan. This was extremely useful when it came to discussing regional co-operation and our ideas of an Asia Pacific Community. We also talked about the internal politics of nations in the region. We both understood that there was really no such place as 'Asia'; that all the countries in the region differed significantly. We knew, for example, that the Philippines, then the most successful economically, was more Latin American than Asian and that it had almost nothing in common with, say, Laos or Thailand.

But what I learned, I think first from him and later others, was that despite these differences in every country of Southeast and East Asia power ultimately rested directly or indirectly with the military, that is the people with the guns. This was true even of Singapore and Malaysia, countries with overtly civilian governments, developed political parties, elected governments and effective civilian bureaucracies. In Malaysia, the military is 95% Malay. There is no way the Malays will allow any Chinese to hold guns, even today. But it is not only guns that have given the military political clout. Historically they have been among the most cohesive forces in these societies, along with some religions. The reason for that is that they trained and went to the same military academies together enabling them to build some measures of trust and understanding among themselves lacking in other areas of society even if some of them ended up in different factions of their respective military organisations. In a basic analysis, we can extend this to the Southeast Asian/East Asian region generally for military officers from various countries throughout this region often were educated together in Western military academies in the US, Europe and Australia and consequently regional networks developed among them. In their respective days, Moertopo and Moerdani were seen to be the military kings of Southeast Asia to whom generals throughout the region deferred and consulted in times of national or military crisis or personal need. This was because Indonesia was seen to be the predominant nation in the region and Moertopo and Moerdani strong personalities with an ability to deliver across the region.

Soedjono and I covered many other subjects, including Australian politics and politicians, the role of trade unions, the origin and nature of Australian political parties, the strategic significance of the Australian-American alliance and, at his initiative, the Australian education system. I hope he took all of this into account when he visited Australia in 1973 and met Prime Minister Gough Whitlam in Canberra. We also discussed religion and philosophy. I don't know what he thought about my comments, but I know his explanations of his and Soeharto's Javanese *Kebatinan* mystical beliefs were beyond my comprehension. Because of what was often called in diplomatic circles his *Kebatinan* dress, black Sobranie cigarettes and his role as Soeharto's mystical advisor, he was labelled 'Rasputin' by many locally based Western diplomats and journalists. But this was to thoroughly misunderstand him. He was a very decent man totally loyal to Soeharto until his death in Tokyo in 1986.

This makes Soeharto's dismissive treatment of him in his 1988 autobiography (*Soeharto: My thoughts, Words and Deeds, An Autobiography*, Pt. Citra Lamroro Gung Persada, 1991) quite appalling. The same book fails adequately to credit the men who put him into power or even to mention Ali Moertopo at all who admittedly, unlike Soedjono, was a political player and at one point a competitor for the presidency. Perhaps that is even more reprehensible. This book was heavily influenced by Soeharto's daughter 'Tutut' and her radical Muslim friends who ultimately sought to destroy the CSIS and its wide band of associates including liberal Christian, abangan and moderate Muslim leaders such as Abdurrahman Wahid. This book, originally published in Indonesian in 1988, soon after the 1987 elections, was a turning point in the history of the Soeharto regime, and incensed CSIS people clearly saw it to be that at the time. The ten year-two elections strategy, led reluctantly and sadly by Moerdani, to remove the rapacious Soeharto and his family was already under way.

8
Soeharto Visits Australia (1972).
A Brief for Soeharto

On February 7, 1972, Indonesian President Soeharto arrived in Australia for a four-day state visit. He visited Canberra, Melbourne and Sydney and met Prime Minister William McMahon. He arrived in my home town Melbourne on February 8 where he met various dignitories at Government House. He was accompanied on this visit by Adam Malik, the Indonesian Minister of Foreign Affairs, Professor Widjojo Nitisastro, the Minister for National Development, and Major General Umar Wirahadikusumah, the Army Chief of Staff. That was the official party. But also accompanying Soeharto was Major General Ali Moertopo and his assistant Jusuf Wanandi. Moertopo sat lower in the bureaucratic ranks than the others who accompanied Soeharto, but he was far more important and influential than any of them as he was still a Special Assistant to the President for Political Affairs.

Wanandi arrived in Australia on January 14 well in advance of the visit. He and Ali had prepared for the visit long beforehand having asked me in December 1971 to prepare a "Brief for Soeharto" on Australian political developments and the economic situation including key personal profiles and any other material I thought appropriate. In the end I produced, gratis, a sixty-one page, single-spaced document (copy available in the Frank Mount Papers). It included a "highly confidential" paper on the "current political situation" which had been written by Bob Santamaria as a briefing paper to the leaders of his National Civic Council, an excellent contribution on the Australian economy written, I think, by economist Margaret Broadbent, and a long background comment on all current Australian political parties and selected politicians written, diplomatically, by me. I have no idea what use, if any, the Indonesians made of this paper. I also wrote three brief speeches for Soeharto one for each capital city he was visiting so that he might comment on some distinctive historical or architectural feature of them. All of this was done simply in the interests of better Australian-Indonesian relations.

Apart from the brief, Ali and his staff asked if I could organise welcoming demonstrations in each capital city. While that could have been done easily, I said that wasn't my business. However, I said that if the Left and the pro-Communist unions came out demonstrating against Soeharto, I was sure there would be a counter action. As it turned out, the Left, surprisingly, did almost nothing. When Soeharto's entourage drove quietly down Swanston Street in Melbourne on its way to Government House, I was standing on the Collins Street corner outside the Melbourne Town Hall with Wanandi and a few friends. Moertopo waved to us as he went past. There wasn't a demonstrator in sight.

9
Flight to Phnom Penh

It was November 1968 and I had a personal invitation from Prince Norodom Sihanouk to join him in Phnom Penh for Independence Day and the Water Festival. This came about since the previous year I had attempted to enter the country but was rejected at the airport because, as mentioned earlier, Australian passports then listed one's occupation which said I was a journalist and journalists had to have an invitation or special visa. This meant that once back in Australia, as mentioned earlier, I had to write an obsequious letter to Sihanouk, pledging my great respect and asking him for a special favour. After many months he replied arrogantly acknowledging my request and in high regal tones he invited me to join him personally, as if we were already friends, to the Independence Day and Water Festival celebrations in November (copies of all correspondence in the Frank Mount Papers).

At around 7am on November 8 Ted Serong dropped me off at Saigon's Tan Son Nhat airport for the flight. I was the only passenger on the Air Cambodge DC4 flight. A smiling female attendant showed me to a seat. After I got settled I realised that the seat, which was much like an ordinary chair, was loose on the floor and consequently rocking a bit. I pointed this out to her and she said, "Way, Way". She came back and handed me a spanner and a screw driver and said "fick it". It was to be another three hours before we took off with me sweating profusely in the unbearable heat because the American pilot, who kept walking around outside and under the aircraft, said there were a couple of engine problems that were "no nos". Whether or not this was ever true I'll never know, but I assume he was in contact with Phnom Penh airport. The flight time between Saigon and Phnom Penh's Pochentong airport in a jet aircraft is about twenty minutes and in a four engine propeller driven one like the DC4 about 45 minutes. We flew up the Bassac River a few feet above the water as if we were in a helicopter. We rose up when we got to Phnom Penh, briefly circled the city and landed. As we taxied to the terminal I could see that buildings and aircraft were either in flames or smouldering with columns of black smoke all over the place. Every plane on the ground was burning. As I looked out my window I could see dozens of Air Cambodge staff waving excitedly at our aircraft, some of them carrying buckets of water to wash it. This was because ours was the only Air Cambodge aircraft left in existence. As I got off the aircraft a pretty girl put a garland of frangipani around my neck and escorted me to the terminal with a wonderful smile. When I got into the concrete terminal, full of smoke, I found there were no customs or immigration officers anywhere because of the presumably VC/Khmer Rouge attack which had occurred a few hours earlier. And there were still rockets exploding here and there. I refused to move until an immigration officer came out to the airport to stamp my passport. I had no intention of spending the rest of my life stuck in a Cambodian immigration-police bureaucratic nightmare. By this time they had delivered my suitcase. I was also carrying my Adler typewriter and an overnight bag. It was to be four hours before an immigration officer appeared. Eventually they got me a taxi into the Hotel Le Royal, where I showered and relaxed with a couple of beers and a pipe.

The Independence Day and Water Festival festivities involved a series of pleasant and splendid affairs. After one spectacular pageant at the main stadium, I was heading off up a boulevard in search of a taxi or a cyclo to take me back to my hotel when a Black Mercedes pulled alongside of me. A rear window opened and a man in a bright white Admiral's uniform and cap asked in excellent English if he could give me a lift. A little hesitantly, I accepted. After exchanging pleasantries, mainly about where I came from, he looked me in the eye as we drove through the police-lined streets, and said: "This man has to go. He and his wife are selling us out to the Vietnamese communists." Then he mentioned the Ho Chi Minh Trail. As I got out of the car at the Le Royal, he reminded me with a wave of his hand, "He has to go". He never told me his name and I never met him again, despite subsequent visits. But when Sihanouk was ousted by the Cambodian National Assembly on March 18, 1970, in favour of General Lon Nol, I clearly remembered his words, and his courage.

10
Whitlam, Khemlani and the CIA

In November 1974, when the Labor Government led by Prime Minister Gough Whitlam was in crisis due its own political incompetence and maladministration, a Pakistani 'commodities trader' named Tirath Hassaram Khemlani flew into Australia. He said he worked for the respectable London company Dalamal and Sons. He'd heard through his contacts among commodities and arms traders in Europe and Hong Kong that Australian government ministers were looking for large loans to finance a number of huge, "reforming", "nation building" projects, including a natural gas pipeline grid across and around the nation. He'd also been told that they wanted these massive foreign loans paradoxically to buy out the interests of foreign mining and energy companies. With the Middle East awash with petro-dollars following the quadrupling of oil prices in 1973-4, Khemlani said he had easy access to between $4 billion and $8 billion US dollars. Through contacts, he was ushered into the offices of the Australian Treasurer Dr. Jim Cairns, and the Minister for Minerals and Energy, Rex Connor, a thuggish and crazy ultra-Australian nationalist who was over the moon at the prospect of Khemlani's billions financing his fanciful grandiose schemes.

On Friday, December 13, 1974, the Labor Government's then 'Gang of Four', and Commonwealth Executive Council representatives Whitlam, Cairns, Connor and Attorney General Lionel Murphy authorised Connor to negotiate a $4 billion, 20 year loan for "temporary purposes" without the knowledge of the ALP caucus and the parliament and without the approval of the Loans Council thereby making it illegal and unconstitutional. From this moment to November 1975, Khemlani would wreak havoc on the government and the ALP at a time they were reeling from other consequences of their inability to govern effectively. It was not long before they realised that Khemlani was a con man and was lying about the money. But they kept communicating with him in the hope there was something there and he kept stalling them.

As the year went on, Connor and others said they had ceased talking to Khemlani in May 1975. But in October 1975 he flew back into the country with a load of documents proving that they hadn't stopped talking to him, which he leaked to the press. That was the end of Connor who was forced to resign. Cairns had months earlier been sacked as Treasurer for misleading the parliament, although he remained Deputy Prime Minister! After Connor resigned, the Leader of the Liberal Party Opposition, the determined, ambitious and impatient Malcolm Fraser, said that the Senate, which the Liberals controlled, would delay passage of the Appropriation Bills (often referred to as the Supply Bills or Money Bills), until Whitlam called an election. Whitlam refused indicating that his government was prepared to rule without Supply by borrowing internationally. That is, it would ignore parliament thereby creating a constitutional crisis. The Governor General, Sir John Kerr, a Whitlam appointee, stepped in and dismissed Whitlam as Prime Minister and asked Fraser to form a government pending elections – which Fraser won in a landslide. In the meantime, Khemlani had disappeared into the obscurity from which he came.

Khemlani was a strange and eccentric little will o' the wisp. In a recent issue of the Melbourne newspaper *The Age* (May 1, 2010) a review of a book dealing with the Loans Affair, or Khemlani Affair as it became known, said, "Unable to raise the finance from conventional lenders in Australia, Cairns had turned to a network of uncredentialled fringe financiers, who hoodwinked him into believing that they could tap into the hundreds of billions of dollars in windfall profits which were pouring into the Middle East following the oil shocks of the early 1970s. The key figure in this was Khemlani, a tiny man nicknamed 'Old Rice and Monkey Nuts', whose diet consisted almost entirely of potato chips, salted peanuts and cigarettes, and who spent his life jetting around the world with his documents secured in a bag strung around his neck, looking for deals – or so *The Age* gleefully reported at the time."

But who was Khemlani really? Brian Buckley, Press Secretary to the Liberal Party Opposition Shadow Treasurer at the time, Phillip Lynch, and later a senior member of Lynch's staff when he was Treasurer, said in his book *Lynched* (Salzburg Publishing, Melbourne 1991), that Khemlani had told him personally and no doubt others that he had connections with the CIA and other intelligence services around the world and kept them informed of some things. None of that is surprising. One would think it usual for a Middle Eastern commodities financier moving in those circles. But from the outset I saw something else from my own experiences and from what he said and didn't say about international finance that led me to tell Bob Santamaria and John Maynes that I thought he was a CIA actor sent to destabilise the Whitlam government with the hope of destroying it. At the time, Santamaria had an excellent working relationship with Malcolm Fraser and John Maynes was a major right-wing, social democratic, power broker in the trade union movement and a good mate and drinking partner of mine. Of the people I knew personally in this power play, Maynes had a much greater influence on events leading to the removal of Whitlam than anybody else.

The Americans had many reasons to be concerned about Whitlam and his government. Apart from the fact that the Labor movement still housed many pro-communist, pro-Soviet, pro-Mao, anti-American elements, Whitlam and a number of his ministers had made comments over the previous couple of years suggesting they were in favour of throwing out the global strategic signals and other US bases at Pine Gap, North West Cape and Nurrungar. Described as the "Family Jewels" in US intelligence and military circles, these bases were major facilities helping the US to monitor Soviet and Chinese missile launches and military movements generally and many forms of telecommunications. The Americans had not forgotten that shortly after the Whitlam government came to power, Attorney General Murphy led an extraordinary raiding party on ASIO headquarters in Melbourne, carting off boxes of secret files and communications partly in an effort to damage Australian-American intelligence co-operation.

While Malcolm Fraser's political pressures and machinations, along with the Khemlani Affair, were crucial elements in Whitlam's ultimate fall, just as important, if not more important, were the behind the scenes activities of a number of anti-communist, social democratic ALP and trade union machine men. They could see the damage that Whitlam and some of his left wing and/or incompetent ministers were doing to the party and the nation and decided that changes had to be made, including the removal of Whitlam if necessary. I would be very surprised if Khemlani hadn't found his way to Connor and Cairns through one of these people. At the same time it should be said that the NCC's Maynes, who was the National President of the Federated Clerks Union, had maintained an effective and influential information gathering network within the ALP ever since the 1955 split with the aim of one day going back in. I know from conversations with him in a few bohemian taverns around town that he was insistent that Whitlam had to go and that he was concerned especially with the damage that Whitlam's Minister for Labor, Senator Jim 'Diamond' McClelland, was doing on almost a daily basis.

11

Santamaria and Malcolm Fraser

In his book *Malcolm Fraser: The Political Memoirs*, co-written with Margaret Simons (The Miegunyah Press, Melbourne, 2010), Malcolm Fraser says he first met Bob Santamaria in late March or early April 1971. According to his biographer, Philip Ayres, this took place at his initiative, in Santamaria's office, after his resignation as Defence Minister on 8 March following a conflict with Prime Minister John Gorton (see Philip Ayres, *Malcolm Fraser, A Biography*, William Heinemann, Melbourne 1987, p.190). In my view it's likely they would have met a lot earlier than that. In 1971, Fraser had been Minister of Defence since November 11, 1969, and before that he had been Minister for the Army and before that Minister for Education and Science in charge of State Aid to non-government schools. I had myself met Fraser briefly in his Canberra office in 1967 when he was Minister for the Army in connection with business relating to the Defend Australia Committee's Vietnam Civil Aid Campaign and at the time assumed he knew Santamaria. But maybe I was wrong and they communicated through other people. I can think of many people who might have performed this function, among them a few 'knights of the realm', including Sir John Anderson and Sir Wilfrid Kent Hughes.

Whenever they first met – and light might be thrown on this in Santamaria's appointment diaries which one would expect to find in *The Santamaria Papers*, in the archives of the State Library of Victoria

– the point I want to make here is that Bob was greatly enamoured of Fraser from an early stage. I can remember sitting in the back seat of his car at his house waiting to head off to a football match with him. In the front passenger seat sat his first wife, Helen. Bob was still inside the house somewhere when Helen turned to me and said, "What do you think of Malcolm Fraser, is he someone special?" I replied, "No, I think he's just another Lib". She then said, "Bob thinks he will be the saviour of Australia; that he stands for most of the family, social, defence, religious and other values we do and that everything must be sacrificed for him."

This was Saturday, September 26, 1970, and we were on our way to the famous VFL Grand Final between Carlton and Collingwood. Bob was a Carlton member who was regularly invited by the former great Liberal Party Prime Minister Sir Robert Menzies, the club's No. 1 member, to join him at the game (and in later days at his home in the suburb of Malvern when he was immobilised by strokes). While I was also a Carlton member who often stood in the outer at Prince's Park with Bob, he had obtained for me a special Grand Final ticket which he said would see me seated next to another and more famous Carlton supporter, the historian Manning Clark, to whom Geoffrey Fairbairn had introduced me many years before and we had subsequently met on a number of occasions. In the event, Clark didn't turn up and I found myself seated next to a then famous 58 year old journalist Dick Whitington and his latest, very much younger, blonde floosie. In fact she looked about my age. Dick had written many books with the cricket great Keith Miller, most of them prefaced by Sir Robert Menzies – but that's another story.

I had come by Bob's house in Kew to collect the ticket having flown in from Indonesia that morning. Fraser was also a senior Carlton member, and later the No. 1, and would almost certainly have been in the Carlton Members rooms at the same time as Menzies and Bob at many games, including, I suspect, this Grand Final and it is hard to think they would not have met at least socially on these occasions. In the days following the great match which saw the most famous Carlton come-from-behind victory, I began thinking about what "sacrificing everything" really meant. As the days went by I came to think that it included the DLP and, if necessary, the NCC itself.

Why did Fraser pursue a relationship with Santamaria, particularly if it is true that they first met, at least seriously, at his initiative in 1971? Fraser had lost his cabinet position and it seems he was looking for support and useful allies wherever he could find them. Ayres says that Fraser saw Santamaria's NCC as the think tank of the Catholic right and that it had very good trade union connections. Ayres says that Fraser saw Santamaria as a man of influence in many places and that he agreed with many of the opinions Santamaria was expressing. Ayres argues that Santamaria gave Fraser a new following with the DLP supporting the idea of a Fraser-led Liberal Party or even a new conservative coalition. It is hard not to come to the conclusion that Fraser also saw that a relationship with Santamaria might give him a line of intelligence on what was happening in the ALP and the trade union movement, and even in some parts of the Liberal Party and the rural Country/National Party as well.

After the ALP's victory on December 5, 1972, which made Whitlam prime minister, Bob seemed to me to have become obsessive about Fraser especially after he was elected a couple of years later as Leader of the Opposition on March 21, 1975. By then Santamaria and Fraser had developed a good relationship on defence, foreign policy, education and general political matters. As the Whitlam government lurched from crisis to crisis during 1975 Bob strongly urged Fraser to deny Supply in the Senate so as to force an election. He even wrote a speech in September 1975 for Fraser outlining the reasons for denying Supply (see Patrick Morgan, *B.A. Santamaria, Running the Show, Selected Documents: 1939-1996*, Miegunyah Press, Melbourne 2008, p. 364).

After Whitlam's dismissal by the Governor General on November

11, 1975, and Fraser's ascension to the prime ministership the Fraser/Santamaria relationship developed even further and prospered throughout Fraser's time as national leader. They achieved a good deal in a number of fields including regional co-operation regarding which I was able to make a modest contribution. However, when the Liberal Party government was defeated by the Bob Hawke-led ALP in the March 1983 election, Fraser resigned from the leadership of the Liberal Party and on March 31 from the parliament. Santamaria told me in May 1989, when I had occasion to see him in his North Melbourne office, that after his election defeat Fraser, much to Bob's disgust, had never spoken to him again. Looking back on this, I wonder whether this might have been because Bob gave him bad or perhaps no advice on what was happening in the ALP – perhaps as a consequence of Bob losing his ALP Intelligence following the 1981 Split in his own NCC (see below). Fraser had made a monumental mistake in calling an election, almost twelve months before he had to, on the very day that the ALP changed leaders from Bill Hayden – who in Labor circles was believed to be unelectable – to the popular Bob Hawke.

Fraser says that correspondence between himself and Santamaria continued off and on until Santamaria died (*Malcolm Fraser, The Political Memoirs*, op cit, p. 231). But it was to be more off than on. However, one time that it was definitely on was in 1992 when Bob wrote to Fraser about forming a new conservative political organisation or political party to support protectionist and interventionist policies opposing the so-called economic rationalists and free traders which Fraser could lead. Fraser says in his *Memoirs* (p. 719) that this led to a number of gatherings involving Bob and himself as well as La Trobe University academic Robert Manne, sociologist John Carroll and Philip Ayres. Fraser says that while Santamaria might have been searching for new political party, he, himself, saw it only as a possible think tank. Within a year it had all fallen though. Fraser added in his *Memoirs* that he had never been a conservative but always a progressive.

One other thing that should be said here is that after its 1974 disastrous election result, the DLP was formally wound up in 1978 while the NCC continued on, but it was never to be the same again. It has never been the same group I got involved with in the early sixties with only one major aim – to defeat the influence of communist totalitarian forces in Australia and the world. I wanted to play a part, however small, in the greatest historic issue of the twentieth century – the conflict between the forces of totalitarianism – both Nazism and communism (which were two sides of the same socialist coin) – and liberal democracy. All the rest of what the NCC and its associated organisations went on with was far less important to me. I joined it because it was the most effective anti-communist, anti-totalitarian force in the country around which we could attract many other people across religious, social and political spectrums. I ran the DLP Club at Melbourne University on the same basis and with the help of one of my best friends, the eccentric but wonderful agnostic Jewish philosopher Dr. Frank Knopfelmacher, we ended up persuading the whole executive of the Rationalist Society, that is the agnostic/atheist club, to defect from the ALP Club to the DLP Club. It was one of my most satisfying moments, only to be surpassed when John Johnston, the President of the ALP Club also defected to the DLP Club. While this was intellectually courageous for these people to do in the context of the times, I always recognised that they were all Arthur Koestler/George Orwell type intellectuals and that they would all eventually move this way anyway. I just happened to be in the right place at the right time and was able to massage and seduce a bit. In the meantime the Liberal Club, run by the Kemp brothers was nowhere to be seen in this great struggle, the Vietnam debate or anything else.

12
A Champagne Breakfast with Lon Nol and Sirik Matak

After the 1970 Annual Pacific Institute Conference wound up in Hong Kong on October 23, Bob Santamaria, Fr. Bill Smith SJ and I flew out to Saigon on October 25 for a four day visit where Ted Serong, Foreign Minister Tran Van Lam and Information Minister Ngo Khac Tinh, all Pacific Institute members, were our hosts. We stayed at the non-air conditioned Jesuit residence and complex on Yen Do Street courtesy of Fr. Henri Forrest SJ. After many briefings, meetings and state functions, which I may have described elsewhere in this book, we left for Phnom Penh on an Air Vietnam flight. There we stayed, as I had often, in cavernous, high ceilinged rooms in the gracious old colonial Hotel Le Royal. I had laid the groundwork for Bob to meet the Prime Minister, General Lon Nol and his Deputy Prime Minister, Prince Sisowath Sirik Matak, during a visit the previous August when I had met and interviewed Lon Nol and Sirik Matak separately. The meeting was confirmed in early October through the office of Lt. General Sosthene Fernandez, Commander in Chief of the Khmer National Armed Forces (FANK). I had first met all three of these people when they held high offices when Prince Sihanouk was Head of State. (When I first met Fernandez, who was of Khmer Krom-Filipino origin, he was the Chief of the National Police). Shortly after being met at Pochentong Airport by Cambodian foreign office officials and garlanded by nubile Khmer maidens, we were informed that the three of us were invited to attend a breakfast with Lon Nol and Sirik Matak the following morning.

We were picked up the next morning and driven down the wide, quiet tree-lined Monivong Boulevard to the Royal Palace. We drove through high ornate gates into the lush tropical palace gardens which housed a complex of buildings of mostly traditional Khmer-Angkor architecture. We pulled up in front of a relatively westernised building with, from memory, a high colonnaded front entrance. From there, we were escorted to a large sprawling marble terrace overlooking the Tonle Sap (River Sap) a short distance from where it joins the mighty Mekong. On white clothed tables and glinting in the morning sun sat various pieces of crockery and five magnificent silver goblets of seemingly ancient vintage. We were asked to take a seat among the large cushioned high-backed cane chairs where we awaited our hosts Lon Nol and Sirik Matak. They eventually arrived, welcomed us, introduced themselves and invited us to join them in a chicken and champagne breakfast. They brought along an interpreter as I expected they would as their English, while acceptable, was not perfect and in any case it gave them extra time to formulate what they wanted to say.

It was a commonplace practice around the world and I had encountered it often before, including in my previous meetings with these two gentlemen. However, the interpreter soon proved to be unnecessary as Bob began speaking in fluent French (as he did when he and I met President Thieu in Saigon a couple of years later) and that is how the conversation continued. Bill Smith and I sat back puffing our pipes and sipping our goblets of cold, toasty Pol Roger while Bob, Lon Nol and Sirik Matak conducted a long earnest conversation. Although I had some basic French and could manage reasonably well around Paris, I could understand only a little of what was being said. But as I sat there it was interesting to see Sirik Matak emerge as the leading participant making many firm, confident points and explaining them at length. Lon Nol spoke occasionally, but most of the time nodded his flabby head in agreement with Sirik Matak. It also struck me that the thin, fit-looking and seemingly decisive Sirik Matak was acting more like a leading general than a Cambodian prince, while the chubby, darker skinned indolent looking General Lon Nol, whom I knew to be a ruthless anti-Vietnamese character, seemed more like a Khmer playboy prince. Sirik Matak always impressed me as a patriotic, anti-communist Khmer liberal who worked the corrupt system he was given as well as he could. As we got up to leave, I handed Lon Nol and then Sirik Matak copies of the 1970 conference update of the 1969 Pacific Institute Resolution, along with an introductory comment. I had given them copies of the original on a previous visit.

When we got back to the hotel, Bob explained around the swimming pool what Sirik Matak had been telling him. Bob said he had made three main points and this sort of summary was something Bob was always superb at. The three points were:

Firstly, the US, instead of just bombing the Ho Chi Minh Trail in Cambodia and Laos from South Vietnam and Guam and conducting occasional incursions across the border in support of South Vietnamese troops, should come into Cambodia properly and purposefully and drive the 50,000 North Vietnamese Army (NVA) invaders out of the north east provinces of his country and thereby cut the Ho Chi Minh Trail which was sustaining the war in the South Vietnamese central highlands and the Mekong Delta. In effect, Sirik Matak said that Cambodia was not a 'sideshow' to the Vietnam War, as was later claimed by some misguided observers including British journalist William Shawcross, but an integral part of the second Indo-China War prosecuted by the Indo-Chinese Communist Party led by Ho Chi Minh (not just the Vietnamese Communist Party).

In hindsight, we can now say that had the US done what Matak was suggesting (and which Averell Harriman stopped) in the mid-1960s, there would have been no 1968 Tet Offensive, no 1972 Easter NVA Offensive, no 1975 collapse of South Vietnam and the North

Vietnamese communists could not possibly have won the war under any circumstances – as the North Vietnamese leadership conceded following the war. South Vietnam today would be a thriving capitalistic democratic state. Sirik Matak told Bob that Sihanouk had to go after he, Sirik Matak, discovered on a visit to Hanoi that Sihanouk had signed documents allowing the NVA free access to the north east provinces and to a number of ports, including Sihanoukville, to support the war in South Vietnam.

Secondly, Cambodia wanted massive US economic aid to help resuscitate a nation destroyed economically by Sihanouk's dissolute incompetence. (For more on the parlous state of the Cambodian economy see Milton Osborne, *Sihanouk, Prince of Light, Prince of Darkness*, Allen and Unwin, Sydney, 1994).

Thirdly, Sirik Matak emphasised that at this time, they were fighting for the survival of the Khmer race against Vietnamese communists.

Bob told Sirik Matak and Lon Nol that he would personally talk to the leaders of the Australian government, including Defence Minister, Malcolm Fraser, about all of these matters. I subsequently sent a summary to Ted Serong for his friends, to Monty Rodulfo who passed it onto MI6, while some friends of mine in Canberra and elsewhere also got copies. As far as I know, nothing ever happened.

As we sat around the wonderful pool under tamarind and flame trees in the oppressive heat, Bob went into one of his rigmaroles about having to get home to Melbourne to his family as soon as possible. He did this every time he travelled in Asia. He didn't like Asia and especially Southeast Asia and in particular French Indo-China. He couldn't stand the French and couldn't get out of Vietnam fast enough. This is despite the bizarre report of him telling a group of Vietnamese Australians many years later that he loved Vietnam and wished to be buried there! On this occasion we were scheduled to fly from Phnom Penh to Bangkok and then down to Singapore for two days where Bob was scheduled to meet the Prime Minister, Lee

Kuan Yew, the foreign minister and the president. After that, Bob and I were to go on to Jakarta for another two days where Harry Tjan had arranged many important appointments for him before heading down to Melbourne.

Bob wanted to ignore all of this, stand up all of these people and fly home straight to Melbourne that day. He asked me to rearrange his schedule, while Bill Smith and I could do whatever we wanted. In the next six to eight hours I had him on flights all around Asia and the Pacific to get him as soon as possible to Melbourne, including a UTA flight from Phnom Penh via Saigon and New Caledonia into Sydney and then Melbourne. No sooner had I made a booking on one flight than he had me cancel it as unsatisfactory. I think I booked and cancelled about a dozen flights that day.

Watching all of this nonsense, a bemused Bill Smith suggested I should keep a detailed log of it all for my memoirs. Thinking memoirs of mine were a bit fanciful, I unfortunately didn't take his advice. As all of this was going on by the pool, the beautiful quiet Kate Webb came wandering along out of the greenery in bone-coloured jeans and a loose lemon blouse. Another fluent French speaker, she was now UPI Bureau Chief in Cambodia having succeeded Frank Frosch who had been killed by the communists a couple of weeks earlier while covering a story. I was able to introduce her to Bob of whom she'd read so much, courtesy of her late father, Professor Leicester Webb. She soon started flirting with me, and the chain-smoker in her led her to ask if she could borrow my "crummy" matches. As she hurried off with them to her office, which was in one of the free standing bungalows set back in the wonderful garden, Bill Smith said to me coldly, "She'd make a bad marriage risk." This time, I didn't have to take Bill's advice as I had come to a similar conclusion many moons before. As indeed had Kate – she had a fine sense of the ridiculous. But she also had a fatalistic streak – whenever a journalist friend would be killed or disappear in action, she'd mumble "you today, me tomorrow" and that went back to the late sixties. Her tomorrow came a few months after this meeting when she was captured by the VC/NVA 56 kilometres out of Phnom Penh on Highway 4 in April 1971.

That evening the three of us, along with Kate and a couple of local journalists dined in the sumptuous hotel restaurant on the far side of the pool. It was truly great French fare. I remember my order well: the best French oven baked onion soup I've ever tasted (and I'd had a few good ones around the Corsican bars of the region), foie gras, superb roast duckling and Roquefort cheese washed down with bottles of excellent St. Emilion red and graciously served by waiters in immaculate white jackets and black Chinese slippers.

In the end, Bob, Fr. Smith and I flew to Bangkok and then Singapore where Bob cancelled all of his appointments and rebooked himself and Smith straight to Melbourne. I went on the Jakarta as originally planned, but now essentially to apologise for Bob.

13

My Take on the 1981 NCC Split

In the late 1970s a serious and acrimonious argument developed within the Australian National Civic Council (NCC) between Bob Santamaria and his supporters on the one hand and John Maynes and his supporters on the other which eventually led to a split in the organisation in 1981. Patrick Morgan in the book he edited on the Santamaria documents concluded that Santamaria had initiated and sustained the conflict, changing the issues involved and eventually asserting it was about his leadership. Morgan says Santamaria's purpose in all of this is not clear and speculates that Santamaria feared from the start that his command of the NCC was under threat (see *B.A. Santamaria, Running The Show, Selected Documents: 1939-1996*, The Miegunyah Press, Melbourne, 2008, Ch. 12).

Of course he always felt there was a challenge to his command from Frank Maher in the fifties to Gerard Henderson in the sixties and beyond. But I suspect this split had little to do with that. Bob and I spent many hours seated next to each other flying around Australia and Southeast Asia in the sixties and early seventies. We had some wonderful conversations and times together both in the air and on the ground in places like Hong Kong, Singapore, Saigon and Phnom Penh. I can remember Bob, Ted Serong and I dancing and singing on a long table in a laid back Hong Kong Italian restaurant. One of the things Bob said to me a number of times during this period, first of all in early seventies if not before, was that there was a "natural division" in the NCC between the trade union or 'industrial' wing led by Maynes and the think tank or ideas wing led by himself and including their news magazine *News Weekly*, and that one day they would go their own ways. It was obvious that he was talking about himself and Maynes – and his own, thinly disguised, dislike of trade unionists. He also said to me not once but at least a dozen times over the years that "life was meaningless without a good fight." Put it all together and you get the 1981 split which ultimately reduced the NCC to nothing politically, especially after the Maynes-led NCC/DLP unions re-affiliated with the ALP.

14

'Asia Pacific Report' and George Bush

Asia Pacific Report (APR) had a great run. The first issue appeared in February 1998 and dealt with Indonesia and the challenge to Soeharto, whose removal or overthrow I knew was coming as you will appreciate from what I have written earlier. Our sources on this, based on thirty year old friendships and political collaboration with people around Benny Moerdani were unsurpassed. So APR grew from this. It started out as a fax newsletter sent out to my contacts in Asia and Australia, the latter growing through constant networking mainly in Melbourne. Although I was doing much less travel than in the past, and most of it on frequent flyer points, I still had a good base of operating contacts in Asia who were knowledgable in behind-the-scenes developments while my own accumulated knowledge was still current and broad enough to have a good intuitive feel for what might be really happening.

In January 1999 APR became an email newsletter which revolutionised both the production and distribution of it. At its height there were nearly a thousand people and organisations on my address list. This included not only people I knew or communicated with as a result of meeting them at conferences in Australia and abroad, but every member of the Australian Federal Parliament, every relevant embassy in Canberra, senior figures in all the major international and security departments and agencies in Canberra, and in the armed forces as well as major commercial corporations across the land. Many of them sent it on to others whose numbers can only be guessed at. Similar things happened overseas. In Washington, a retired US Navy commander emailed it throughout the Pentagon, the CIA, Congress and elsewhere; in San Diego a retired, famous US Marines officer, a wonderful friend who sat paralysed in bed as a result of an aircraft accident, sent it on to all his friends who included most serving US Marine generals and officers around the world; in London an old friend from *The Economist* sent it on to all sorts of highly placed people in government, the military and the intelligence services; and in Asia much the same thing happened in Tokyo, Beijing, Manila, New Delhi, Singapore and Jakarta.

All of this was great and APR was, without doubt, having an influence on thinking, foreign policy formulation and operational planning in all of those places – including I might say on counter-insurgency planning and practices in Iraq if only because the Australian Colonel David Kilcullen, a key advisor to the US General David Petraeus, was a regular APR reader and a long time student of Australian and Serong counter-insurgency doctrines and practices. One of the downsides of this widening and wonderful email readership was that I started getting emails from academics and post graduate students throughout the US and Europe asking for me details on many of the subjects I had written about or touched upon, for example, the South Vietnamese Police Field Force. They sent long questionnaires. Others, both in Australia and overseas, simply wanted to argue with what I was saying. I appreciated all of that. But had I indulged it, I would not have had time for anything else for they were endless and persistent in their argumentation. So I adopted early on the usual journalists' policy of no response. Had I not, this book would not be here.

Over the ten years it ran, APR covered many issues following the fall of Soeharto in 1998. They included the liberation of East Timor; radical Islamism and its threats to Indonesia, Asia and the world;

regional co-operation – including ASEAN, APEC and the ASEAN East Asia Summit (EAS); Taiwan and China; the future of Japan; the rise of India; a range of intelligence and counter-insurgency issues; and the fundamental global and strategic importance of protecting the Sea Lanes of Communication (SLOCS) running through the Indonesian waterways, the South China Sea and the South Pacific islands.

Early in the piece, a Melbourne website called PWHCE (Perspectives on World History and Current Events) run by a group of Melbourne University students and post-graduates asked if it could carry excerpts from APR with appropriate acknowledgement. I agreed and it was great stuff but it led to even more people emailing me from around the world because APR was now everywhere. I began to get emails from places like Holland about Fr. Beek. The academics and young students who ran PWHCE, whom I hardly knew, promoted APR as follows: " … the Report provides insights into Asian political developments which are simply not available from most mainstream media … the *Asia Pacific Report's* list of readers reads like a Who's Who of Foreign Affairs in the Australia-Asia Pacific region … " These APR excerpts can still be accessed on the internet even though the PWHCE website has closed down as a result of its bright editors moving on to greater things around the world. (If interested, you can google www.pwhce.org/apr).

In 2004 on a visit to Washington with Eileen, I met a US Army colonel in the bar of the Army and Navy Club on Farragut Square where we were staying. We enjoyed a few beers and he told me he worked in a senior strategic and security affairs position in the White House just a few blocks away. We exchanged cards and I began emailing him APR. For a couple of years he sent me Christmas cards from the White House. I never thought much about it. Then in 2006 a very close friend of ours in San Diego was invited to the White House to meet President George Bush. This friend, Eric Hayes, from a solid

Marines family and a regular APR reader, was America's most famous survivor of Crohn's disease having endured something like twenty operations yet still able to play tennis in his fifties. On Crohn's Disease Day he was invited to the White House, partly because a George Bush brother who worked in the White House also suffered from Crohn's disease. In the end, Eric, a highly engaging fellow, got an hour with the President. In the course of their conversation he mentioned that he read this Australian newsletter *Asia Pacific Report* and thought that the President might be interested in it. Bush's assistants interrupted and said he already got it and produced downloaded copies to show Eric. When Eric told me this, I got a good kick out of it. But it just shows that in this Internet age you never know where your emails might end up.

15

For the Good Times

In the dying days of the Republic of South Vietnam in April 1975, I was heading for one of my occasional restaurants in Saigon. It didn't have the finest food in town by a long chalk, but in the good old days it had served the best Colorado Steak outside of the US Army facilities and a very acceptable American red wine from the Napa Valley when any decent wine was generally hard to get anywhere in Asia. It was an American-Vietnamese restaurant called the Viet My in Thai Lap Thanh, a narrow street off Tu Do. One of its attractions was that it featured some wonderful background Vietnamese and Chinese cabaret-style female singers who normally you didn't notice too much as they warbled songs mostly from what today is called the American songbook. As I sat in the restaurant with Ngo Khac Tinh with his family in tears over the collapse of South Vietnam and what might befall them, a beautiful Chinese Vietnamese singer, whom I'd flirted with on happier occasions, came down off the stage. Carrying a small South Vietnamese flag and wearing a magnificent, sexy pastel-coloured Ao Dai, she strolled towards me with tears flowing down her face as she sang in broken English the Kris Kristofferson/Perry Como song *For The Good Time*s. "Don' look so sad. I know its over …". There wasn't a dry eye in the place.

"Don' look so sad, we get along, we find an offer," she whispered as she kissed me lightly on the cheek. I have rarely felt so moved. A nation was about to disappear and millions of fun-loving Vietnamese feared for their future under a brutal, dour communist conquerer from the North. But knowing their flair, and that among them were the best of the industrious North who had fled from Ho Chi Minh in 1954, including the best of the North's French trained Confucian bureaucracy, I always felt that 'South Vietnam' would be hard to kill off. And today the South Vietnamese defiantly and overwhelmingly still call Ho Chi Minh City "Saigon". To do otherwise would be something like my city of Melbourne accepting, after a Labor Party victory, being called "Gough Whitlam City".

Aboriginal Art at 30,000 feet

One of my first flights out of Australia in the mid-sixties was on a Qantas Boeing 707 bound for Singapore. It was bright cloudless sunny day and I sat at a window seat for I loved looking out at the world below whether over land or sea. The flight from Sydney took us straight across the dead red heart of the continent over Alice Springs and Ayer's Rock both of which were clearly visible from 30,000 feet. But what also struck me as I gazed down on hundreds of miles of red, burgundy and yellow rocky ridges, dried rivers, dying blue lakes and dead straight sand coloured roads and various other formations and features was how much of it was redolent of aboriginal art.

16
Jesuits in Asia

For many decades Jesuits in Asia have played a significant role in the development of liberal and democratic institutions in the region. As a part of that they have educated not only Catholics, but thousands of non-Catholic and non-Christian students – Muslims, Hindus, Confucianists, Buddhists, Taoists, Javanese mystics and others – in the principles of modern, Westernised civil society. As one Indonesian Cabinet minister said to me, "I might be a Muslim, but I'm a Westernised Jesuit sufi Muslim", having been educated in a Jesuit school and having known many liberal Catholics in his political career.

In Australia, I have never had any significant involvement with members of the clergy, let alone bishops. In Asia things were different. This was because many foreign missionaries and local clergy there were extremely well informed on what was happening politically, socially and economically. Some of them had been living in the same places for up to thirty years. So if I went to Muslim Mindanao in the Philippines, northeastern Thailand, or rural parts of Indo-China, for example, among the first people I'd seek to talk with were the local foreign missionaries and native clergy who were also often members of foreign missionary orders. Many of the foreign missionaries, predominantly from Europe, Canada and America, were highly and sometimes university educated articulate men with whom it was an utter joy to spend an hour or three in conversation over a drink or a meal in a hot tropical dining room. I can remember discussing English literature in the Mekong Delta in the midst of the war. While they knew the ins and outs of local politics and socio-economic affairs they were also able to stand back from the local societies and understand them historically and contemporally. These men helped change the face of Asia. Obviously, I am talking not only of Jesuits here, but members of dozens of different orders including the Dominicans (who established the first university in the region, the University of Santo Tomas in Manila, in 1611 which still flourishes today), Oblates, Passionists, Redemptorists, Vincentians, Salesians, and so on. But overall the Jesuits were by far the most politically significant across the region. There were also a few influential, political nuns from various orders, but the best of them, given the times, operated in the background.

Alongside the activities of people like Fr. Beek in Indonesia and the historian Horacio de la Costa in The Philippines, which I have already described in this book, across the region Jesuits trained thousands of young people in what we might call the liberal democratic political arts. Apart from their universities, they also ran trade union educational centres and political-civic educational groups, a number of which I participated in in the Philippines, Taiwan, Hong Kong and Thailand. In Taiwan they ran the Rerum Novarum Labor Center which trained trade union leaders many of whom ran the machine backbone of the Democratic Progressive Party (DPP) which came to power defeating the KMT in 2000 during an historic period of democratic transition (see *Asia Pacific Report,* No. 23, April 10, 2000, titled "The New Taiwan: The KMT, DPP and the Democratic Deliverance or How the KMT helped the DPP into Power"). In Hong Kong, the effervescent Father McGovern SJ trained trade union leaders, some of whom have been among the major pro-democracy stirrers and shakers in the former British colony. In Japan they were always very highly influential through, among many other channels, Sophia University which helped the Japanese in the areas of imagination and innovation, two things that appear to be lacking today in China as a result of its self-imposed cut-off from Western influence and thought, and which could inhibit its future prospects. And then, of course, there were the Jesuits throughout Indo-China, like Henri Forrest in Saigon, who was later employed in the deepest dungeons of the Vatican reputedly on foreign aid work.

As I travelled around the region meeting all of these extraordinary people, I discovered that those in one country had no idea what those of even the same religious order were doing in other countries, and that this applied most significantly to the Jesuits. In fact, in most cases they had never even heard of their other country counterparts. So on the margins of Pacific Institute conferences, I set about trying to bring them together so that they might know of each other's existence and learn a little from each other's experiences.

* * *

The Hong Kong based Hungarian Jesuit Laszlo La Dany was a fascinating man and a powerful intellect. For over thirty years he produced a weekly newsletter called *China News Analysis* based on his daily 24 hour listening to radio broadcasts across the closed China nation – nothing but impeccable Chinese sources. He became the quintessential China expert and China watchers throughout the world read him religiously and quoted him, almost always without attribution. But that never worried him. He attended many Pacific Institute conferences delivering papers and I lunched with him in Hong Kong and elsewhere often. On the last occasion in July 1990, a few weeks before he died of lung cancer on September 23, he took me for a memorable lunch in one of those exquisite little Chinese restaurants I could never find on my own. I knew he was ailing, but his death still came as a surprise.

I asked him over the lunch "Who runs China today?" I meant what individual or factions at this time. However, he took it more broadly and said in effect the following. It's the Communist Party of course, but it's a different sort of Communist Party to that in the West – Italy or Australia. The Chinese Communist Party is really another Chinese secret society like the Shanghai Green Gang that ran China under Chiang Kai-shek (and like those that have run China and Japan for centuries to this day). It operates like these underworld gangs through extortion, bribery, murder, and smuggling. And just like the gangs, it is next to impossible to know what is happening inside the Communist Party. For some periods it has been impossible even to tell who the party leaders were. La Dany reminded me that when Mao Tse Tung died in September 1976 and was succeeded by Hua Guofeng, Henry Kissinger had said that the Americans knew nothing about Hua, not even where he lived.

Then many years later in mid-2010 I was at a lunch with a former very senior Australian mining executive who had dealt with and traded with China for 30 years. When I asked who made the major economic and trading decisions in China and in what parts of the governing apparatus they were taken, he said he had no idea, that he was only concerned with receiving the cheques. Another interesting observation La Dany made was that during the Cultural Revolution which began in the mid-sixties, all education at all levels across the board, including schools, universities, museums and libraries closed for ten years while millions of books were destroyed. Teachers were run out of town as was anyone wearing spectacles to read. This he said had produced a generation or two of illiterates. The oldest of these people would today be in their late-fifties. What, if any, significance does this have for China today and the near future – for its educational system, bureaucracy, government and Communist Party leadership? Did all military educational institutions also close?

* * *

Legend has it that liberal Jesuits brought radical liberation theology to the Philippines and the region. But that is not true. Radical liberation theology came to The Philippines, surprisingly enough, through the

Divine Word missionaries. The liberal Philippine Jesuits, thanks to de la Costa, saw what it was and opposed it. Having much smarter philosophers, like Antonio Lambino and Felipe Gomez, than the old and even younger Philippine left, and certainly better associated political operatives, the Jesuits won in the end in 1986 when they outmaneovred the communist front Bayan in the lead up to the election of that year which saw Marcos ousted (see Part I, Chapter 3). This was well before the collapse of the Soviet Union in 1989. Yet it is worth noting that with the collapse of the Soviet Union, liberation theology, radical or otherwise, suddenly disappeared from the scene. It makes one wonder who was financing it all.

I have to say one other thing here. Having spent the best part of thirty years travelling around Asia during which time I met many bishops and all sorts of other Catholic clergy, male and female, I never ran into anything that could be called the "Vatican Intelligence Service". It just doesn't exist, otherwise I would have encountered it. Certainly Apostolic Delegates report back to Rome on political, social and economic developments but I have yet to meet any of these clerical diplomats with any real political nous and I'd be more than most surprised if any of them had an organised intelligence network of any kind at their disposal.

17

Two Adventures

I: "The Human Fly" Escapes in Bangkok

In March 1971, I spent three weeks visiting regions of Thailand – north, south and east – affected by insurgencies of various kinds. I had based myself in the modest five story Imperial Hotel in Bangkok in a Soi off Sukumvit Road behind the colonial Erawan Hotel (now the Grand Hyatt Erawan Hotel) which in those days was not far from the British Embassy and a number of American military institutions involved in the Vietnam War. The Imperial was flanked by a very expensive, modern red brick ten story apartment block on one side and a hardly noticeable sprawling very up-market very Thai tropical massage parlour on the other.

After a week moving around Southern Thailand on a tour organised by a good political contact, the country's only Muslim senator, Leck Vanich Angkhul, during which I met the leaders of many rebel organisations including the Pattani United Liberation Organisation (PULO), I was tired, sore and in need of soothing. I headed straight off to my bedroom for a long warm shower and a good sleep. At around four in the morning I was awakened by voices shouting in the night and then the faint smell of acrid smoke. I got up and from the smell and the shouting realised there was a fire in the hotel. Because of the Bangkok heat I was wearing only a pair of shorty pyjamas. I tried to turn on the lights but the power had gone – the first thing that happens in a serious fire. I grabbed the torch I always carried, opened the door and stepped into the pitch dark corridor. I nearly choked in the incredibly acrid thick smoke and immediately reached back for my door which was just in the process of closing, about to click. Had it done so I'd be dead. It was one of those cylindrical door knobs that didn't turn but you opened with a long key – and I didn't have the key with me; it was still in the room.

When I got back into the room I had to think carefully. The only way out was through a similar door onto the balcony and then over the balcony somehow. I looked over the balcony and couldn't see much below at all. Then I noticed that the room beside me had a large grill across the front of its balcony and the room below it was the same. These grills were designed to stop thieves climbing into the rooms. But only two out of three rooms in this hotel had them and mine was one that didn't. All those people in rooms with them died that night because they couldn't get out, including the man in the room next to me. I also noticed that there were water or drainage pipes running down the outside of the hotel, fortuitously right past my room. What I did next to save my life, I could not possibly have done had I also had to look after anybody else, say a wife or a girl friend. With the torch still stuck in my shorts I ventured out on to the grill next door and started slowly to work my way down the outside of the hotel from the fifth floor using the water pipe between floors. As I did so people were screaming into the night and jumping off the scorching roof to their deaths. Unknown to me at the time, a well known Thai TV journalist and photographer who lived in the fancy apartments next door, was photographing the fire and me working my way down the outside of the hotel. When I had gone down three – or was it in my mind four – floors I couldn't feel any more grills under my feet and looked down again and couldn't see much. So I shone the torch down and it reflected in water. I thought, "Ha, that's the ground". It was hard to know how far it was, but in my mental calculations it was maybe eight feet or so, but in any case, I had no choice. So I let go. Bang cluck! Shit! An enormous shudder ran through my body. It was only three to four feet and I was on the concrete roof of a ground floor extension. Running all around my feet was a network of water pipes and I'd miraculously landed between. Had I hit any of them I'd have broken a leg. When I climbed off the roof, I walked through the fancy apartments in shorty pyjamas and ran into the journalist mentioned above who gave me his card. I then wandered out the front of the hotel.

Thousands of local Thais, including girls from the massage parlour next door, had poured into the street to see the fire for they never thought a concrete building could burn. Yet there it was a truly spectacular sight of blue, yellow, green and other technicoloured flames, crackling explosions and thick billowing white and black smoke. That people were dying, some of them screaming and jumping off the roof of hotel into the carpark, seemed to be of little or no interest to them and the massage girls laughed at me in my shorts and made some obviously ribald comments in Thai. When news of the fire reached the radio news, other people started turning up after daybreak including many of my contacts who knew I was staying in the hotel. So there I was half naked hiding in a little street side shop from various representatives of the Thai government, the Burmese government, the Cambodian government, various Burmese rebel organisations, the US embassy, the British Embassy, the Laotian government, the Pathet Lao, the Kuomintang, the South Vietnamese embassy, Phoumi Nosavan's emissaries and others. After they'd gone, presumably thinking I was dead, I managed, eventually, to get in touch with the Australian Embassy where an Australian voice told me they knew nothing of the fire. I told them to look out the window. Eventually many hours later, in mid-morning, an embassy car turned up and took me to the nearby Amarin Hotel, where I had stayed often. I must be one of the few people in history ever to walk into a four star hotel in nothing but a pair of shorty pyjamas and ask for a room. Of course, on the way up in the lift, I was offered any number of girls. While I showered, an embassy officer went off and bought me some basic clothing. I can't remember his name, but if he's reading this book I'd be delighted to buy him a beer.

I'd survived, but sadly this was not true of most of the guests of the hotel. There were about a hundred and sixty guests and only four of us survived. There were some horrible deaths. A young American military mother and her two of her children boiled to death in their bath. Others died screaming at those grills, grilled to death in effect like a piece of steak. The four of us who survived had incredible stories and met briefly afterwards in the Amarin. A United Arab Airlines pilot was the only member of his male and female crew to survive. He jumped out of his room and landed on a corrugated iron roof between two horizontal wooden beams and was cushioned by the iron sheets in his fall. With a few cuts and bruises he was immediately on his feet. An American major jumped off the roof and landed in a coconut tree. He grabbed a branch which swayed up and down a few times, but then gently put him down and he walked away totally unscathed. An Englishman in his fifties who had been a rescue officer during the bombing of London in World War II was in a room on the other side of the building to me and at a level just below mine. His room didn't have a grill. It took him no time to tie his sheets together, securely fasten them to a solid window upright and scale down to the ground.

The next day there were photographs of the fire on the front pages of all the Bangkok newspapers including *The Bangkok World* which under the heading "The Human Fly" had a photograph of a fortunately unrecognisable me climbing down the drainpipe. Later that day I returned to the hotel to meet the TV journalist who had given me his card and presumably had taken the photographs about which my instincts told me to say nothing. From his luxury apartment, we could look down into my hotel room. The windows were smashed, it all looked hot and dark and gallons of water had been poured into the room by the fire brigade which was still around. I thanked him for his help, said we should get together sometime for a meal, and left. The next day I returned to the hotel and was able to climb the internal stairs in considerable heat and smoke to my room where I was able to retrieve my thoroughly drenched briefcase containing files and notes, my Adler typewriter and a number of water damaged books which sit on my bookshelves to this day. The following day I awoke to read in *The Bangkok World* that the journalist who had helped me was claiming he had seen the fire brigade steal thousands of dollars of photographic equipment from my room and he named me since I had introduced myself to him. As I knew the Bangkok Fire Department was run by the Bangkok Police Department, neither of which I had any desire to involve myself with, I immediately packed, took a taxi to the airport and flew out to Singapore and shortly thereafter Melbourne where Eileen was preparing for our marriage. For me, every day since that fire has been a bonus, for I was literally one second from certain death.

II: A Pen-Pal "Bride"

One afternoon in 1978 I was sitting at the desk in my home office in Manila when the door bell rang. I opened the door and there stood a man I knew from the National Civic Council and whom I hadn't seen for some years. He'd got my address from Bob Santamaria. He was in his mid-thirties which made him about the same age as me. I knew him to be what we might call a very conservative Tasmanian Catholic who had never travelled out of Australia before. For the purpose of this story, I'll call him Harry. I invited him in and he told me his story. He said he had been writing for more than a year to a young and beautiful female pen-pal in Cotobato in the southern Philippine province of Mindanao. They'd exchanged photographs, and so on and he had now come to meet her in the hope of taking her back to Australia to marry her. He showed me the photographs and said he would be flying down to Cotobato the next day. I said "good luck" and off he went.

    A couple of weeks later there was an almighty banging on our front door in the middle of the night. I got out of bed and there was tall, gaunt Harry. He was exhausted. When he settled down and had a couple of coffees he explained. The girl was as beautiful as anyone he had ever seen. For four or five days they had wonderful times together. Then it all turned sour when it eventuated that she was a mistress of the most powerful and brutal Philippine constabulary general in the region who had told his thugs to run Harry out of town or kill him. He immediately fled. He said it had taken him over week to get back to Manila, dodging the general's goons and ferry-hopping between islands. Then he looked at me with a smile and a sad eye and said, "I came here here expecting a Roman Holiday, but I've ended up in a Humphrey Bogart movie". Fortunately he'd kept his passport and as I was the Executive Secretary of the Australian Business Group in the Philippines, I was able to get him out of the country on a flight the next morning.

18

Why I Parted Company with Bob Santamaria

Bob Santamaria and I had some great times together in Australia and Asia. In Australia, we worked together politically from the time I was at university where I established the Melbourne University DLP Club. The DLP Club then spawned two nationwide organisations the Defend Australia Committee and the Wheat for India Campaign, both of which I've written about earlier in this book. Bob supported both and I started writing articles for his paper *News Weekly*, which I'd read for more than a decade, and speeches for various DLP and Liberal Party politicians. At the same time, Sibnarayan Ray had me writing for Indian newspapers. Sometime early in 1965 when I was 23 years of age, I was elected to the Victorian State Executive of the DLP, but retired from that position in 1968 as a result of my extended, six months long, overseas tours of Southeast Asia. Apart from these political associations Bob and I were also friends on account of the fact that I went to Melbourne University at the same time as three of his daughters which brought us all into social contact, sometimes in Bob's home. Following that, as you know, Bob and I co-operated politically in Asia over many years.

He cut a remarkable figure. Graham Freudenberg, Gough Whitlam's press secretary, said in his 1977 biography of Whitlam that Santamaria was unique in Australian history being its only political intellectual in the high European tradition. Through his outstanding intellect and determination, said Freudenberg, he created and sustained a political movement which influenced events for a generation. He was a brilliant writer and the best television commentator of his time (see Graham Freudenberg, *A Certain Grandeur: Gough Whitlam in Politics*, Sun Books, Melbourne 1977, p. 12.). He was certainly unique in my world. In the early to mid-sixties we young Melbourne University anti-communist student political activists were heavily influenced by a combination of Bob's high Western European thought and commitment to action on the one hand, and the extraordinary Frank Knopfelmacher's high and at times cutting East European political thought and demand for action by us on the other. It was a heady mix and it changed us, at least politically.

Bob Santamaria had many great achievements both at home and abroad. At home, he led the fight for State Aid to church and independent schools for years before his DLP associates negotiated breakthrough deals with the ruling Liberal Party leaderships in Canberra and Melbourne. In the foreign policy, defence and intelligence areas, he initiated and achieved a number of major things through the threat of DLP preference deals, including the establishment of the Australian naval base at Cockburn Sound. In social policy, he and the DLP repeatedly won advances in child endowment and equal pay for women. In industrial relations, he and his trade union allies fought bravely for years against communist/ALP unity tickets and eventually achieved secret ballots in trade union elections. They also fought against communist and criminal thuggery on the waterfront and in the Seaman's Union, some of their colleagues meeting with serious 'accidents' of a death-intended nature. In economic policy, Bill Crowe, the NCC's economics advisor and commentator, invented the productivity wage index.

Internationally, Santamaria with his associates, principally me, helped take Australia into Southeast Asia in a new way in the sixties through the Pacific Institute which in conjunction with its Indonesian associates helped develop new forms of regional co-operation and ultimately APEC. But overall, Santamaria and the NCC/DLP complex in Australia was organisationally the most effective and influential liberal democratic, anti-communist force committed to fighting and defeating communist forces in Australia and overseas. When the Soviet Union ultimately collapsed in 1989, Santamaria and John Maynes in Australia had won, the DLP/NCC complex had won, and we anti-communists all over the world had won a victory of historic proportions against the forces of global communist totalitarianism. Despite the problems of the world today, we continue to bask in that.

Bob Santamaria and I had some very good times socially and privately especially when we travelled together in Southeast Asia. Delightful and charming as he was, sometimes while sitting for hours together on an aircraft he would talk with and confide in me over a drink or two. Apart from discussing regional and global strategic matters, he would speak about his problems involving political colleagues, allies and enemies, himself, his wife and his family and how he might deal with it all. Many of these things he said to me in confidence – and I respect that – but many others weren't. However I have excluded most of them here as they are not relevant to this book. One thing I can say quite safely is that I never remotely thought at any time in my long association with Bob that I was engaging with a saint and I say that strongly because of some moves in Australian Catholic circles to promote him as such.

Throughout our association there were many things I disagreed with him about and these ranged from people, theological matters, social policy issues, economic policy, local and national political assessments to international judgements. But, like others, I let them all go in the much larger interest of the great struggle of our age, that against communist totalitarianism. After the electoral defeat of the DLP in 1974, the removal of the Whitlam government in 1975, the gradual weakening of communist influence in Australia and the fall of Vietnam in 1975, all of which coincided with Bob's growing disinterest in trade union affairs, Bob turned to other areas of interest for his weekly newspaper commentaries. It might have been thought that he would continue to take an interest in Australia's engagement with Asia and regional co-operation, but after the fall of South Vietnam he lost interest in both. In the late seventies I asked him why and replied, "What's in it for me?" (a question he had asked on a number of occasions in the past when I had put various possible projects to him). Apart from adopting an increasingly anti-American posture after Vietnam, he decided to become an economic commentator while maintaining his national and general international political analysis. In the background he supported the National Party and the Joh Bjelke-Petersen for Canberra movement and later, in a desperate bid for political relevance, turned full circle and proposed to his supporters that they infiltrate the ALP (see Patrick Morgan, *B.A. Santamaria, Running the Show, Selected Documents: 1939-1996*, op cit, p. 400).

Bob had no understanding of economics. He had never studied it and year eleven students knew more than he did. For example, he misunderstood what economists meant by the terms microeconomics and macroeconomics. He thought a bank's assets were its liabilities and vice versa. He'd never heard of the trade cycle. On top of that he was a strong protectionist, on one occasion writing that tariffs were "an inherent good" so the more we had of them the better. This was despite the fact that the 1970 Pacific Institute Resolution was a significant free trade document whose economic section was written by one of the greatest free trade economists of all time, his great friend Colin Clark. In the end, he betrayed Clark. He thought, wrongly, that tariffs and other forms of protection helped farmers. None of this stopped him lecturing prime ministers, treasurers and Reserve Bank governors. It was all embarrassing.

In his commentaries he regularly attacked international traders, bankers, financiers and "speculators" in "the global economy". You can imagine my surprise when I discovered that he and one of his brothers had established a merchant bank in Collins Street, Melbourne, called Melbank for the purpose of investing and speculating in the global economy. Not surprisingly, the bank did not do well and lost a lot of money. But at least it explained why some years earlier he had asked me, "What's a merchant bank? What does it do?" I laughed.

As his intolerable economic nonsenses appeared week after week I began to feel a deep unease that some people might actually think, given our past associations, that I agreed with what he was saying, if indeed I wasn't writing it for him. I'd wake up in the morning thinking, "God, I hope nobody thinks I agree with that crazy irrational stuff." So I just started moving away from him by ceasing contact. There were never any sharp words between us – although he did make some unacceptable demands about my continuing friendship with John Maynes, an old Mount family friend – and I just drifted away. It wasn't easy because in so many ways I loved the man and he haunted my dreams generously for a very long time. Even today he appears occasionally.

Apart from these economic and other policy issues the greatest problem I had with Bob throughout our association was that he was not always a man of his word. For example, he'd agree on a deal over lunch and perhaps shake your hand on it and a few days, weeks or months later deny it that the conversation had ever happened. He didn't always do this, but it occurred often. Others had the same experience, regularly. NCC officials like Norm Lauritz and Gerald Mercer and the DLP senators put up with it during the long fight against communist totalitarianism, but when that faded, the situation changed. All but one of the five DLP senators, while they were senators, broke with Bob over this issue, as did independent Senator Brian Harradine (see Morgan, *Documents*, pages 377-381). This was a pity because at various times of his career Bob, while a complex man, was a truly great and courageous politician and churchman who, to say the least, had a wide and lasting influence and major achievements to his name. For me, the Pacific Institute, his concept of the Pacific Community and what it led to were among the greatest. The good memories linger.

Select Bibliography

A: BOOKS

All the books listed below form a part of Frank Mount's private library. They were either written in or relate to the period of the memoirs.

AUSTRALIA and ASIA and REGIONAL CO-OPERATION

Byrnes, Michael, *Australia and the Asia Game*, Allen & Unwin, 1994.

D'Alpuget, Blanche, *Hawke the Prime Minister*, Melbourne University Press, 2010.

Garnaut, Ross, *Australia And The Northeast Asian Ascendency*, Australian Government Publishing Service, Canberra, 1989.

Gyngell, Allan & Wesley, Michael, *Making Australian Foreign Policy*, Cambridge University Press, Melbourne 2003.

Keating, Paul, *Engagement, Australia Faces the Asia-Pacific*, Macmillan, Sydney, 2000.

Moertopo, Ali, *Indonesia in Regional and International Co-operation: Principles of Implementation and Construction*, CSIS, Jakarta, 1973.

Walker, David, *Anxious Nation: Australia and the Rise of Asia, 1850-1939*, University of Queensland Press, 1999.

The US and ASIA

Fifield, Russel H., *Southeast Asia in United States Policy*, Praeger, New York, 1963.

Gurtov, Melvin, *Southeast Asia Tomorrow – Problems and Prospects for US Policy*, Johns Hopkins Press, Maryland, 1970.

Haig, Alexander M. Jr., with Charles McCarry, *Inner Circles: How America Changed The World, A Memoir*, Warner Books, New York, 1992.

GUERRILLA WARFARE and COUNTER-INSURGENCY:

Chapman, F. Spencer, *The Jungle is Neutral*, Chatto & Windus, London, 1949.

Fairbairn, Geoffrey, *Revolutionary Warfare and Communist Strategy*, Faber and Faber, London, 1968.

Greene, T.N. (Ed.), *The Guerrilla – And How To Fight Him, Selections from the Marine Corps Gazette*, Praeger, New York, 1962.

Grivas George, *Guerrilla Warfare and Eoka's Struggle*, Longmans, London, 1964.

Guevara, Ernesto Che, *Episodes of the Revolutionary War*, International Publishers, New York, 1968.

Heilbrunn, Otto, *Partisan Warfare*, Praeger, New York, 1962.

Mao Tse Tung, *On Guerrilla Warfare*, Praeger, New York, 1965.

Nasution A.H., *Fundamentals of Guerrilla Warfare*, Pall Mall, London, 1965.

Sinclair, Andrew, *Guevara*, Fontana, London, 1970.

Thompson, Robert, *Revolutionary War in World Strategy 1945-1969*, Secker and Warburg, 1970.

Trinquier, Roger, *Modern Warfare – A French View of Counterinsurgency*, Pall Mall, London, 1964.

Truong Chinh, *Primer for Revolt*, Praeger, New York, 1963.

Valeriano, Napoleon and Bohannan, Charles, *Counter-Guerrilla Operations, The Philippine Experience*, Praeger, New York, 1962.

STRATEGY and STRATEGIC THOUGHT

Beaufre, Andre, *Introduction to Strategy*, Faber and Faber, London, 1965.

Kennedy, Paul, *Strategy and Diplomacy 1870-1945: Eight Studies*, George Allen and Unwin, London, 1983.

Kissinger, Henry A., *Nuclear Weapons and Foreign Policy*, The Norton Library, New York, 1969.

Kissinger, Henry, *Diplomacy*, Simon & Schuster, New York, 1994.

Liddell-Hart, B.H., *Strategy: The Indirect Approach*, Faber and Faber, London, 1967.

Rapoport, Anatol (Ed), Carl Von Clausewitz, *On War*, Penguin, Middlesex, England, 1967.

Strause-Hupe, Robert and others, *Protracted Conflict, A Challenging Study of Communist Strategy*, Harper & Brothers, New York, 1959.

VIETNAM and THE VIETNAM WAR:

Barr, Marshall, Surgery, *Sand and Saigon Tea: An Australian Army Doctor in Vietnam*, Allen & Unwin, Sydney, 2001.

Bui Diem, *In the Jaws of History*, Houghton Mifflin, Boston, 1987.

Burchett, Wilfred, G, *Vietnam, Inside Story of the Guerilla War*, International Publishers, New York, 1965.

Butler, David, *The Fall of Saigon*, Sphere, London, 1986.

Davies, Bruce and McKay, Gary, *The Men Who Perservered*, Allen & Unwin, Sydney, 2005.

Duiker, William J., *Ho Chi Minh*, Theia Books, New York, 2000.

Duncanson, Dennis J., *Government and Revolution in Vietnam*, Oxford University Press, London, 1968.

Fall, Bernard, *The Two Viet-Nams, A Political and Military Analysis*, Pall Mall Press, London, 1963.

Fitzgerald, Frances, *Fire in the Lake, The Vietnamese and the Americans in Vietnam*, Macmillan, 1972.

Gettleman, Marvin. E. (Ed), *Vietnam: History, Documents, and Opinions on a Major World Crisis*, Penguin, London, 1966.

Grandin, Bob, *The Battle of Long Tan as Told by the Commanders*, Allen and Unwin, Sydney, 2004.

Halberstam, David, *The Making of a Quagmire*, The Bodley Head, London, 1964.

Ham, Paul, Vietnam, *The Australian War*, Harper Collins, Sydney, 2007.

Hammer, Helen J., *The Struggle for Indo-China*, Stanford University Press, Stanford, 1954.

Hammer, Helen, *Vietnam, Yesterday and Today*, Holt, Rinehart & Winston, New York, 1966.

Herr, Michael, *Dispatches*, Alfred A. Knopf, New York, 1977.

Hickey, Gerald Cannon, *Village in Vietnam*, Yale University Press, 1964.

Higgins, Marguerite, *Our Vietnam Nightmare*, Harper & Row, New York, 1965.

Honey, P.J., *Communism in North Vietnam*, An Ampersand Book, London, 1963.

Honey, P.J., *Genesis of a Tragedy: The Historical Background to the Vietnam War*, Ernest Benn, London, 1968.

Karnow, Stanley, *Vietnam, A History: The First Complete Account of Vietnam at War*, The Viking Press, New York, 1983.

Koch, Christopher, *Highways to a War*, William Heinemann, Australia, 1995.

Kolko, Gabriel, *Vietnam, Anatomy of War 1940-1975*, Allen and Unwin, London, 1986.

Lancaster, Donald, *The Emancipation of French Indo-China*, Oxford University Press, London, 1961.

Lanning, Michael Lee and Cragg, Dan, *Inside the VC and the NVA: The Real Story of North Vietnam's Armed Forces*, Ivy Books, New York, 1992.

Lansdale, Edward Geary, *In the Midst of Wars, An American's Mission to Southeast Asia*, Harper & Row, New York, 1972.

Lunn, Hugh, *Vietnam, A Reporter's War*, University of Queensland Press, 1985.

McKay, Gary, *Australia's Battlefields in Viet Nam*, Allen & Unwin, Sydney, 2003.

Meray, Tibor, *On Burchett*, Callistemon Publications, Melbourne, 2008.

Perry, Roland, *The Exile, Burchett: Reporter of Conflict*, William Heinemann, Australia,

Pike, Douglas, *Viet Cong*, Massachusetts Institute of Technology, US, 1966.

Pike, Douglas, *War, Peace and the Viet Cong*, The M.I.T. Press, US, 1969.

Ray, Sibnarayan (Ed), *Vietnam: Seen from East and West*, Thomas Nelson, Melbourne, 1966.

Shaplen, Robert, *The Lost Revolution: Vietnam 1945-65*, Andre Deutsch, London, 1966.

Sheehan, Neil, *A Bright Shining Lie*, Jonathon Cape, London, 1989.

Syme, Anthony, *Vietnam: The Cruel War*, Horwitz Publications, London, 1966.

Tanham, George, *War Without Guns, American Civilians in Rural Vietnam*, Praeger, New York, 1966.

Thompson, Robert, *No Exit from Vietnam*, Chatto & Windus, London, 1969.

Vo Nguyen Giap, *Big Victory, Great Task*, Pall Mall Press, London, 1968.

Warner, Denis, *The Last Confucian*, Penguin, UK, 1964.

Webb, Kate, *On the Other Side: 23 Days with the Viet Cong*, Quadrangle Books, New York, 1972.

Westmoreland, General William C., *A Soldier Reports*, Doubleday, New York, 1976.

SANTAMARIA and ASIA:

Ayres, Philip, *Malcolm Fraser, A Biography*, William Heinemann Australia, Melbourne, 1987.

Morgan, Patrick (Ed), *B.A. Santamaria, Your Most Obedient Servant, Selected Letters, 1938-1996*, The Miegunyah Press, Melbourne, 2007.

Morgan, Patrick, (Ed), *B.A. Santamaria, Running the Show, Selected Documents, 1939-1996*, The Miegunyah Press, Melbourne, 2008.

Santamaria, B.A., *Against the Tide*, Oxford University Press, Oxford, 1981.

SERONG and the VIETNAM WAR:

Blair, Anne, *There to the Bitter End, Ted Serong in Vietnam*, Allen & Unwin, Sydney, 2001.

Blair, Anne, *Ted Serong, The Life of an Australian Counter-insurgency Expert*, Oxford University Press, Melbourne, 2001.

Ham, Paul, *Vietnam, The Australian War*, Harper Collins, Sydney 2007.

McAULEY:

Ackland, Michael, *Damaged Men, The Precarious Lives of James McAuley and Harold Stewart*, Allen & Unwin, Sydney, 2001.

Coleman, Peter, *The Heart of James McAuley, Life and Works of the Australian Poet*, Connor Court Publishing, Melbourne, 2006.

McAuley, James, *Collected Poems*, Angus & Robertson, Sydney, 1994.

McCredden, Lyn, *James McAuley*, Oxford University Press, Melbourne, 1992.

Pybus, Cassandra, *The Devil and James McAuley*, University of Queensland Press, 1999.

SOUTHEAST ASIA – GENERAL AND HISTORICAL:

Bloodworth, Dennis, *An Eye For The Dragon*, Secker & Warburg, London, 1970.

Brimmell, J.H., *Communism in South East Asia, A Political Analysis*, Oxford University Press, London, 1959.

Coedes, G, *The Making of South East Asia*, Routledge & Kergan Paul, London, 1966.

Crozier, Brian, *South-East Asia in Turmoil*, Penguin, 1965.

Elegant, Robert, *Pacific Destiny, Inside Asia Today*, Crown, New York, 1990.

Estelle Holt, *Asia and I*, Putnam, London, 1958.

Gordon, Bernard, *The Dimensions of Conflict in Southeast Asia*, Prentice Hall, New York, 1966.

Manglapus, Raul, *Will of the People: Original Democracy in Non-Western Societies*, Freedom House, New York, 1987.

Meyer, Milton, *Southeast Asia: A Brief History*, Littlefield, Adams & Co, New York, 1965.

Osborne, Milton, *Region of Revolt, Focus on Southeast Asia*, Pergamon Press, Australia, 1970.

Pearn, B.R., *An Introduction to the History of South-East Asia*, Longmans of Malaya, Kuala Lumpur, 1963.

Saidenfaden, Erik, *The Thai Peoples*, The Siam Society, Bangkok, 1963.

Sanders, Sol, *A Sense of Asia*, Charles Scribner's Sons, New York, 1969.

Scalapino, Robert A. (Ed), *The Communist Revolution in Asia; Tactics, Goals and Achievements*, Prentice-Hall, New York, 1965.

Shaplen, Robert, *Time Out of Hand: Revolution and Reaction in Southeast Asia*, Andre Deutsch, London, 1969.

Singh, Patwant, *The Struggle for Power in Asia*, Hutchinson of London, 1971.

Steadman, John M., *The Myth of Asia*, Simon and Schuster, New York, 1969.

Tarling, Nicholas, *Southeast Asia, Past and Present*, Cheshire, 1966.

Tinker, Hugh, *Reorientations: Studies on Asia in Transition*, Pall Mall Press, London, 1965.

Wilson, Dick, *Asia Awakes: A Continent in Transition*, Weidenfeld and Nicolson, London, 1970.

Young, Gordon, *The Hill Tribes of Northern Thailand*, The Siam Society, Bangkok, 1962.

SOUTHEAST ASIA – NATIONS

Indonesia:

Barton, Greg, *Gus Dur: The Authorized Biography of Abdurrahman Wahid*, Equinox Publishing, Jakarta, 2002.

Brackman, Arnold C., *Indonesian Communism, A History*, Praeger, New York, 1963.

Brackman, Arnold C., *The Communist Collapse in Indonesia*, Asia Pacific Press, Singapore, 1970.

Coppel, Charles A., *Indonesian Chinese in Crisis*, Oxford University Press, Oxford, 1983.

Crouch, Harold, *The Army and Politics in Indonesia*, Cornell University Press, 1970.

Elson, R. E., *Suharto, A Political Biography*, Cambridge University Press, 2001.

Feith, Herbert and Castles, Lance (Ed), *Indonesian Political Thinking, 1945-1965*, Cornell University Press, Ithaca, 1970.

Grant, Bruce, *Indonesia*, Melbourne University, 1964.

Jenkins, David, *Suharto and His Generals, Indonesian Military Politics, 1975-1983*, Cornell Modern Indonesia Project, New York, 1984.

Kartodirdjo, Sartono, *Modern Indonesia: Tradition and Transformation*, Gadjah Mada University Press, Jogjakarta, 1991.

Laksono, P.M., *Tradition in Javanese Social Structure Kingdom and Countryside*, Gadjah Mada University Press, Jogjakarta, 1990.

Lee Khoon Choy, *Indonesia: Between Myth and Reality*, Nile & Mackenzie London, 1976.

Lowry, Robert, *The Armed Forces of Indonesia*, Allen & Unwin, Sydney, 1966.

Lubis, Mochtar, *Twilight in Jakarta*, Hutchinson of London, 1963.

May, Brian, *The Indonesian Tragedy*, Routledge & Kegan Paul, London, 1978.

McDonald, Hamish, *Suharto's Indonesia*, Fontana Books, Melbourne, 1980.

Moertopo, Ali, *The Acceleration and Modernisation of 25 Years' Development*, CSIS Jakarta, 1972.

Pour, Julius, Benny Moerdani, *Profile of a Soldier Statesman*, Jakarta 1993.

Roeder, O.G., *The Smiling General: President Soeharto of Indonesia*, Gunung Agung, Jakarta, 1969.

Soeharto, *My Thoughts, Words and Deeds, An Autobiography*, P.T. Citra Lamtoro Gung Persada, Jakarta, 1991.

Suryadinata, Leo, *Military Ascendancy and Political Culture: A Study of Indonesia's Golkar*, Ohio University Center for International Studies, 1989.

Williams, Maslyn, *Five Journeys From Jakarta*, Collins, Sydney, 1966.

Vietnam – See Above

Cambodia:

Leifer, Michael, *Cambodia: The Search for Security*, Pall Mall Press, London, 1967.

Osborne, Milton, *Sihanouk, Prince of Light, Prince of Darkness*, Allen & Unwin, 1994.

Williams, Maslyn, *The Land in Between: The Cambodian Dilemma*, William Collins, Sydney, 1969.

Laos:

Dommen, Arthur, *Conflict in Laos: The Politics of Neutralization*, Praeger, New York, 1964.

Langer, Paul F., and Zasloff, Joseph J., *North Vietnam and the Pathet Lao: Partners in the Struggle for Laos*, Harvard University Press, 1970.

Sisouk Na Champassak, *Storm Over Laos, A Contemporary History*, Praegar, New York, 1961.

Toye, Hugh, *LAOS, Buffer State or Battleground*, Oxford University Press, London, 1968.

The Philippines:

Burton, Sandra, *The Impossible Dream: The Marcoses, the Aquinos, and the Unfinished Revolution*, Warner Books, New York, 1999.

De la Costa, Horacio, SJ, *Readings in Philippine History*, Bookmark, Manila, 1965.

Farwell, George, *Mask of Asia: The Philippines*, Cheshire, Melbourne, 1966.

Gowing, Peter G. and McAmis, Robert D., *The Muslim Filipinos: Their History, Society and Contemporary Problems*, Solidaridad Publishing House, Manila, 1974.

Joaquin, Nick, *The Aquinos of Tarla: An Essay on History as Three Generations,* Solar Publishing, Manila, 1983.

Karnow, Stanley, *In Our Image*, Random House, New York, 1989.

Lachica, Eduardo, *HUK: Philippine Agrarian Society in Revolt*, Solidaridad Publishing House, Manila, 1971.

Manaput, Ricardo, *Some are Smarter than Others: The History of Marcos' Crony Capitalism*, Aletheia Publications, New York, 1991.

Marcos, Ferdinand E., *Revolution from the Center: How the Philippines is Using Martial Law to Build a New Society*, Raya Books, Hong Kong, 1978.

Marcos, Ferdinand, *Towards a Filipino Ideology*, Publisher, Ferdinand Marcos, Manila, 1979.

Montemayor, Jeremias U., *Ours to Share: An Approach to Philippine Social Problems*, Rex Book Store, Manila, 1966.

Montemayor, Jeremias U., *The Philippine Agrarian Reform Program*, Rex Book Store, Manila, 1976.

Nakpil, Carmen Guerrero, *A Question of Identity*, Vessel Books, Manila, 1973.

Pedros, Carmen Navarro, *Imelda Marcos*, St. Martins Press, New York, 1987.

Psinakis, Steve, *Two Terrorists Meet*, Alchemy Books, San Francisco, 1981.

Rempel, William C., *Delusions of a Dictator: The Mind of Marcos as Revealed in His Secret Diaries*, Little, Brown and Company, Boston, 1993.

Saulo, Alfredo B., *Communism in the Philippines*, Ateneo Publications Office, Manila, 1969.

Seagrave, Sterling, *The Marcos Dynasty*, Harper & Row, New York, 1988.

Thompson, Mark R., *The Anti-Marcos Struggle*, New Day Publishers, Manila, 1996.

Yabes, Criselda, *The Boys from the Barracks: The Philippine Military After EDSA*, Anvil Publishing, Manila, 1991.

Hong Kong:

Hughes, Richard, *Hong Kong: Borrowed Place – Borrowed Time*, Andre Deutsch, 1968.

Morris, Jan, *Hong Kong, Epilogue To An Empire*, Penguin, 1988.

Burma:

Butwell, Richard, *U Nu of Burma*, Stanford University Press, Stanford, 1963.

Trager, Frank N., *Burma from Kingdom to Republic, A Historical and Political Analysis*, Praeger, New York, 1966.

Woodman, Dorothy, *The Making of Burma*, The Cresset Press, London, 1962.

Thailand:

Busch, Noel F., *Thailand: An Introduction to Modern Siam*, D. Van Nostrad Company, 1964.

Darling, Frank C., *Thailand and the United States*, Public Affairs Press, Washington, 1965.

Lomax, Louis E., *Thailand: The War That Is, The War That Will Be*, Vintage Books, New York, 1967.

Riggs, Fred.W., *Thailand, the Modernisation of a Bureaucratic Polity*, East-West Center Press, Honolulu, 1966.

Silcock, T.H. (Ed), *Thailand: Social and Economic Studies in Development*, Australian National University Press, Canberra, 1967.

Wilson, David A., *Politics in Thailand*, Cornell University Press, New York, 1962

Malaysia:

Boyce, Peter, *Malaysia and Singapore in International Diplomacy: Documents and Commentaries*, Sydney University Press, 1968.

Brackman, Arnold C., *Southeast Asia's Second Front: The Power Struggle in the Malay Archipelago*, Praeger, New York, 1966.

Clutterbuck, Richard, *The Long War: The Emergency in Malaya 1948-1960*, Cassell, London, 1967.

Mahathir bin Mohamad, *The Malay Dilemma*, Asia Pacific Press, Singapore, 1970.

Rahman, Tunku Abdul, *May 13, Before and After*, Utusan Melayu Press, Kuala Lumpur, 1969.

Ryan, N.J., *The Cultural Background of the Peoples of Malaya*, Longmans, London, 1962.

Stewart, Ian, *The Mahathir Legacy: A nation divided, a region at risk*, Allen & Unwin, Sydney, 2003.

Tregonning, K.G., *Malaysia and Singapore*, Cheshire, Melbourne, 1964.

Van Der Kroef, Justus M., *Communism in Malaysia and Singapore: A Contemporary Survey*, Martinus Nijhoff, The Hague, 1967.

Singapore:

Huxley, Tim, *Defending the Lion City, The Armed Forces of Singapore*, Allen & Unwin, 2000.

Josey, Alex, *Democracy in Singapore: The 1970 By-Elections*, Asia Pacific Press, Singapore, 1970.

India:

Bhattacharyya, G.F., *M.N. Roy and Radical Humanism*, Wadia, Bombay, 1961.

B: JOURNAL and MAGAZINE ARTICLES, PAMPHLETS, PAPERS, DOCUMENTS, REPORTS and NEWSLETTERS

Vietnam and the Vietnam War

Douglas Pike, *The Viet-Cong Strategy of Terror*, the United States Mission, Viet-Nam, 1970.

Keesing's Research Report No. 5, *South Vietnam: A Political History 1954-1970*, Charles Scribner's Sons, New York, 1970.

Mount, Frank, "The Paris Agreement and the Future of Vietnam", *South-East Asian Spectrum*, Vol. 1, No. 3, April 1973, the journal of the South-East Asia Treaty Organisation (SEATO), Bangkok, Thailand (also produced unedited in the Pacific Institute's private circulation newsletter Pacific News, No. 53, April 1973).

Mount, Frank, "The Situation in Vietnam", *Quadrant*, Sept-Oct, 1970, Australian Association for Cultural Freedom, Sydney.

Mount, Frank, "Vietnam", A *News Weekly* pamphlet-supplement, Melbourne, June 1966.

Sheehan, Paul and others, *The Pentagon Papers*, Bantam Books, New York, 1971.

US State Department Documents on Vietnam War, Extensive Collection (Frank Mount Papers).

Regional Co-operation – Pacific Community, APEC, ASEAN

Mount Frank, *The Genesis of APEC, An Australian Viewpoint*, Occasional Paper Series, The United States Global Strategy Council, Washington, June 1994.

Mount, F.J., *Some Economic Aspects of the Pacific Community*, Proceedings of a Seminar on The Concept of a Pacific Community, Renown Press, Melbourne, March 1967.

Mount, Frank, "Australia, APEC and ASEAN: A Strategy for Australia", *Australia and World Affairs*, No. 36, Autumn 1998, Quarterly Journal of the Council for the National Interest, Melbourne.

Santamaria, B.A., "A Pacific Confederation", *Quadrant*, Number 21, Summer, 1962.

Santamaria, B.A., *A Pacific Community: The Basic Document*, Proceedings of a Seminar on The Concept of a Pacific Community, Renown Press, Melbourne, March 1967.

Southeast Asia – General

Documents on Australian Foreign Policy, Australia and the Indonesian Incorporation of Portuguese Timor 1974-1976, Department of Foreign Affairs and Trade, Canberra, Melbourne University Press, 2000.

Frank Mount, "The Prussians of Southeast Asia: Can They Be Stopped?", *Asian Affairs, An American Review*, Vol. 6, No. 6, July August, 1979, American-Asian Educational Exchange, New York.

Mount, Frank, "Indonesia: Forces of Instability", *Pacific Community*, Number 1, June 1969, Quarterly Journal of the Pacific Institute, The Hawthorn Press, Melbourne.

Mount, Frank, "Indonesia: Security and Defence Implications for the South-west Pacific", *Defender*, Vol. XV, No 2, Winter 1998, the National Journal of the Australia Defence Association, Melbourne.

Mount, Frank, "Indonesia: The 1971 Elections", *Pacific Community*, No. 7, Summer 1970, Quarterly Journal of The Pacific Institute, The Hawthorn Press, Melbourne.

Mount, Frank, "South-east Asia 1972: Year of the Rat", *News Weekly*, January 10, 1973 (whole issue), National Civic Council, Melbourne.

Mount, Frank, "South-East Asia's Global Strategic Context", *South-East Asian Spectrum*, Vol. 2, No. 4, July 1974, Journal of the South-East Asia Treaty Organisation (SEATO), Bangkok, Thailand.

Mount, Frank, "The Changing Church in the Philippines", *Social Survey*, March 1981, Journal of the Institute of Social Order, Melbourne.

Mount, Frank, "The Fading Mirage of the Promised 'Golden Era'; A Review of World Affairs", *News Weekly*, January 8, 1975, (whole issue), National Civic Council, Melbourne.

Mount, Frank, "The Philippines,1980", *Asian Affairs, An American Review*, Nov-Dec, 1980, American-Asian Educational Exchange, New York.

Mount, Frank, "The World and South-East Asia", *News Weekly*, January 9, 1974 (whole issue), National Civic Council, Melbourne.

Mount, Frank, "Malaysia: The May 13, Post-Election Riots", *Pacific Community*, Number 3, Summer, 1969, Quarterly Journal of the Pacific Institute, The Hawthorn Press, Melbourne.

Rodulfo, A.M., "Ethnic and Religious Minorities in South-East Asia", *Pacific Community* No. 5, Winter 1970, Quarterly Journal of the Pacific Institute, The Hawthorn Press, Melbourne.

Rodulfo, A.M., "Villages in the Shadow of China", *Pacific Community*, Number 2, Spring, 1969 Quarterly Journal of the Pacific Institute, The Hawthorn Press, Melbourne.

Serong, Brigadier F.P., "Communist Military Strategy and Doctrine in Southeast Asia", *Pacific Community*, Number 1, June 1969, Quarterly Journal of the Pacific Institute, The Hawthorn Press, Melbourne

Serong, F.P., "Urban Insurgency in South-East Asia", *South-East Asian Spectrum*, Vol. 2, No. 4, July 1974, journal of the South-East Asia Treaty Organisation (SEATO), Bangkok, Thailand.

China

China News Analysis, a weekly newsletter, produced by Laszlo La Dany SJ.

C: JOURNALS and MAGAZINES carrying articles on the Southeast Asian region over this period of potential interest to students of the region – a selection:

Asia Magazine (Hong Kong), *Current Affairs Bulletin* (Sydney), *Asian Affairs* (New York), *Asiaweek* (Hong Kong), *Australian Outlook* (AIIA, Melbourne), *Bulletin of Indonesian Economic Studies* (ANU Canberra), *Foreign Affairs* (New York), *Foreign Report* (*The Economist*, London), *Hemisphere* (Melbourne), *News Weekly* (Melbourne), *Orbis* (Philadelphia), *Pacific Affairs* (Vancouver), *Pacific Community* (Melbourne), *Quadrant* (Sydney), *Quest* (New Delhi), *Social Survey* (Melbourne), *Solidarity* (Manila), *South-East Asian Spectrum* (SEATO, Bangkok), *The Bulletin* (Sydney), *The Economist* (London), *The Far Eastern Economic Review* (Hong Kong), *To The Point International* (Antwerp), *Vietnam Digest* (Sydney),

D: PRIVATE PAPERS:

The Frank Mount Papers, including:

Correspondence between Frank Mount and Bob Santamaria, 1967-1986.

Confidential Reports to Bob Santamaria and other clients, 1967-72, 1972-2004.

Correspondence, general, 1967-81.

Frank Mount Diaries, 1960 – .

B.A. Santamaria files.

James McAuley files.

Ted Serong files.

Pacific Institute files.

Asia Pacific Report files.

Defend Australia Committee files.

DLP Files.

Wheat for India files.

Special Papers and Notes on countries and issues in the region.

Voluminous articles and newspaper/ magazine cuttings on the region and many of the persons mentioned in *Wrestling with Asia*.

Index

A Certain Grandeur: Gough Whitlam in Politics (Freudenberg), 344
AAP (Australian Associated Press), 168
ABRI (Armed Forces of Indonesia), 118, 122–124, 175, 239, 271–272, 274, 285
ABRI's Socio-Political Unit (SOSPOL), 122
Abu Bakar Bashir, 111, 115, 230, 265–268, 288
ACFOD (Asian Conference for Development), 291
Ackland, Michael, 154
Adenauer, Konrad, 17
ARVN Popular Forces (PF), 79
Agence France Presse (AFP), 79
Agent Orange, 99–100, 272
Aidit, Dipa Nusantara, 115
Air America, 44, 76, 85, 248
Air Defence Exercises (ADEXs), 211
Al Qa'ida, 111, 265–266
Albert, Charlie, 64, 108, 136
Alcoholics Synonymous, 157
ALP (Australian Labor Party), 17, 78, 82, 85, 113–115, 142–144, 191–194, 206, 262, 307–308, 310, 313–315, 324, 344, 346
ALP Club, Melbourne University, 78, 85, 113, 142–144, 315
Alwi, Des, 285
Ananda Bazaz Patrika, 46
Anderson, Sir John, 94, 311
Anglipay sect, 67

Anglipay, Gregorio, 67
Anglo-Malaysian Defence Agreement (AMDA), 54, 210
Anwar, Rosihan, 125
APEC (Asia Pacific Economic Cooperation), 6–7, 14, 112, 122, 183–199, 240, 327, 345
Appropriation Bills, 308
April 6 Liberation Movement (A6LM), 71
Aquino, Benigno (Ninoy), 71
Aquino, Benigno III, 74
Aquino, Cory, 66, 69, 71
Araneta, Rev. Francisco, 13, 64
Ardnt, Heinz, 120
Armed Forces of Indonesia (ABRI), 118, 122–124, 175, 239, 271–272, 274, 285
Arndt, Heinz, 190
Arthur, Lou, 51
ARVN Regional Forces (RF), 79
ASEAN (Association of Southeast Asian Nations), 6–8, 14, 54–57, 95, 112, 122, 135, 159, 185–188, 191, 195–197, 204, 237, 268, 294, 327
ASEAN East Asia Summit (EAS), 14, 196, 327
ASEAN Free Trade Area (AFTA), 186
ASEAN- Pacific Co-operation (APC), 190
ASEAN Regional Forum (ARF), 14
Asia and I (Holt), 40
Asia Foundation, 98, 181

Asia Pacific Economic Co-operation (APEC), 6–7, 14, 112, 122, 183–199, 240, 327, 345

Asia Pacific Report (APR), 66, 94, 241–242, 272, 277, 290–292, 325–328

Asia Pacific Strategy Council (APSC), 241–242

Asia Pacific Triangle, 187–189

Asian Bureau, 64, 254

Asian Development Bank (ADB), 7, 59, 159

Asian Financial Crash, 285

Asian Student Centre Melbourne, 27

Asintelhankam (Assistant for Intelligence, Hankam or Head, Indonesian Military Intelligence), 239

ASIS (Australian Secret Intelligence Service), 8, 147, 238

Asper, Tony, 268

ASPRI (Presidential Assistants), 119

Ateneo de Manila University, 63–64, 135, 253, 263

Atma Jaya University, 280

Austasia Consultants, 240

Austin, Dick, 51

Australian Army, 15, 17

Australian Army Jungle Training Centre, 17, 22

Australian Army Training Team Vietnam (AATTV), 18, 21, 141, 178

Australian Association for Cultural Freedom (ACF), 146, 148

Australian Business Group in the Philippines (ABG), 342

Australian Department of Defence, 241

Australian Joint Intelligence Organisation (JIO), 53

Australian Labor Party (ALP), 17, 64, 78, 82, 85, 113–115, 142–144, 157, 191–192, 262, 307–308, 310, 313–315, 324, 344, 346

Australian National University (ANU), 62, 149

Australian Secret Intelligence Service (ASIS), 8, 147, 238

Australian-Thai Chamber of Commerce, 142

Avila, Charles, 64, 108, 136, 138, 156

Ayres, Philip, 311, 313–314

B.A. Santamaria, Running the Show; Selected Documents; 1939-1996 (Morgan), 17, 313, 323, 346

B.A. Santamaria, Your Most Obedient Servant; Selected Letters:1938-1966 (Morgan), 114, 255

Bagong Alansang Makabayan (BAYAN), 65, 72, 335

BANDILA, 72–73

Bandung Institute of Technology (BIT), 293

Barich, John, 149

Barisan Sosialis Party, Singapore, 52

Barker, Garry, 53

Basis, Jesuit journal, 257

Batubara, Cosmas, 285

Bauer, Clyde, 75–76, 85, 101, 163, 170, 206, 248

Beech, Keyes, 159

Beek Organisation, The, 5, 253–263

Beek, Joop SJ (aka Jopie, Joseph), 5

Bjelke-Petersen, Joh, 346

Belo, Carlos, 258, 275

Bennett, Tony, 154

Bennetts, John, 53

Benson, Sam, 142

Berjaya (United Malaysian Peoples' Organisation), 107
Berkeley Mafia, 119
Bhadra, Sushil, 47
Binh Xuyen, 77
Birch, Michael, 168
Black Panther Company (Hac Bao Company), 174–175
Black Thursday, 279
Black Tuesday, 279
Blair, Anne, 18–19, 222
Bloodworth, Dennis, 53, 159, 181
Boom and Bust, 60
Bowan, John, 194
Bradman, Sir Donald, 56
Brando, Marlon, 83, 155
British Advisory Mission (BRIAM), 99
Broadbent, Margaret, 302
Brookes, Alfred, 237–238
Browning, Bob, 113, 130
Brynner, Yul, 157
Buckley, Brian, 309
Buckley, Vincent, 5, 142–144, 154
Buddhism, 36, 111
Bui Cong Tuong, 245–246, 249
Bui Diem, 213–214
Bui Tin, 95
Bunker, Ellsworth, 212
Burchett Wilfred, 139, 245–251
Burdick, Eugene, 83
Burgess, Guy, 3, 157
Burma, 18, 23, 26–27, 32–33, 43
Burton, Sandra, 71
Bush, President George, 325–328
Cabot Lodge, Henry, 18
Caduad (Strategic Reserve), 17

Cairns Group, 186, 192
Cairns, Jim, 9, 85, 141, 307–308
Cameron, Clyde, 85
Camm, Henry, 159
Can Lao Party, 25, 83
Cantwell, John, 168
Cao Dai, 78, 84
Cao Van Vien, 247
Carlton ALP Branch, 143
Carroll, John, 314
Catholic Action, 17, 65, 253, 255, 261
Cawthorn, Sir Walter (Bill), 8–9, 11, 47, 136, 199
Census, Grievance and Revolutionary Development Cadre Program, 79
Central Intelligence Agency (CIA), 8, 18–20, 34, 44, 68, 76, 80–81, 85–87, 98, 121, 148, 185, 202, 220, 238, 241, 245–251, 291, 307–310, 326
Centre for Strategic & International Studies (CSIS), Indonesia, 122, 124–125, 184, 187–189, 191, 193, 195, 231–232, 235–236, 262–263, 267, 269, 281–282, 285, 288, 291, 298, 300
Chamberlin, Sir Michael, 51
Chanoff, David, 214
Chantarasay, Tienthone, 41, 147
Charter Change (Cha Cha), 74
Chat Chavangkul, General, 31, 181
Cheviot Beach, 145
Chieu Hoi (Open Arms) Program, 81
Chin Peng, 98
China News Analysis, 333
Christian Social Movement (CSM), Philippines, 5, 64
Christian Social Week, 6

CIA (Central Intelligence Agency), 8, 18–20, 34, 44, 68, 76, 80–81, 85–87, 98, 121, 148, 185, 202, 220, 238, 241, 245–251, 291, 307–310, 326

CIA Directorate of Intelligence, 80

CIA Weekly Summary, 80, 87

Civil Air Transport (CAT), 76

Clark, Cecilia, 59, 61, 63

Clark, Christopher, 59, 197

Clark, Colin, 5, 8, 47, 49, 59–63, 108, 132, 136, 138, 153, 186, 190, 346

Clark, Manning, 312

Cline, Ray, 185, 202, 230, 241, 248

Cockburn Sound, 344

Codd, Mike, 194

Cody, Matt, 51

Coffey, Ray, 159

Commission on Elections (COMELEC), 71

Communism and Democracy in Australia (Webb), 97–98

Communist China, 44, 46, 82

Communist Party of China (CPP), 77

Conditions of Economic Progress (Clark), 60–61

Congress for the Defence of Australia (CDA), 9

Connery, Sean, 157

Connolly, Richard, 152

Connor, Rex, 307

Control Risks, 237

CORDS (U.S. Civil Operations and Revolutionary Development Support), 20

Cosgrove, Peter, 88

COSVN (North Vietnam's Central Office South Vietnam), 91–92, 220

COSVN Resolution 12, 217–218

Counter-insurgency (CI), 4, 18, 20–21, 56, 78, 81, 88, 95, 98–100, 132, 166, 170, 272, 326–327

Country Party, 148

Crawford, Sir John, 62, 120, 162, 189–190

Crowe, Bill, 344

Crozier, Brian, 177–178

Crozier, Laurie, 177, 180

Cultural Revolution, 334

D'Alpuget, Blanche, 193–194

Dai Viet, 78, 84

Dalamal & Sons, 307

Damaged Men: The Precarious Lives of James McAuley and Harold Stewart, 154

Dan Chu Party, 89, 202, 204

Dan Tu Do (Freedom or Tu Do Party), 89

Danaher, Tom, 51

Dang Dan Chu (Democratic or Dan Chu Party), 89

Dang Van Quang, 89, 208, 247

Dang Van Sung, 87

Darling, Frank C., 197

Darul Islam, 254, 265

David, Neil, 82

Davies, Bruce, 19

Davies, Derek, 49

Davis, Neil, 82

De Gasperi, Alcide, 17

de la Costa, Rev. Horacio, 8, 13, 57, 63–64, 70, 108, 135, 332, 335

De Silva, Jack, 24–25, 57, 165–169

Defence Intelligence Organisation (DIO), 76, 85

Defend Australia Committee (DAC), 4, 9–10, 54, 77, 85, 138–143, 145, 149, 152, 311, 343, 366

Deliverance: The Inside Story of East Timor's Fight for Freedom (Greenless & Garran), 277
Democratic Action Party (DAP), 55–56
Democratic Labor Party (DLP), 4–5, 17, 27, 45, 77, 138, 141–143, 145, 149, 152, 157, 191, 206, 221, 245, 313, 315, 324, 343–345, 347, 366
Diponegoro Division, 117, 295, 297
District Intelligence Operations Coordination Centers (DIOCC), 79
Djiwandono, Soedjati, 109, 122, 125, 189
Djojohadikusomo, 119
DLP Club (Melbourne University Democratic Labor Party Club), 45, 78, 143, 315, 343
DLP Victorian State Executive, 4, 138, 343
Dommen, Arthur, 159
DPP (Democratic Progressive Party), 332
DPR (House of Representatives), 288
Draw, Henry, 225
Drysdale, Peter, 120
Duke of Gloucester Ball, 104
Duncanson, Denis, 159
Dutch East India Company, 105
Dutch Television, 39, 125, 147
Dwipayana, G., 124

East Asia Summit (EAS), 14, 196, 327
East Timor, 53, 111, 120, 169, 204, 229, 247, 258, 269–277, 283, 289, 296, 326
Edhie, Sarwo, 115, 117, 285
Elegant, Robert, 19, 158, 160
Enrile, Juan Ponce, 71
Ern Malley Hoax, 150
Evans, Graham, 94

Evans, Ray, 142
Ex Bersama Padu, 211

Fairbairn, Geoffrey, 47, 54, 149, 153, 156–157, 312
FAO (Food and Agriculture Organisation), 291
Far Eastern Economic Review, 26, 49, 126
Farrago, 78, 96
Federated Clerks' Union, 191, 310
Federated Ironworkers' Association, 142
Federation of Free Farmers (FFF), Philippines, 5, 62, 64, 138, 254
Federation of Free Workers (FFW), 8, 64, 254, 268
Feith, Herb, 6
Fernandez, Sosthene, 181, 317
Fernando, Rev. Dudley, 49
Ferrier, Noel, 281
Fighting Words, 9
Five Power Defence Arrangements (FPDA), 95, 210–212
Fleming, Ian, 157
Focus (DLP journal), 245
Ford, Gerald President, 206, 269
Ford, Maggie, 292
Foreign Affairs, 49
Forrest, Henry SJ, 317, 333
Forum Demokrasi, 286
Four Corners, 9, 138
Frank Mount Papers, 24, 83, 89, 93, 136–137, 198, 206, 208, 216, 221, 246, 250, 257–261, 271, 274, 301, 303
Frankel, Peter, 139–142
Fraser, Malcolm, 147, 189–190, 308–315
Freudenberg, Graham, 343–344

Functional Groups (Sekber Golkar), 122, 257

Gair, Vince, 60, 245, 251
Garnaut, Ross, 190, 192, 194–195, 231
Garran, Robert, 277
Gartner, John, 51, 197
Geldorp, Rev, 257
General Agreement on Tariffs and Trade (GATT), 186, 192
Geneva Agreement 1962, 40
Gerakan Party, 55–56
Gibson, Donald, 33
Gibson, Mel, 281
Glang, Alunan, 230
Gleeson, Eileen, 33, 201
Golden, Jerry SJ, 143–144
Golkar, 70, 122–123, 259, 261, 284
Golkar Party, 8, 257, 286–287, 289
Gomez, Felipe SJ, 335
Gonzales, Norberto, 137, 268
Gorton, John, 148–149, 311
Green, Marshall, 213
Greene, Graham, 16, 83
Greenlees, Don, 277
Groupers, 157
Gumelar, Agum, 274, 285, 289–290

Ha Nhu Chi, 84, 203, 206
Habibie, B.J., 262, 275–276, 283, 285, 287, 290
Haig, Alexander, 93, 212–213, 224–227
Ham, Paul, 19, 21, 79, 141
HANKAM (Department of Defence & Security), 274, 282–283, 285
Hanoi Politburo, 218

Harian Kompas, 125, 204
Harkins, Paul D., 18
Harmoko, 284
Harper Smith, Patrick, 249
Harradine, Brian, 347
Harries, Owen, 139
Harriman, Averell, 40, 43, 96, 219, 319
Hartono, Raden, 284, 287, 289
Hasan, Bob, 284
Hasluck, Paul, 149
Hastings, Peter, 158
Hawke: The Prime Minister (D'Alpuget), 193
Hawthorn Press, 197
Hayden, Bill, 314
Hayes, Eric, 327
Henderson, Dikko, 157
Henderson, Gerard, 323
Highways to a War (Koch), 82, 97
Hitchcock, Alfred, 157
Hitchcock, Lionel, 21–22
HMI (Himpunan Mahasiswa Islam or Islamic Students' Association), 282
Hmong, 84
Ho Chi Minh, 46, 319, 329–330
Ho Chi Minh Trail, 35, 44, 82, 93, 95–96, 180, 305, 319
Hoa Hao, 78, 84
Hoang Duc Nha, 89, 221, 246
Hoemardani, Soedjono, 109, 115, 117, 119–122, 187, 189, 204, 235, 285, 295, 297–300
Hollway, Sandy, 193–194
Holt, Estelle, 40, 42
Holt, Harold, 144–149
Honey, P.J., 197
Honey, Patrick, 159

Hook, Don, 158
Horwood, John, 113, 130
Howard, John, 276–277
Hua Guofeng, 334
Huber, Rev., 257–258
Hughes, Richard, 156–159, 281
Hung, N.T., 213
Hyland, Keith, 98, 177, 199, 206, 221

ICMI (Indonesian Association of Muslim Scholars), 287, 289
Idris, Kemal, 115, 285
IGGI (International Governmental Group on Indonesia), 119
IMF (International Monetary Fund), 291
Impossible Dream: The Marcoses, The Aquinos and the Unfinished Revolution (Burton), 71
In the Huon Valley (McAuley), 151
Indian Communist Party, 46
Indonesia in Regional and International Cooperation: Principles of Implementation and Construction (Moertopo), 188
Indonesian Armed Forces (ABRI later TNI), 271, 274–276, 279, 283
Indonesian Catholic Party (Partai Katolik), 120, 123, 254
Indonesian Communist Party (PKI), 8, 94–95, 109, 113–117, 121, 254–255, 259
Indonesian State Intelligence Coordinating Board (BAKIN), 24, 119, 123, 125, 239, 259, 282, 293, 298
Indonesian Students' Action Front (KAMI), 113
Inner Circles, How America Changed the World: A Memoir (Haig), 93
Institute of Social Order – Australia, 6
Institute of Social Order (ISO), 64, 254

Integrated Air Defence System (IADS), 210–211
INTERFET (International Force East Timor), 276–277
Internal Security Department (ISD), Singapore (Special Branch), 204
International Control Commission (ICC), 41
Islamism, 266, 326
ISO (Institute of Social Order), 64, 254

James, Frank, 51
Jemaah Islamiyah, 265
Jess, John, 140
Joeseof, Daoed, 122
Joewono, Clara, 189
Johnson, Lyndon President, 146–147, 203
Johnson, U Alexis, 213–214
Jose, Francisco Sionel (Frankie), 58
Josey, Alex, 53, 181, 197
Journey Without Arrival: The Life and Writing of Vincent Buckley (McLaren), 143
Jusuf, Mohammad, 239

Kamayaan, 156
Kampi (Partner of the Free Filipinos), 156
Kane, Jack, 245–246, 251
Karennis, 27, 31
Karnow, Stanley, 21–22, 80–81
Kebatinan sect, 67
Kelly, Peter, 149
Kennedy, Robert, 95
Kent-Hughes, Sir Wilfred, 140, 145, 211, 311
Kerr, Sir John, 308
Keynes, John Maynard, 60–61, 132

Khalid Shaikh Mohammad, 230
Khemlani Affair, 308, 310
Khemlani, Tirath Hassaram, 307–310
Khmer National Armed Forces (FANK), 317
Khmer Rouge, 45, 94, 173, 228, 304
Khoman, Thanat, 39, 147
Kilcullen, David, 18, 326
King of Malaysia, Sultan of Kedah, 107
Kintner, William, 248
Kissinger, Henry, 21, 82, 99, 204–205, 212–214, 216, 226, 269, 293, 334
Klausner, Bill, 98, 181
KMT (Kuomintang), 332
Knopfelmacher, Frank, 5, 17, 47, 78, 140, 158, 315, 344
Koch, Christopher, 82, 97, 281
Koch, Phil, 158
Koestler, Arthur, 315
Kolko, Gabriel, 175–176
Konfrontasi, 117, 209
Kopkamtib (Operational Command for the Restoration of Security and Order), 123, 239
Kostrad (Army Strategic Reserve), 116, 274, 283, 285, 289, 297
Kouprasith Abhay, General, 42
Kraal, Ivor, 105
Kristiadi, Joseph, 281
Krygier, Richard, 146, 148
Kun Vououraj, 43
Kurukulasuriya, Giom, 49
Kusumaatmadja, Mochtar, 190

La Dany, Laszlo SJ, 333–334
Lagdameo, Luis Amado, 64
Lakas-CMD (Lakas- Christian Muslim Democrats), 156
Lambert, Ted, 101
Lambino, Antonio SJ, 335
Langford, Mike, 82
Laramy, Ronald, 169
Latif, Widya, 119
Lauritz, Norm, 347
Le Carre, John, 157
Le Duc Tho, 212–213
Leck Vanich Angkhul, 29, 57, 102, 142, 337
Lederer, William J., 83
Lee Kuan Yew, 51, 69, 147, 171
Lewis, Sir Arthur, 61
Liberal International, 113
Liberal Party of Australia (LP), 27, 32, 138, 140–141, 148–149, 190, 210, 221, 308–309, 312–314, 343–344
Liberation Theology, 69–70, 73, 334–335
Light-A-Fire Movement, 229
Lim Bian Kie (Jusuf Wanandi), 108, 120, 136, 204, 255–257, 260, 262
Lim Bian Koen (Sofyan Wanandi), 120, 298
Lim Kit Siang, 55–56
Lim Sioe Liong, 295
Lim Yew Hock, 52
Lomas, Frederick, 17, 22
Lon Nol, 181, 305, 317–322
Lopulissa, Leo, 274
Los Angeles Times, 158, 292
Lubis, Mochtar, 53, 125
Lunn, Hugh, 158
Lynch, Phillip, 140, 309
Lynched (Buckley), 309

Macapagal, Diosdado, 14, 68

Macapagal-Arroyo, Gloria, 68, 74, 108, 137, 156, 268
MacDonald, Ramsay, 60–61
Machmud, Amir, 259
Maclean, Donald, 3, 157
MACV (US Military Assistance Command Vietnam), 20, 165, 167
Madden, Ted, 148
Malaysian Chinese Association (MCA), 102, 136
Malcolm Fraser, A Biography (Ayres), 311
Malcolm Fraser: The Political Memoirs (Fraser and Simons), 311, 314
Malik, Adam, 39, 125, 147, 301
Manahan, Manuel, 64, 136
Manglapus, Raul, 5, 8, 13–14, 64, 66, 108, 136
Manne, Robert, 314
Mannix, Daniel, Archbishop, 144
Mao Tse Tung, 334
MAPHILINDO, 14
Marcos, Ferdinand, 67
Marcos, Mariano, 67–68
Mastura, Michael, 230
Matak, Prince Sirik, 44, 181, 228, 317–322
May, Brian, 261–262
Maynes, John, 9, 47, 140, 191–192, 309–310, 323–324, 345, 347
McArthur, George, 159
McAuley, James, 5, 144, 150–154
McAuley, Katherine, 150
McAuley, Norma, 150, 152
McAuley, Philip, 150
McCawley, Peter, 120
McClelland, 'Diamond' Jim, 310
McCoy, Alfred, 44

McEwen, John, 148
McGovern, Rev. SJ, 332
McKay, Gary, 19
McLaren, John, 143
McMahon, William, 210–211, 301
McNamara, Robert, 76, 99
Megawati, Sukarnoputri, 286, 288, 290
Melbank, 347
Melbourne Club, 8, 138, 238
Melbourne University Newman Society, 143
Mendis, Noel, 49
Menik, Mrs, 281
Menzies, Robert, 312
Menzies, Sir Robert, 145, 312
Meray, Tibor, 251
Mercer, Gerald, 140, 347
Merrick, Ron, 101
Mexican Communist Party, 46
MI6 (British Secret Intelligence Service – SIS), 15, 23, 130, 158, 320
Miller, Keith, 312
Minh 'Big', 87, 223
Moerdani, L.B. (Benny), 24–25, 109, 117, 124–125, 232, 239, 261–262, 266, 269, 271, 273–274, 283, 285–287, 289–290, 296, 299–300, 325
Moertopo, Ali, 14, 24–25, 53, 55, 109, 115–122, 124–125, 134, 184, 187–190, 209, 230, 235, 247, 255, 257–263, 265–268, 271, 273, 282, 285, 293–296, 298–302
Mohammad, Goenawan, 125
Mojuntin, Peter, 107–108
Molyneux, Bing, 51
Montemayor, Jeremias (Jerry), 5, 8, 13–14, 62–64, 66, 108, 136, 138
Moorabbin News, 81

Morgan, Patrick, 17, 86, 113–114, 139, 142, 207–208, 255, 313, 323, 346
Morley, Robert, 157
Morris, Malcolm, 199
Morse, Bob, 101
Mounier, Emmanuel, 84
Mount, Eileen, 131
Mount, Frank, senior, (author's father) 51
Mount, Lucy, 237
Mount, Patrick, 237
Muhammadiyah, 254
Murphy & Moloney, solicitors, 246
Murphy, Lionel, 307
Murray, Robert, 17
Mustapha, Tun, 106–107, 273
Myint, John, 26, 32, 39, 45, 113, 181, 201
Myint, Terry, 27, 31–32
Myrdal, Gunnar, 61

Na Champassak, Sisouk, 41, 57, 147
Nadhlatul Ulama (NU), 53, 116
Naro, Johnny, 125, 262
Nasution, Abdul Haris, 115, 117–118
Nathan, S.R., 53, 183, 204, 247, 273
National Catholic News Agency (NCNA), 181
National Civic Council (NCC), 3–4, 10, 17, 27, 46, 140–142, 150, 221, 228, 237, 254, 270, 310, 313–315, 323–324, 344–345, 347
National Democratic Front (NDF), 65, 72
National Liberation Front (NLF), 218
National Movement for Free Elections (Namfrel), 71
National Party, 313, 346

National Social Democratic Front (NSDF), 87
Nationalista Party, 70
Ne Win, General, 26–27, 31
New People's Army (NPA), 65, 68, 72
New Society Movement (KBL), 70
New South Wales Labor Party, 142
New York Times, 175
New Yorker, 158
Newman College, 143–144
News Weekly, 3–4, 10–11, 53, 100, 104, 126, 145, 147–148, 220, 240, 270, 324, 343
Newsweek, 49
Ngo Dinh Diem, President, 15, 25, 83, 85, 173, 179, 213
Ngo Dinh Nhu, 83
Ngo Dinh Thi Hiep, Elizabeth, 173
Ngo Khac Tinh, 8, 25, 57, 84, 86–89, 108, 133, 136, 164, 170, 172, 174, 176, 184, 228, 236, 247, 251, 317, 329
Ngo Quang Truong, 207
Ngo Quoc "Mike' Phong, 203
Nguyen Cao Ky, 24, 88
Nguyen Ngoc Bich, 246
Nguyen Ngoc Linh, 199, 203, 246
Nguyen Ngoc Phac, 246
Nguyen Thi Dinh, Madame, 225
Nguyen Van Chau, 90, 203
Nguyen Van Ngan, 89
Nguyen Van Thieu, President, 8, 24, 69
Nguyen Van Thuan, Bishop (later Cardinal), 25, 85, 132
Nhan-Xa Party, 8, 19, 25, 75–98, 133–134, 136, 139, 164–165, 169–181, 205, 208–209, 235–236
Nitisastro, Widjojo, 301

Nixon, Richard President, 93, 204–206, 213–214, 216
No Exit from Vietnam (Robert Thompson), 180
Nolting, Frederick, 18
Noone, Dick, 98
North Vietnam, 9, 20, 41, 44, 90, 93, 96, 141, 165, 180, 185, 208, 212
North Vietnamese Army (NVA), 22–23, 44, 79–83, 88–89, 91–92, 97, 141, 163–167, 169, 171–175, 177, 179–180, 201–202, 207, 213, 216–220, 319–320, 322
Nung, ethnic group, 178–179
NVA Easter 1972 Offensive, 82

O'Brien, Paddy, 142
O'Connor, Rev. Patrick, 181
Ohira, Masayoshi, 189
Ojong, P.K., 125–126, 204
Old Craw, 157
On Burchett (Meray), 251
On the Other Side: 23 Days with the Viet Cong (Webb), 97
ONA (Office of National Assessments), 238–242
Ondaatje, Michael, 49
Operation Komodo, 273
Operation Seroja, 273
OPSUS (Army's Special Operations), 24, 117–119, 123–124, 134, 257, 260, 293, 298
Ortiz, Rev. Pacifico, 64, 108
Orwell, George, 315
Osborne, Milton, 7, 106, 320
Oudone Sananikone, General, 40
Ouane Rattikone, General, 42–43

Ours to Share, An Approach to Philippine Social Problems (Montemayor), 63

Pacific Affairs, 49
Pacific Basin Economic Council (PBEC), 189
Pacific Community, 3, 6–7, 11, 53–54, 62, 135, 137, 145, 184, 189–191, 195–198, 203, 348
Pacific Destiny: Inside Asia Today (Elegant), 160
Pacific Economic Co-operation Council (PECC), 14, 184, 189–192, 195
Pacific Institute, 1–242
Pacific Institute: Vietnam Chapter, 199
Pacific News, 197
Pacific Trade and Development Conference (PAFTAD), 189
Pacification Program, 16, 81, 83, 209
Packer, Sir Frank, 51
Palmos, Frank, 169
Pangestu, Mari, 189
Papal encyclicals, 17
Paris Agreement, January, 1973, 21, 91, 93, 212, 217–219
Paris Peace Accords, 82
Parkindo, 123
Partai Katolik, 120, 123, 254
Partai Nasional Indonesia (PNI), 123
Partai Sosialis Indonesia (PSI), 123, 254, 258–259
Pasquarelli, Jack, 237
Pathet Lao (PL), 40–41, 44, 339
Pattani United Liberation Organisation (PULO), 102, 337
PDI (Indonesian Democratic Party), 123, 286, 288, 290

PDI-P (Indonesian Democratic Party-Struggle), 290
Peace with Freedom (PWF), 10, 61, 138, 149
Peacock, Andrew, 140
Pelaez, Manuel, 64, 108
Pentagon, The, 20, 220, 326
People's Action Party (PAP), Singapore, 52
People's Daily, 95
People's Liberation Army (PLA) in Vietnam, 20
People's Progressive Party (PPP), 64, 66, 123, 125, 286, 288–289
Perfectly Frank (Bennett), 154
Peter Mojuntin, the golden son of the Kadazan (Sta. Maria), 107
Petersen, Barry, 178
Petreaus, David, 18
Pham Van Dong, 89, 178, 199
Phan Quang Dan, 199, 250
Philippine Communist Party (CPP), 65, 72–73, 77
Philippine National Intelligence & Security Authority (NISA), 64, 108, 136
Phoenix Program, The, 8, 15, 21, 79, 132, 163
Phoumi Nosavan, General (Ret), 42, 101, 339
Phung Nhat Minh, 199
Pierce, Eric, 146
Pigott, Bruce, 168
Pike, Douglas, 248
Pizzinelli, Corrado, 176
PKI (Indonesian Communist Party), 8, 94–95, 109, 113–117, 121, 254–255, 259

Pohla, Patrick, 21–23, 32, 130, 163
Pol Pot, 21, 45, 94, 228
Police Field Force (PFF), 16, 21–23, 76, 81, 130, 132, 170, 181
Polkam (Co-ordinating Ministry for Politics & Security), 283
Port Phillip Coast Guard Auxiliary, 148
Portrait of a Cold Warrior (Smith), 68
PPP (United Development Party), 286
Prabowo Subianto, 283, 285, 289–290
Pramoj, Kukrit, 159
Pranarka, A.M.W., 281
Prapat Charusatien, 36
Prawiro, Radius, 119
Pringowirono, Colonel, 282
Progressive Party of the Philippines (PPP), 64, 66, 123, 125, 288–289
Provincial Reconnaissance Units (PRU), 79, 81
PSI (Indonesian Socialist Party), 123, 254, 258–259
PULO (Pattani United Liberation Organisation), 102, 337
PWHCE (Perspectives on World History and Current Events) website PWHCE.org, 327
Pybus, Cassandra, 154

Quadrant, 6, 144

Race, Jeffrey, 197
Radical Humanist Society, 46–47
Radical Islam, 230, 241, 259, 265–266, 290, 326
Radical Liberation Theology, 73, 334
Rahman, Tunku Abdul, 55, 103, 106
Rais, Amien, 290

Rajaratnam, Sinathamby, 39, 53, 273
Ramadhan, K.H., 124
Ramos, Fidel, 69–71
Ramos, Narciso, 147
Rationalist Society, 315
Ray, Sibnarayan, 5, 343
Reform the Armed Forces Movement (RAM), 71–72
Region of Revolt: Focus on Southeast Asia (Osborne), 7
Rerum Novarum, 66, 254, 332
Rerum Novarum Labor Center, 332
Reuters, 169, 219
Revolutionary Guerrilla Warfare, 78, 100
Riggs, Fred. W., 36
Rochlen, Don, 248
Rodulfo, Algernon Montague ('Monty'), 15, 22, 47, 99, 130, 158, 163, 169, 176–177, 197, 320
Roh Tae-woo, President, 194
Romulo, Carlos P., 39, 138, 273
Rostow, W.W., 61
Roy, M.N., 46–47
Royal Laotian Government (RLG), 40, 42–43
Rubinstein, Arthur, 151
Rukmana, Siti Hardiyanti 'Tutut', 284, 287
Running in the Family (Ondaatje), 49
Ryan, John, 220
Salim, Emil, 119
Salleh, Datuk Seri Harris, 107
Samuel, Peter, 60, 146, 149, 245, 251
San Juan, Rev Vicente, 64
Sanders, Sol, 94, 159
Sanderson, John, 94
Santa Cruz Massacre, 283

Santamaria, Anne, 131
Santamaria, B.A. (Bob), 3, 9, 11, 16–17, 26–27, 39, 42, 49, 51, 53, 57, 60, 62, 77, 83, 86, 88–89, 108, 113, 129, 131, 136, 139, 141, 145, 147–148, 153, 157, 183, 187, 189, 191, 194–195, 206–207, 210, 212, 216, 221–222, 228, 230, 237–238, 245, 250, 255, 258, 262, 269–270, 302, 309, 311, 317, 323, 341, 343–348
Santamaria, Bernadette, 139
Santamaria, Helen, 131, 183, 206–207, 312
Scalapino, Robert, 159
Schecter, Jerrold L., 213
Schumann, Robert, 17
Sea Lanes of Communication (SLOCS), 6, 54, 112, 186–187, 212, 272, 327
Seagrave, Sterling, 68
Second Indo-China War, 76, 319
Secret Intelligence Service (SIS), 23, 130
Security Challenges (Thayer), 212
Senanayake, Dudlay, 49, 60
Serong, Francis Philip ('Ted'), 8–9, 15, 17–18, 22, 57, 75, 77, 81, 83, 86, 90, 95–96, 130–131, 137, 151, 154, 163, 165–166, 169, 177–178, 180, 187, 199, 202–203, 206, 208, 216, 220, 222, 228, 230, 234, 245, 248–249, 303, 317, 320, 323
Severino, Rodolfo, Jnr, 197
Shafie, Ghazali, 14, 54, 135, 260
Shan State Army (SSA), 28, 33, 181
Shaplen, Robert, 158
Shawcross, William, 319
Shinawatra, Thaksin, 37
Shop Distributive & Allied Employees Association (SDA), 191
Short, Laurie, 142

Sihanouk, Prince Norodom, 303
Sihanouk, Prince of Light, Prince of Darkness (Osborne), 320
Silalahi, Harry Tjan, 47, 109, 122, 125, 193, 232
Sin, Jaime Cardinal, 70
Sinatra, Frank, 154
Singapore Foreign Intelligence (SID), 53, 204, 273
Sirik Matak, Prince, 44, 181, 228, 317–322
Sisouk na Champassak, 41, 57, 147
SLOCS (Sea Lanes of Communication), 6, 54, 112, 186–187, 212, 272, 327
Smith, Joseph, 68
Smith, Rev. W.G. (Bill), 6, 131, 136, 183, 197, 206, 317–318, 321
Soe Hok Djie, 285
Soeharto, 25, 62, 69, 109, 115–119, 120, 122–124, 171, 187, 209, 259, 262, 266, 269, 273–275, 279, 282–291, 293–295, 297–298, 300–302, 325–326
Soeharto, President, 14, 67, 134, 187, 190, 235, 296, 301
Soeharto: My Thoughts, Words and Deeds, An Autobiography (Soeharto), 124, 300
Soemitro, General, 123–124
Soerono, 274
Soesastro, Hadi, 122, 189, 267, 282
Solidaridad Bookshop, 58
Solidarity journal, 58
Soliven, Maximo, 63
Sophia University, 332
SOSPOL (Indonesian military's Social & Political Affairs Department), 122, 290
South East Asia in Turmoil (B. Crozier), 178
South Vietnam, 8–9, 16, 18–19, 24, 41, 44, 51–52, 77, 79–84, 86, 88, 90–95, 99, 108, 129–131, 133, 134, 136, 139, 147, 149, 155–156, 165, 167, 170, 178–180, 184, 191, 202–203, 205–208, 212–213, 215–216, 218–219, 222–223, 226, 236, 247, 251, 254, 271–272, 282, 319–320, 329–330, 346
South Vietnamese Government (GVN), 23, 216, 218
South Vietnamese Military Intelligence, 247
Southeast Asia Treaty Organisation (SEATO), 98, 362
Souvanna Phouma, Prince and Prime Minister, 40
Souvanna Phouma, Prince Panya, 40–41
Soviet Comintern, 46, 77
Soviet Union, 73, 77–78, 82, 92–94, 96, 215, 272, 335, 345
Special Branch, Thailand, 30–32
Special Operations (OPSUS) – ABRI Indonesia, 24, 117–119, 123–124, 134, 257, 260, 293, 298
Spectrum (SEATO), 98
Springsteen, Bruce, 154
Spry, Charles, 147
Sta. Maria, Bernard, 108
Stanford University, 101
Stephens, Dato Donald, 106–107
Storm Over Laos, A Contemporary History (Sisouk), 41
Strong, Ben, 225
Students' Representative Council (SRC), 78
Subchan, Zainuri Echsan, 114
Sugama, Yoga, 117, 119, 125
Sullivan, William H., 213, 219–220
Sulong, Zainal, 247
Supersemar, 118

Suryo, 119
Sydney Morning Herald, 169

Tai, Paul, 102, 136
Tan Chee Khoon, 55
Tan, Juan C. (Johnny), 8, 47, 64, 108, 136
Tanaka, Kakuei, 124
Tanham, George, 98, 181
Tanjung, Feisal, 283, 287, 289, 296
Taruc, Luis, 138
Tawi Sli, Datuk Pemghuli, 105
Tay Seoh Huah, 53
Taylor, Maxwell, 214
Taylor, Rosemary, 86
Ted Serong: The Life of an Australian Counter-Insurgency Expert (Blair), 18
Tempo magazine, 286
Tet Offensive, 1968, 19, 23, 79–81, 92, 97, 133, 149, 156, 163–181, 203, 319
Thai Border Patrol Police (BPP), 101
Thai Intelligence, 29–30
Thai Special Branch, 32
Thailand: The Modernization of a Bureaucratic Polity (Riggs), 36–37
Thanh Thai, Emperor, 173
Thanom Kittickachorn, 36
Thayer, Carlyle, 211–212
The Age, Melbourne, 308
The Anti-Marcos Struggle: Personalistic Rule and Democratic Transition in the Philippines (Thompson), 71
The Australian Security Intelligence Organisation (ASIO), 147, 267, 310
The Devil and James McAuley (Pybus), 354
The Economist, 49, 178, 326
The General Theory of Employment, Interest and Money (Keynes), 60

The Good Life (Bennett), 154
The Hawke Memoirs (Hawke), 192
The Hindu, 46
The Hindustan Standard, 46
The Honourable Schoolboy (Le Carre), 157
The Indonesian Tragedy (May), 261
The Jaws of History (Diem & Chanoff), 214
The Marcos Dynasty (Seagrave), 68
The Men Who Persevered (Davies and McKay), 19
The National Income of Australia (Clark and Crawford), 62
The Observer, 53
The Palace File (Hung & Schecter), 213
The Politics of Heroin in Southeast Asia (McCoy), 44
The Quiet American (Greene), 16, 83
The Radical Humanist, 46–47
The Santamaria Papers (National Library of Victoria), 83, 311
The Split: Australian Labor in the Fifties (Murray), 17
The Statesman, 46–47
The Straits Times, 55
The Times of India, 46
The Ugly American (Burdick and Lederer), 83
The Way of Hope (Thuan), 228
The Wild One film, 155
The Year of Living Dangerously (Koch), 18
There to the Bitter End: Ted Serong in Vietnam (Blair), 18
Thompson, Mark R., 71, 229
Thompson, Robert, 98–100, 132, 180, 216
Thomson, George, 52–54, 57, 137, 181, 247, 273
Thought, 46
Time, 168

Tifverman, Larry, 248
Tjan, Harry (also Harry Tjan Silalahi), 47, 53, 109, 120, 122, 125, 137, 193, 204, 232, 239, 247, 255, 257, 262, 268–271, 273–274, 281–282, 285, 287, 289, 297, 321
To Minh Trung, 249
Tobin, Terry, 139
Tommy Makin and the Clancy Brothers, 144
Ton That Dinh, 15
Ton That Thien, 159, 197
Too, C.C., 102–106
Trager, Frank N., 197
Traill, John, 246, 249–250
Tran Kim Phuong, 199, 204
Tran Ngoc Phung, 226, 228
Tran Quoc Buu, 202–203
Tran Thien Khiem, 205, 207, 250
Tran Van Do, 147
Tran Van Dong, 89
Tran Van Lam, 15, 25, 87, 89, 129, 164, 177, 199, 204, 207, 213, 247, 249, 317
Tribal Research Centre, Thailand, 33
Trisakti University, 279–280
Trumbull, Robert, 159
Truong Cong Cuu, 25, 57, 83, 108, 133, 136, 170, 172, 176, 235
Tun Abdul Razak, 55
Tung, Major, 174–175

U.S. Consulate, Melbourne, 85
U.S. Global Strategy Council, 184, 195, 241
U.S. National Security Committee, 95
U.S. Special Forces Intelligence, 101
U.S. State Department, 20, 76, 205
United National Kadazan Organisation (UNKO), 106
United Press International (UPI), 19, 97, 104, 321
United Sabah National Organisation (USNO), 106–107
United States Aid (USAID), 34, 43, 76, 85
United States Global Strategy Council (GSC), 184, 195, 241
United States Information Service (USIS), 34
University of Dalat, 171
University of Melbourne, 60
University of Santo Tomas, 64, 332
US 31st Marine Expeditionary Unit (MEU), 276
US Congress, 92–93, 208
US News and World Report, 49
USAID, 34, 43, 76, 85
USS Belleau Wood, 276–277

van der Kroef, Justus M., 197
Vatican Intelligence Service, 335
Ver, Fabian, 68, 70
Victorian Labor Party, 142
Vietcong Ben Tre Province Party Committee, 245
Vietcong Infrastructure (VCI), 21, 77–81
Vietnam (Mount) *News Weekly* Supplement, 10
Vietnam Civil Aid Campaign, 311
Vietnam Kuomintang (VNQDD), 78, 84, 88
Vietnam Nhan-Xa Cach Mang Dang (Vietnam Social Humanist Revolutionary Party or Nhan-Xa Party), 8, 25

Vietnam Prognosis, April, 1974 to Mid-1975: Eight Scenarios (Mount), 83, 216, 219

Vietnam, A History; The First Complete Account of Vietnam at War (Karnow), 22

Vietnam, Anatomy of War, 1940-1975 (Kolko), 175

Vietnam: The Australian War (Ham), 19, 141

Vietnamisation, 21, 81, 209

Vo Nguyen Giap, 100, 165

Vu Quy Ky, 91, 203, 208, 248

Wadjdi, Firdaus, 282, 285

Wahid, Abdurrahman, 114, 116, 125, 234, 262, 267, 285–291, 300

Walkinsaw, Bob, 85

Wanandi, Jusuf, 55, 108–109, 120–123, 125, 136, 184, 189, 191, 193, 195, 204, 208–209, 231, 239, 247, 255, 258–259, 262, 276, 281–282

Wanandi, Marcus SJ, 258

Wanandi, Sofyan, 120–121, 282, 285, 298, 301–302

Ward, Ian, 53, 158

Wardhana, Ali, 119

Warfe, George, 17, 22

Warner, Denis, 158, 250

Watergate, 20, 82–83, 90, 92–93, 95, 206, 209, 215–216, 222, 251

Webb, Kate, 19, 96, 104, 134, 164, 291–292, 321

Webb, Leicester, 97, 321

Westmoreland, William, 95, 166

Weyard, Frederick, 166

Wheat for India Campaign, 4, 45–46, 77, 143, 343

White, Brian, 142

Whitington, Dick, 312

Whitlam, Gough, 82, 206, 270–271, 300, 307–310, 313, 330, 343, 345

Wilson, David, 33, 49

Wilson, Harold, 147

Wirahadikusumah, Umar, 301

Wiranto, General, 274, 279, 283–285, 289–290, 296

Woolcott, Richard, 137, 269–270

Wright, Tommy, 22, 163

Yani, Achmud, 115, 117, 285

Ying Sita, Princess, 181

You Only Live Twice (Fleming), 157

Young Liberals, 81

Young, Guilford, Archbishop, 153

Young, Mike, 85

Yudhoyono, Susilo Bambang, 233, 274, 285, 289

ZOPFAN (Zone of Peace, Freedom and Neutrality), 55

Zulharmans, 285

www.ingramcontent.com/pod-product-compliance
Lightning Source LLC
Chambersburg PA
CBHW052055300426
44117CB00013B/2136